D0533906

'Migration is one of the most specta⟨ in the world economy, and also one o⟩ ⟨...stood. in this new⟩ book, Paul Collier, Professor of Economics at Oxford University and a former director of Development Research at World Bank, sets out to wrestle it to the ground' Robert Calderisi, *The Tablet*

'Gracefully written and elegantly argued' Kenan Malik, *Independent*

'Collier is sensitive to cultural considerations . . . doesn't shy away from controversy . . . As an economist who has studied migration, Collier has a solid grasp of its supply and demand' Eric Kaufmann, *Literary Review*

'Collier modestly admits that he does not have all the answers, but has simply tried to give readers enough building blocks to think about the issue for themselves. *Exodus* is certainly an intelligent and stimulating contribution to this often toxic debate – and underlines Collier's reputation as an economist who writes books that non-economists can actually understand' Andrew Lynch, *Sunday Business Post Magazine*

'Paul Collier's new book on international migration is magisterial. It offers a sophisticated, comprehensive, incisive, multidisciplinary, well-written balance sheet of the pros and cons of immigration for receiving societies, sending societies, and migrants themselves. For everyone on all sides of this contentious issue, Exodus is a "must-read"' Robert D. Putnam, Professor of Public Policy, John F. Kennedy School of Government, Harvard University

'Paul Collier has done it again. *Exodus* is his latest effort to subject taboo topics to straightforward questions that most other scholars shrink from asking. This time Collier considers the effects of migration on the departing peoples' new homes, their old homes, and the emigrants themselves. Collier's framework for thinking about the topic is valuable; his explanation of past research is insightful; and his agenda for further studies displays his aptitude for considering big topics while pressing for detailed research. Moreover, he courageously interconnects different fields of scholarship – addressing problems that don't fit neatly into academic categories. This book is a true achievement' Robert B. Zoellick, Former President of the World Bank Group, U.S. Trade Representative, and U.S. Deputy Secretary of State

'At a time when debate over immigration policy is polarizing public opinion, there could be no better guide to the issues involved than Paul Collier. He is lucid, undogmatic, convinced of the potential benefits of immigration but aware that these benefits can be put at risk if the process is managed indiscriminately or thoughtlessly. This important book will not end the debate but will help steer it' Paul Seabright, Toulouse School of Economics and Director of the Institute for Advanced Study in Toulouse

'An economist and expert on the world's poorest populations analyses who migrates, why, and the effects on host societies . . . Valuable reading for policymakers' *Kirkus*

ABOUT THE AUTHOR

Paul Collier is Professor of Economics and Director of the Centre for the Study of African Economies at Oxford University and a former director of Development Research at the World Bank. He is the author of, among others, the award-winning *The Bottom Billion* and *The Plundered Planet*.

PAUL COLLIER

Exodus
*Immigration and Multiculturalism
in the 21st Century*

PENGUIN BOOKS

PENGUIN BOOKS

Published by the Penguin Group
Penguin Books Ltd, 80 Strand, London WC2R ORL, England
Penguin Group (USA) Inc., 375 Hudson Street, New York, New York 10014,
USA Penguin Group (Canada), 90 Eglinton Avenue East, Suite 700, Toronto, Ontario, Canada M4P 2Y3
(a division of Pearson Penguin Canada Inc.)
Penguin Ireland, 25 St Stephen's Green, Dublin 2, Ireland (a division of Penguin Books Ltd)
Penguin Group (Australia), 707 Collins Street, Melbourne, Victoria 3008, Australia
(a division of Pearson Australia Group Pty Ltd)
Penguin Books India Pvt Ltd, 11 Community Centre, Panchsheel Park, New Delhi – 110 017, India
Penguin Group (NZ), 67 Apollo Drive, Rosedale, Auckland 0632, New Zealand
(a division of Pearson New Zealand Ltd)
Penguin Books (South Africa) (Pty) Ltd, Block D, Rosebank Office Park, 181 Jan Smuts Avenue,
Parktown North, Gauteng 2193, South Africa

Penguin Books Ltd, Registered Offices: 80 Strand, London WC2R ORL, England

www.penguin.com

First published in the United States of America by Oxford University Press 2013
First published in Great Britain by Allen Lane 2013
Published in Penguin Books 2014
008

Copyright © Paul Collier, 2013

The moral right of the author has been asserted

Printed in Great Britain by Clays Ltd, St Ives plc

978-0-141-04216-9

www.greenpenguin.co.uk

Penguin Books is committed to a sustainable
future for our business, our readers and our planet.
This book is made from Forest Stewardship
Council™ certified paper.

For Pauline, my rootless cosmopolitan

Contents

Prologue 3

Part 1 *The Questions and the Process*
Chapter 1: The Migration Taboo 11
Chapter 2: Why Migration Accelerates 27

Part 2 *Host Societies: Welcome or Resentment?*
Chapter 3: The Social Consequences 57
Chapter 4: The Economic Consequences 111
Chapter 5: Getting Migration Policy Wrong 135

Part 3 *Migrants: Grievance or Gratitude?*
Chapter 6: Migrants: The Winners from
                  Migration 145
Chapter 7: Migrants: The Losers from
                  Migration 169

Part 4 *Those Left Behind*

Chapter 8: The Political Consequences *179*

Chapter 9: The Economic Consequences *195*

Chapter 10: Left Behind? *217*

Part 5 *Rethinking Migration Policies*

Chapter 11: Nations and Nationalism *231*

Chapter 12: Making Migration Policies Fit for Purpose *245*

Notes *275*

References *283*

Index *293*

EXODUS

Prologue

HE FACES ME AS I WRITE THIS: KARL HELLENSCHMIDT. No longer the penniless young immigrant, by the time of the photograph he has a suit, an English wife, and six young children. He looks confidently into the camera, unaware that his family is about to be wrecked by the anti-immigrant racism of the First World War. Britain is soon fighting to defend civilization from the barbaric Huns. He is one of them. Civilization, in the guise of the gutter rag *John Bull*, includes Karl Hellenschmidt in its trumped-up list of enemy agents. By night a civilized mob attacks his shop. A representative of civilization tries to strangle his wife. He is interned as an enemy alien; his wife succumbs to terminal depression. Twelve-year-old Karl Hellenschmidt Jr. is pulled out of school to run the shop. And then, barely twenty years later, another war: Karl Hellenschmidt Jr. moves home and changes his name. He becomes Charles Collier.

Many of us are the descendants of immigrants. Natural sentiments of belonging can easily be tipped into the visceral cruelty of which my family was a victim. But such responses to immigrants are not universal. By chance this year I met someone whose father had been on the other side at that anti-German riot. The recognition that innocent immigrants had been wronged had descended down his family as it has down mine.

My grandfather migrated from a poverty-stricken village in Germany, Ernsbach, to what was then the most prosperous city in Europe: Bradford. That move, not just country to country but village to city, typifies modern migration from poor countries to rich ones. But once he arrived in Bradford, my grandfather's sense of youthful adventure reached its limit: he went straight to a district already so packed with other German immigrants that it was known as Little Germany. The same limits to adventure characterize today's migrants. A century on, Bradford is no longer the most prosperous city in Europe: in a reversal of fortunes it is now far less prosperous than Ernsbach. It has remained a city of arrival, and it has remained a city of tensions. Elected by immigrant votes, Britain's only member of Parliament who belongs to the Respect Party, essentially a party of Islamic extremists, is from Bradford. This time, some of the immigrants really are enemy agents: four of them committed the terrorist suicide bombings that killed fifty-seven people in London. Immigrants can be perpetrators of visceral cruelty as well as its victims.

This book is in part a continuation of my work on the poorest societies—the bottom billion. People's struggle to migrate from these countries to the rich West is both of professional and personal moment. It is a difficult but important question whether the resulting exodus is beneficial or harmful to those left behind. These are the poorest societies on earth, and yet the West's policies on immigration create effects on them that are both inadvertent and unrecognized. We should at least be aware of what, in an absence of mind, we are doing to these societies. I also see my friends torn between their duty to remain home and their duty to make the most of opportunities.

But the book is also a critique of the prevailing opinion among liberal thinkers, a group of which I am a member, that modern Western societies should embrace a postnational future. In view of my own family circumstances, I might be expected to be an enthusiast for that new orthodoxy. At borders we present three different passports: I am English, Pauline is Dutch but brought up in Italy, while Daniel, born in the United States, proudly sports his American passport. My nephews are Egyptian, their mother is Irish. This book, like my previous ones, is written in France. If ever there was a postnational family, mine is surely it.

But what if everyone did that? Suppose that international migration were to become sufficiently common as to dissolve the meaning of national identity: societies really became postnational. Would this matter? I think it would matter a great deal. Lifestyles such as that of my family are dependent, and potentially parasitic, on those whose identity remains rooted, thereby providing us with the viable societies among which we choose. In the countries on which I work—the multicultural societies of Africa—the adverse consequences of weak national identity are apparent. The rare great leaders such as Julius Nyerere, the first president of Tanzania, have struggled to forge a common identity among their people. But is national identity not toxic? Does it not lead back to that anti-Hun riot? Or worse: Chancellor Angela Merkel, Europe's preeminent leader, has voiced fears that a revival of nationalism would risk a return not just to race riots but to war. I recognize that in espousing the value of national identity I must credibly allay these fears.

Even more than with my other books I am dependent upon an international array of other scholars. Some are my colleagues and partners in research; others I have never even met but can benefit from through their publications. Modern academic endeavor is organized into a vast array of specialists. Even within the economics of migration, researchers are highly specialized. For this book I needed the answers to three clusters of questions: What determines the decisions of migrants? How does migration affect those left behind? How does it affect indigenous populations in host countries? Each of these questions has distinct specialists. But I came increasingly to realize that migration is not primarily about economics: it is a social phenomenon, and as for academic specialism, this opens Pandora's box. Surmounting these different analyses was an ethical question: by what moral metric should the various effects be judged? Economists have a glib little ethical toolkit called utilitarianism. It works a treat for the typical task, which is why it has become standard. But for a question such as the ethics of migration it is woefully inadequate.

The resulting book is an attempt to generate a unified analysis of a wide array of disparate specialist research, across social science and moral philosophy. Within economics my key influences have been the writings of George Akerlof through his innovative ideas on identity, and Frédéric Docquier for his rigorous investigation of the migration process, and especially discussion with Tony Venables both on economic geography and as a sparring partner for the model that is the analytic workhorse of this book. In social psychology I have drawn on discussions with Nick Rawlings and the works of Steven Pinker, Jonathan Haidt, Daniel Kahneman, and Paul Zak. In philosophy I have learned from discussions with Simon Saunders and Chris Hookway and from the writings of Michael Sandel.

The book is an attempt to answer this question: what migration policies are appropriate? Even to pose this question requires a degree of courage: if ever there was a hornet's nest it is migration. Yet while the topic is regularly around the top of voter concerns, with rare exceptions, the literature on it is either narrow and technical or heavily filtered by advocacy for some strongly held opinion. I have tried to write an honest book that is accessible to all: it is therefore short and the style is nontechnical. Sometimes the argument is speculative and unorthodox. Where this happens I say so. My hope at such stages is that it will both provoke and stimulate specialists to do the work that is needed to determine whether these speculations are well founded. Above all, I hope that the evidence and arguments in this book will open popular discussion of migration policy beyond views that are theatrically polarized and stridently expressed. The issue is too important to stay that way.

PART 1

The Questions and the Process

CHAPTER 1

The Migration Taboo

MIGRATION OF POOR PEOPLE TO RICH COUNTRIES is a phenomenon overloaded with toxic associations. The persistence of mass poverty in the societies of the bottom billion is an affront to the twenty-first century. Aware of a richer life elsewhere, many young people in these societies are desperate to leave. By means legal and illegal, some of them succeed. Each individual exodus is a triumph of the human spirit, courage and ingenuity overcoming the bureaucratic barriers imposed by the fearful rich. From this emotive perspective any migration policy other than the open door is mean-spirited. Yet that same migration can also be cast as selfish: responsibilities to others in yet more desperate circumstances are being ignored, as workers abandon dependents and the enterprising desert the less able to their fate. From this emotive perspective, migration policy needs to bring back into account the effects on those left behind that migrants themselves discount. The same migration can even be cast as an act of imperialism in reverse: the revenge of the once-colonized. Migrants build colonies in host countries that divert resources from, compete with, and undermine the values of the indigenous poor. From this emotive perspective, migration policy needs to protect those who remain in place. Migration is emotive, but emotive reactions to presumed effects could drive policy in any direction.

Migration has been politicized before it has been analyzed. The movement of people from poor countries to rich ones is a simple economic process, but its effects are complex. Public policy on migration needs to come to terms with this complexity. Currently, policies toward migration vary enormously, both in countries of origin and host countries. Some governments of countries of origin actively promote emigration and have official programs maintaining connections with their diasporas, whereas others restrict exits and regard their diasporas as opponents. Host countries vary enormously in the overall rate of immigration they permit, from Japan, which has become one of the richest societies on earth while remaining completely closed to immigrants, to Dubai, which has also become one of the richest societies on earth by means of immigration so rapid that its resident population is now 95 percent nonindigenous. They vary in how selective they are in the composition of migration, with Australia and Canada being much more educationally demanding than America, which is in turn more demanding than Europe. They vary in the rights of migrants once in the country, from granting them legal equality with the indigenous, including the right to bring in relatives, to being contract workers, subject to repatriation and without any of the rights of citizens. They vary in the obligations of migrants, from being directed to live in particular locations and required to learn the local language, to being free to congregate in own-language clusters. They vary in whether assimilation should be encouraged or cultural differences preserved. I can think of no other area of public policy where differences are so pronounced. Does this diversity of policy reflect sophisticated responses to differences in circumstances? I doubt it. Rather, I suspect that the vagaries of making policy on migration reflect a toxic context of high emotion and little knowledge.

Migration policy has been fought over using competing values rather than competing evidence. Values can determine analysis in both a good sense and a bad sense. The good sense is that until we have resolved our values, it is not possible to make normative assessments, whether concerning migration or anything else. But ethics also determines analysis in a bad sense. In a revealing new study, the moral psychologist Jonathan Haidt demonstrates that although people's moral values differ, they tend to cluster into two groups.[1] Devastatingly, he shows that depending upon the cluster of values to which people belong their moral judgment on particular issues shapes their reasoning, rather than the other way round. Reasons purport to justify and explain judgments. But in fact, we grasp at reasons and pull them into service to legitimize judgments that we have already made on the basis of our moral tastes. On no significant issue is all the evidence exclusively lined up on only one side of the argument: it certainly isn't on migration. Our ethics determine the reasoning and evidence that we are prepared to accept. We give credence to the flimsiest of straws in the wind that are aligned with our values, while dismissing opposing evidence with a torrent of contempt and vitriol. Ethical tastes on migration are polarized, and each camp will entertain only those arguments and facts that support its prejudices. Haidt demonstrates that these crude biases apply on many issues, but for migration these tendencies are compounded. In the liberal circles that on most policy issues provide the most informed discussion, migration has been a taboo subject. The only permissible opinion has been to bemoan popular antipathy to it. Very recently, economists have gained a better understanding of the structure of taboos. Their purpose is to protect a sense of identity by shielding people from evidence that might challenge it.[2] Taboos save you from the need to cover your ears by constraining what is said.

Whereas disputes about evidence can in principle be resolved by one party being forced to accept that it is mistaken, disagreements about values may be irresolvable. Once recognized as such, differences in values can at least be respected. I am not a vegetarian, but I do not regard vegetarians as deluded morons, nor do I try to force-feed my vegetarian guests with foie gras. My more ambitious aim is to induce people to reexamine the inferences they draw from their values. As Daniel Kahneman has explained in *Thinking Fast, Thinking Slow*, we tend to be reluctant to undertake the effortful thinking that uses evidence properly. We prefer to rely upon snap judgments, often based on our values. Most of the time such judgments are remarkably good approximations to the truth, but we over rely upon them. This book is meant to move you beyond your snap value-based judgments.

Like everyone else, I came to the subject of migration with value-based prior opinions. But in writing it I have tried to suspend them. From my discussions, migration is a subject on which almost everyone seems to have strong views. People can usually support their views with a smattering of analysis. But I suspect that, consistent with the research of Jonathan Haidt, in large part these views are derived from prior moral tastes rather than from superior command of the evidence. Evidence-based analysis is the strong suit of economics. Like many policy issues, migration has economic causes and economic consequences, and so economics is at the forefront of assessing policy. Our toolkit enables us to get better technical answers to causes and consequences than can be achieved simply by common sense. But some of the effects of migration that most concern ordinary people are social. These can be incorporated into an economic analysis, and I attempt to do so. But more commonly economists have been glibly dismissive of them.

The political elites who actually set policy are caught in the crossfire between the value-laden concerns of voters and the lop-sided models of economists. The result is confusion. Policies not only vary between countries, they oscillate between the open door favored by economists and the closed door favored by electorates. For example, in Britain the door was opened in the 1950s, partially closed in 1968, flung open again in 1997, and is now being closed again. They also migrate between political parties: of these four policy changes, the Labour Party and the Conservative Party are each responsible for one door-opening and one door-closing. Often politicians talk tough and act soft, and more rarely the opposite. Indeed, sometimes they appear to be embarrassed by the prefer-ences of their citizens. The Swiss are unusual in that ordinary people have the power to force referenda on their government. One of the issues on which people used this power was, inevitably, migration. The vehicle for popular concern was a referendum on rules for mosque building. It revealed that a substantial majority of the population opposed mosque building. The Swiss government was so embarrassed about these views that it promptly tried to have the result declared illegal.

Moral positions on migration are confusingly bound up with those on poverty, nationalism, and racism. Current perceptions of the rights of migrants are shaped by guilty reactions to different past wrongs. It is only possible to have a rational discussion of migration policy once these concerns have been disentangled.

There is a clear moral obligation to help very poor people who live in other countries, and allowing some of them to move to rich societies is one way of helping. Yet the obligation to help the poor cannot imply a generalized obligation to permit free movement of people across borders. Indeed, the people who believe that poor people should be free to move to rich countries would likely be the first to oppose the right of rich people to move to poor countries: that has uncomfortable echoes of colonialism. Arguing that because people are poor they have a right of migration confuses two issues that are better kept distinct: the obligation of the rich to help the poor, and the rights of freedom of movement between countries. We don't need to assert the latter to endorse the former. There are many ways of fulfilling our obligation to help the poor: if a society decides not to open its doors to migrants from poor countries, it might opt for more generous treatment of poor societies in other domains of policy. For example, the government of Norway imposes relatively tight restrictions on immigration, but it adopts an aid program that is correspondingly generous.

While the moral obligation to help the global poor sometimes spills over to views on the right to migrate, a more potent spillover is revulsion against nationalism. While nationalism does not necessarily imply restrictions on immigration, it is clearly the case that without a sense of nationalism there would be no basis for restrictions. If the people living in a territory do not share any greater sense of common identity with each other than with foreigners, then it would be bizarre collectively to agree to limit the entry of foreigners: there would be no "us" and "them." So without nationalism it is difficult to make an ethical case for immigration restrictions.

Unsurprisingly, revulsion against nationalism is strongest in Europe: nationalism repeatedly led to war. The European Union has been a noble attempt to put this legacy behind us. A natural extension of revulsion against nationalism is revulsion against borders: a defining achievement of the European Union is the free movement of European people anywhere within the Union. For some Europeans national identity is now passé: one of my young relatives will not admit to a geographic identity beyond that of Londoner. If national identity is best discarded, then there seems little ethical justification for preventing the entry of migrants: why not let anyone live anywhere?

The acceptability of national identity varies enormously. In France, America, China, and Scandinavia national identity remains strong and politically neutral, while in Germany and Britain it has been captured by the extreme political Right and is consequently taboo. In the many societies that have never had a strong national identity, its absence is usually a matter of regret and concern. In Canada, Michael Ignatief recently ignited a storm by admitting that the long attempt to forge a translinguistic sense of common identity between the Quebecois and anglophone Canadians had failed.[3] In Africa, the weakness of national identity relative to tribal identities is widely regarded as a curse that it is the task of good leadership to rectify. In Belgium, which currently holds the world record for the longest period without a government—because the Flemish and Walloons could not agree on one—there has not even been an attempt to forge a common identity. One of Belgium's ambassadors is a friend of mine, and over dinner the issue of his own identity arose. He cheerfully denied any sense of feeling Belgian, but not because he felt either Flemish or Walloon. Rather, he regarded himself as a citizen of the world. Pressed on where he felt most at home, he chose a village in France. I cannot imagine a French ambassador volunteering an equivalent sentiment. Both Canada and Belgium manage to sustain high incomes despite their weak national identities, but their solution has been complete spatial segregation between the different language groups, combined with radical decentralization of political authority to these subnational territories. For practical purposes of public service delivery, Canada and Belgium are four states with cohesive identity, not two states without it. In Britain the acceptability of national identity is confused because of the relatively recent multinational composition of Britain from its component parts: nobody in Britain, except for some immigrants, thinks of themselves as primarily British. In Scotland national identity is openly promoted as part of mainstream culture, whereas English nationalism is subversive: there are far fewer officially flown English flags than Scottish flags.

Nationalism has its uses. Its potential for abuse cannot be forgotten, but a sense of shared identity turns out to enhance the ability to cooperate. People need to be able to cooperate at various different levels, some below the level of the nation and some above it. A shared sense of national identity is not the only solution to achieving cooperation, but nations continue to be particularly salient. This is evident from taxation and public spending: although both functions occur at many levels of government, overwhelmingly the most important is national. So if a shared sense of national identity enhances the ability of people to cooperate at that level, it is doing something truly important.

A shared sense of identity also predisposes people to accept redistribution from rich to poor and to share natural wealth. So the revulsion against national identity is liable to be costly: leading to a reduced ability to cooperate and a less equal society. But despite these benefits, it may nevertheless be necessary to forsake national identity. If nationalism inexorably leads to aggression, then the costs of abandoning it must surely be accepted. Since the decline in European nationalism, Europe has enjoyed a prolonged and unprecedented period of peace. This association has led politicians such as Chancellor Angela Merkel to promote the symbols of European unity, notably the euro, as a defense against the return to war. But the inference that the decline in nationalism has caused the decline in violence gets causality wrong: the revulsion against violence has caused a decline in nationalism. More important, the revulsion against violence has radically reduced the risk of violence. Attitudes to violence have changed so profoundly that European warfare is now unthinkable.

I will suggest that it is no longer necessary to discard national identity in order to guard against the evils of nationalism. If a shared national identity is useful, then it can safely coexist with a nation at peace. Indeed, the Nordic countries surely bear this out. Each society is unashamedly patriotic, extending to rivalry with its neighbors. The region has a history of warfare: Sweden and Denmark have both had long periods of belligerence at the expense of Finland and Norway, respectively. But continued peace is now beyond question. Nor is that peace underpinned by Europe's formal institutions for cooperation. Indeed, those formal institutions have inadvertently divided rather than united the Nordic countries. Norway is not in the European Community, though the other three countries are. But of these three only Finland is in the eurozone. So Europe's institutions of unity split these four countries into three distinct blocs. The Nordic countries have achieved among the highest living standards on earth: not just high private incomes, but social equity and well-functioning public services. The contribution of patriotism and a sense of common identity cannot be quantified, but is surely there.

While the responsibility to the poor and fear of nationalism may both have contributed to confusion over whether societies should have the right to restrict immigration, by far the most potent spill-over to support for freedom of movement between countries as a natural right comes from opposition to racism. Given the histories of racism in both Europe and America it is both unsurprising and fully warranted that opposition to racism is so impassioned. Most migrants from poor countries are racially distinct from the indigenous populations of rich host countries, and so opposition to immigration skates precariously close to racism. In Britain, one high-profile anti-immigrant speech in the 1960s clearly crossed this line: opposing the immigration of people of African and South Asian origin in lurid terms of impending interethnic violence. That foolish speech by a long-dead minor politician, Enoch Powell, closed down British discussion of migration policy for over forty years: opposition to immigration became so indelibly linked to racism that it could not be voiced in mainstream discourse. Powell's manifestly ridiculous prediction of "rivers of blood" not only closed down discussion, it came to define liberal fears: the great lurking danger was supposedly the potential for interracial violence between immigrants and the indigenous. Nothing that could conceivably awaken this dormant dragon was permissible.

The taboo only became breakable in 2010 as a result of mass immigration from Poland. British immigration policy toward the Poles had been distinctive in its liberality. When Poland joined the European Community, transition arrangements gave member countries the right to restrict Polish immigration until the Polish economy had itself adjusted. All major countries except Britain duly imposed entry restrictions. That the British government decided not to do so may have been influenced by a forecast made by the British civil service in 2003 that very few east Europeans—no more than 13,000 a year—would want to migrate to Britain. This forecast turned out to be spectacularly wrong. Actual immigration to Britain from eastern Europe in the following five years was around one million.[4] Immigration on this scale, though warmly welcomed by households such as my own who found the influx of skilled, hardworking artisans

HE NEVER USED THE PHRASE!

very useful, was also widely resented, often by indigenous workers who felt threatened. While both the welcome and the opposition were manifestly self-serving, neither could reasonably be seen as racist: Poles happened to be white and Christian. A decisive and indeed comic moment in the 2010 election was when the prime minister, Gordon Brown, was recorded by a forgotten microphone following a staged talk with an ordinary citizen selected by his staff. Unfortunately, the citizen had chosen to complain about the recent wave of immigration. Brown was recorded berating his staff about their choice, denouncing the woman as "a bigot." The spectacle of a prime minister so manifestly out of touch with concerns widely perceived to be legitimate contributed to Brown's resounding defeat. The new leadership of the Labour Party has apologized, stating that the previous open-door policy was wrong. At last it may have become possible in Britain to discuss immigration without connotations of racism.

But it may not. Since race is correlated with other characteristics such as poverty, religion, and culture, it remains possible that any limitation on migration based on these criteria is viewed as the Trojan horse for racism. If so, then it is still not possible to have an open debate on migration. I only decided to write this book once I judged that it is indeed now possible to distinguish between the concepts of race, poverty, and culture. Racialism is a belief in genetic differences between races: one for which there is no evidence. Poverty is about income, not genetics: the persistence of mass poverty alongside the technology that can make ordinary people prosperous is the great scandal and challenge of our age. Cultures are not genetically inherited; they are fluid clusters of norms and habits that have important material consequences. A refusal to countenance racially based differences in behavior is a manifestation of human decency. A refusal to countenance culturally based differences in behavior would be a manifestation of blinkered denial of the obvious.

While relying on the legitimacy of these distinctions, I am acutely conscious that my judgment may be wrong. The issue matters because, as will become apparent, much of consequence for migration policy turns on income and cultural differences. If this is assumed to be code for racism, then it is best that debate not be attempted, at least in Britain: we may still not be free of the long shadow of Enoch Powell. So my working assumption is that the right to live anywhere is not a logical corollary of opposition to racism. There may be such a right, and I will turn to it, but it does not follow simply from the legitimate concerns about poverty, nationalism, and racism.

Think of three groups of people: the migrants themselves, the people left behind in the country of origin, and the indigenous population of the host country. We need theories and evidence as to what happens to each of these groups. The first of these perspectives, that of migrants, I leave until last because it is the most straightforward. Migrants face costs of overcoming the barriers to movement that are substantial, but they reap economic benefits that are much larger than these costs. Migrants capture the lion's share of the economic gains from migration. Some intriguing new evidence suggests that these large economic gains are partly, or perhaps substantially, offset by psychological losses. However, although this new evidence is striking, there are as yet too few reliable studies to judge the overall importance of the effects it identifies.

The second perspective—that of the people left behind in impoverished countries of origin—was my original motivation in writing this book. These are the poorest societies on earth, which over the past half-century have fallen behind the prospering majority. Does emigration drain these societies of the abilities of which they are already desperately scarce, or does it provide a lifeline of support and a catalyst for change? If the benchmark for the effects of migration on those left behind is the completely closed door, then they are much better off as a result of migration. The same could be said of the other economic interactions between the poorest societies and the rest of the world: trade is better than no trade, and the movement of capital is better than complete financial immobility. But the benchmark of autarchy for the poorest societies is an undemanding and irrelevant hurdle: no serious policy analyst proposes it. The pertinent benchmark, as with trade and capital flows, is the status quo relative not to autarchy, but to either faster or slower emigration. I show that in the absence of controls, emigration from the poorest countries would accelerate: they would face an exodus. But migration policies are set not in poor countries but in rich ones. In determining the rate of immigration into their own societies, the governments of rich countries also inadvertently set the rate of emigration experienced by the poorest societies. While recognizing that current migration is better for these societies than no migration, is the current rate ideal? Would poor countries gain more were migration somewhat faster or somewhat slower than at present? Posed in such a way the question was until recently unanswerable. But new and highly rigorous research suggests that for many of the bottom billion, current emigration rates are likely to be excessive. A decade ago an analogous academic effort laid the groundwork for a policy rethink on capital flows. There are long lags between research and policy change, but in November 2012 the International Monetary Fund announced that it would no longer regard the open door for capital flows to be necessarily the best policy for poor countries. Each of these nuanced assessments will outrage the fundamentalists who derive their policy preferences from their moral priors.

The final perspective, of the indigenous population in host societies, is what is likely to be of direct interest to most readers of this book, and so I start with it. How does the magnitude and pace of immigration affect social interaction, both between the indigenous and immigrants, and among the indigenous themselves? What are the economic effects on different skill and age cohorts among the indigenous? How do the consequences change over time? The same benchmark issue arises for the indigenous population of host countries as for those left behind in countries of origin. The pertinent benchmark is not zero migration but somewhat more than current levels or somewhat less. The answer is evidently country-specific: an underpopulated country like Australia may not arrive at the same answer as a densely populated country like the Netherlands. In trying to answer this question I will argue that social effects are usually likely to trump economic effects, in part because the economic effects are usually modest. For the neediest sections among the indigenous population the net effects of migration are often probably negative.

The long march through these three different perspectives will provide the building blocks for an overall evaluation of migration. But to move from description to evaluation we need both an analytic and an ethical framework. In the typical work of advocacy on migration both the analytics and the ethics trivialize the problem because all the important effects appear to work in the same direction, with opposing effects being dismissed as "controversial," "minor," or "short term." But any honest analysis must recognize that there are both winners and losers, and that even determining the overall effect on a particular group can be ambiguous, depending on how gains are measured against losses. If some people win while others lose, whose interest should prevail? Much economic analysis of migration comes to a clear and powerful answer: the winners gain much more than the losers lose, so hard luck on the losers. Even with the simple metric of monetary income, the gains far outweigh the losses. But economists usually move on from money to the more sophisticated concept of "utility," and by this metric the overall gains from migration are even larger. For many economists that answer settles the matter: migration policy should be set so as to maximize global utility.

In part 5 I challenge this conclusion. I argue that rights should not be dissolved by the sleight of hand involved in "global utility." Nations are important and legitimate moral units: indeed, the fruits of successful nationhood are what attract migrants. The very existence of nations confers rights on their citizens, most especially on the indigenous poor. Their interests cannot lightly be dismissed through the invocation of gains in global utility. The people left behind in countries of origin are in a yet more vulnerable position than the indigenous poor of host countries. They are both more needy and far more numerous than migrants themselves. But unlike the indigenous poor of host countries, they have no prospect of rights over migration policies: their own governments cannot control the rate of emigration.

Migration policies are set not by the governments of countries of origin but by those of host countries. In any democratic society, the government must reflect the interests of the majority of its citizens, but both the indigenous poor and those living in the poorest societies are of legitimate concern to citizens. Hence, in setting migration policy, host governments will need to balance the interests of the indigenous poor against the interests of migrants and of those left behind in poor countries.

A rabid collection of xenophobes and racists who are hostile to immigrants lose no opportunity to argue that migration is bad for indigenous populations. Understandably, this has triggered a reaction:

desperate not to give succor to these groups, social scientists have strained every muscle to show that migration is good for everyone. Inadvertently, this has allowed the underlying question to be set by the xenophobes: "Is migration bad or good?" The central message of this book is that this is the wrong question. Asking this question of migration is about as sensible as it would be to ask, "Is eating bad or good?" In both cases the pertinent question is not bad or good but how much is best. Some migration is almost certainly better than no migration. But just as eating too much can lead to obesity, so migration can be excessive. I show that, left to itself, migration will keep accelerating, so that it is liable to become excessive. This is why migration controls, far from being an embarrassing vestige of nationalism and racism, are going to be increasingly important tools of social policy in all high-income societies. What is embarrassing is not their existence but their inept design. In turn this reflects the taboo that has blocked serious discussion.

This book is an attempt to break that taboo. I am all too aware that, as with all attempts to break taboos, it carries risks. The fundamentalist guardians of orthodoxies stand ready with their fatwas. It is time to get started, and the starting point is to understand why migration accelerates.

CHAPTER 2

Why Migration Accelerates

FOR HALF A CENTURY FOLLOWING the outbreak of the First World War countries closed their borders. Wars and the Depression made migration practically difficult and immigrants unwelcome. By the 1960s people overwhelmingly lived in the country in which they had been born. But during that half-century of immobility, there had been a dramatic change in the global economy: a gulf had opened up between the incomes of countries.

Within a society the distribution of income is hump-shaped: most people are somewhere in the middle, with two tails, one being the rich minority, the other the poor minority. The fundamental statistical reason that the distribution of income usually looks like this is chance: the process of generating income depends upon repeated situations in which people can be lucky or unlucky. A cumulative process of good and bad fortune generates hump-shaped outcomes. If the luck cumulates multiplicatively, as with a rolling bet on horse races, then the tail for the rich minority becomes extended: a few people get very rich indeed. So powerful and universal are these multiplicative forces of income generation that the distribution of income in every country on earth conforms to it.

But by the 1960s the distribution of income *between* countries did not look anything like that. Instead of having a hump in the middle, it had a hump at each end. In technical language it was bimodal; more popularly expressed, there was a rich world and a poor world. The rich world was becoming richer at rates without historical precedent. For example, between 1945 and 1975 French per capita income tripled: the French refer to the period as "the Golden Thirty Years." Economists built Growth Theory to try to understand what was driving this new phenomenon. But the poor world had missed out on growth and was continuing to do so. Economists built Development Economics to understand why such a divide had occurred and why it was persisting.

Four Pillars of Prosperity

In discussing migration policy, much hinges on why some countries are so much richer than others, and so I will now offer a succinct account of how both professional opinion and my own thinking on the issue have evolved. When development economics was in its infancy, the standard explanation for the astounding gap in income was the difference in the endowment of capital. Workers in high-income countries were more productive because they had so much more capital with which to work. This explanation has not been completely abandoned, but one fundamental change that economics has had to come to terms with is that capital has become internationally mobile: there are huge flows between countries. Yet capital is not flowing in significant quantities to the poorest countries. Poor countries still have very little capital, but this can no longer be seen as the primary cause of their poverty; something else must jointly account for both their lack of capital and their poverty. Poor choices in economic policy, dysfunctional ideologies, bad geography, negative attitudes about work, the legacy of colonialism, and a lack of education have all been proposed and investigated as explanations. Most have some reasonable basis for support, but none seems likely to be the ultimate explanation: for example, policy choices do not just happen; they are the result of some political process.

Increasingly, economists and political scientists have coalesced around explanations that focus on how the polity is organized: how political interest groups shape long-lasting institutions that thereafter affect choices.[1] One influential line of argument is that the key initial conditions for prosperity are those in which it is in the interest of political elites to build a tax system: historically in Europe they needed revenues to finance military spending. In turn, a tax system gives a government an interest in enlarging the economy, and so induces it to build the rule of law. The rule of law induces people to invest, confident that productive assets will not be expropriated. Investment drives growth. Onto this secure base for investment, a further layer of institutions addresses the distribution of income. Protest from the many excluded forces the rich to commit to inclusive political institutions: we arrive at property-owning democracy.

A related line of argument is that the key institutional change is the shift in political power from predatory elites bent on extracting revenues from the productive population to more inclusive institutions that protect the interests of the productive. In an important new study, Daron Acemoglu and James Robinson argue that the English Glorious Revolution of 1688, in which power shifted from king to Parliament, was the first such decisive event in world economic history, unleashing the Industrial Revolution and opening the path to global prosperity.

This line of reasoning has given primacy to political and economic institutions. One indication that democratic institutions matter is that a change of leader only makes a significant difference to economic performance if these institutions are weak. Good institutions restrain the vagaries that would otherwise be generated by the character of individual leaders.[2] So formal political and economic institutions matter: high-income countries have better political and economic institutions than low-income countries.

But democratic political institutions only function well if ordinary citizens are sufficiently well informed to discipline politicians. Many issues are complex, as is migration policy itself. Keynes insightfully proposed that ordinary people handle complexity through narratives: readily digestible theories-in-miniature.[3] Narratives spread easily, becoming public goods, but they can stray quite a long way from reality. Narratives of disease are an example. The switch from the narrative that illness is due to witchcraft to one that encapsulates germ theory is fundamental to improvements in public health. It occurred in Europe in the late nineteenth century. In Haiti it is still under way: even in the wake of the earthquake, people were wary of hospitals. Depending on their content, narratives can support, complement, or undermine institutions. The narrative "Germans no longer tolerate inflation" underpinned the deutsche mark. But no equivalent narrative has been built across Europe for the euro. Like the deutsche mark, it has an institutional defense consisting of two fiscal rules; but since its launch in 2001, sixteen of the seventeen member countries, including Germany, have broken them. The euro is a brave, and perhaps foolhardy, attempt to force the differing economic narratives that have prevailed across Europe to adapt to a common new institution. But such adaptation is slow and uncertain. Even by 2012, and despite an unemployment rate of 27 percent, Spanish inflation remained higher than that in Germany, and cumulatively the prolonged higher inflation had drastically undermined the country's competitiveness. Narratives can evolve, but they matter.

Whereas Europe provides an example of differing economic narratives, the contrast between America and South Sudan illustrates differing political narratives. President Clinton famously won an election campaign on the slogan "It's the economy, stupid!" A society in which this sentiment resonates is going to use a given set of political institutions quite differently than one in which the narrative is "The Dinka have been wronged by the Nuer."[4] Similarly, a society that thinks "foreign investment means jobs" is going to run a National Investment Authority rather differently than one that thinks "foreign investment means exploitation." False narratives eventually fade, but they may take a long time a-dying. So one reason for the wide gap in incomes may be that institutions are supported in high-income societies by narratives that are more functional than those prevailing in low-income societies.

But many of the rules that govern economic behavior are informal, so the analysis can be extended beyond institutions and narratives to social norms. Two key norms concern violence and cooperation. In a violent society the rule of law keeps getting overridden: households and firms must divert effort into safety, and in the limit they seek safety through choosing to remain poor so they are less of a target.[5] The capacity to cooperate is fundamental to prosperity: many goods and services are "public goods" that are most efficiently supplied collectively. So the social foundations of peace and cooperation matter for growth and are not direct corollaries of formal institutions. Steven Pinker has convincingly suggested that norms concerning violence have evolved quite radically in distinct steps over many centuries.[6] An early step is the passage from anarchy to centralized power: a passage that Somalia has yet to make. Another is the passage from power to authority: a step that many regimes have yet to manage. A more recent step has been the enhanced ability to empathize with the suffering of others and the demise of codes of clan and family honor, making the infliction of violence less acceptable.

The foundations of cooperation have been extensively studied through game-based experiments and are now quite well understood. Sustained cooperation depends upon trust. The extent to which people are willing to trust each other varies enormously between societies. High-trust societies are better able to cooperate and also face lower costs of transactions because they are less dependent upon processes of formal enforcement. So social norms matter, as well as formal institutions. The norms prevalent in high-income societies support much lower levels of interpersonal violence, and higher levels of trust, than those prevalent in low-income societies.

In turn, institutions, narratives, and norms facilitate the emergence of effective organizations that enable their workforce to be productive. Typically, high productivity depends upon reconciling large size with worker motivation. Economists have long realized that big is productive: large organizations are able to reap economies of scale. But only recently have they developed a convincing analysis of motivation. Incentives are evidently part of the story, but the work of Nobel laureate George Akerlof and Rachel Kranton has opened up a new appreciation of how successful organizations motivate through identity. An effective firm persuades its workers to adopt identities that are conducive to productivity.[7] Akerlof's central idea comes through posing the question "What makes a good plumber?" He argues that the essential step is neither technical training nor incentive pay, but whether the plumber has made the leap of identity: "I am a good plumber." For a plumber who has made this leap, doing anything less than a good job would be inconsistent with his sense of identity. In the private sector, competition forces organizations to make their workers productive. Akerlof and Kranton show that successful firms indeed devote time and effort to persuade their workers to internalize the objectives of the firm: to become "insiders." In the public sector, political accountability forces organizations to do the same. The higher the proportion who become insiders, the more productive is the workforce, so that everyone is better off.

One reason poor countries are poor is that they are short of effective organizations: many are too small to reap scale economies, and many, especially among the public organizations, fail to motivate their workers. For example, teachers in many poor countries typically do not show up for work and have not maintained essential skills such as functional literacy. The consequence for educational standards is disastrous, as revealed by international test scores.[8] Such teachers have evidently not made the crucial leap of identity: "I am a good teacher," and this is, in part, a failure of the organizations that employ them.

I will refer to the combination of institutions, rules, norms, and organizations of a country as its *social model*. Even among high-income countries social models differ considerably. America has particularly strong institutions and private organizations, but somewhat weaker public organizations than Europe, and Japan has much stronger norms of trust than either of them. But though they differ in detail, all high-income societies have social models that function remarkably well. Quite possibly, different combinations work well because the components adapt so as to fit each other: for example, institutions and norms may gradually evolve so as to be well suited given the state of narratives and organizations. But such adaptation is not automatic. On the contrary, hundreds of different societies existed for thousands of years before any of them happened upon a social model capable of supporting the ascent to prosperity. Even the Glorious Revolution was not undertaken with the objective of unleashing prosperity: it was triggered by a mixture of religious prejudice and political opportunism. The English social model that emerged in the eighteenth century was replicated and improved in America. This in turn influenced social revolution in France, which exported its new institutions by force of arms across western Europe. The key point I wish to convey is that the present prosperity enjoyed in the Western world, and which is belatedly spreading more widely, is not the outcome of some inevitable march of progress. For thousands of years until the twentieth century ordinary people were poor, everywhere. A high living standard was the privilege of extractive elites rather than the normal reward for productive work. Had it not been for a fortuitous combination of circumstances that relatively recently produced a social model conducive to growth, this dreary state of affairs would most likely have continued. In poor countries it continues still.

If the prosperity of the high-income world rests on this platform, it has crucial implications for migration. Migrants are essentially escaping from countries with dysfunctional social models. It may be well to reread that last sentence and ponder its implications. For example, it might make you a little more wary of the well-intentioned mantra of the need to have "respect for other cultures." The cultures—or norms and narratives—of poor societies, along with their institutions and organizations, stand suspected of being the primary cause of their poverty. Of course, on criteria other than whether they are conducive to prosperity these cultures may be the equal of, or superior to, the social models of high-income societies. They may be preferable in terms of dignity, humanity, artistic creativity, humor, honor, and virtue. But migrants themselves are voting with their feet in favor of the high-income social model. Recognizing that poor societies are economically dysfunctional is not a license for condescension toward their people: people can as readily earn the right to respect while struggling against a hostile environment as while succeeding in a benign one. But it should put us on our guard against the lazier assertions of multiculturalism: if a decent living standard is something to be valued, then on this criterion not all cultures are equal.

Workers who migrate from poor countries to rich ones are switching social models. As a result their productivity rockets upward. It is possible to get the same productivity gain if functional social models spread to the low-productivity societies, instead of transferring their people to the high-productivity societies. Ideas are ultimately decisive, and they can flow through many channels. Societies do indeed pick up ideas and thereby transform themselves: in my lifetime I have seen several such episodes. Within western Europe in the 1970s Spain, Greece, and Portugal cast off dictatorships and embraced democracy. In 1989 the Soviet empire cast off communism, a transformation that reverberated around other regions as military regimes in Latin America and Africa were toppled. A remarkable wave of transformation is right before our eyes: the Arab Spring, which has transformed Tunisia, Egypt, Libya, and, as I write, shortly Syria. These transformations each demonstrate the potency of the idea of democratic institutions. At the onset of the Cold War the Soviet leader, Stalin, reportedly posed the rhetorical question, "How many divisions has the pope?" His implication that Soviet power trumped religious belief has since been revealed as precisely wrong: ideas beat guns. The question that should have been troubling him was, "Is the communist social model viable?" The transfer of ideas is enabling the rapid convergence of many once-poor countries with high-wage economies. This will reduce the need for migration and may reverse it. But there is no simple institutional blueprint that just needs to be copied. Institutions, narratives, norms, and organizations do not need to look the same everywhere, but they do need to cohere.

The movement of goods can also be a substitute for the movement of people. Indeed, an initial impetus to the migration of workers to high-wage countries was the need to get around the trade restrictions that rich countries imposed on imports from poor countries. In Britain the major clusters of Asian migrants in Bradford and Leicester were initially recruited to shore up the textile factories based there. The factories were no longer able to attract British workers because of rising wages in the rest of the economy. It would have been more efficient to relocate the textile factories to Asia, as indeed happened a decade or so later. But British trade barriers on the import of textiles closed off this option. As a result, the trade protection that temporarily preserved the factories bequeathed a permanent legacy of clusters of Asian immigration. Restricting the movement of goods, as Britain did, thereby inducing an offsetting movement of people, offers no overall economic gains. But it does generate a range of social costs. It is often asserted that increasing migration is an inevitable facet of globalization. But in fact this is just lazy rhetoric. Far from the movement of people being all of a piece with other aspects of globalization, movements in goods, capital, and ideas are all alternatives to moving people.

Where it is possible to reap the productivity gain by moving ideas, goods, or money rather than people, it is surely sensible to do so. Over the time frame of the next century, this is indeed what is likely to happen. But, as I now elaborate, these alternatives to migration are all too slow to close the massive gap in income between the poorest societies and the rich within our own lifetimes.

How the Income Gap Affects Migration

The growth of rich countries during that Golden Thirty Years and the stagnation of the poor are fundamental to understanding the origins of modern migration. The unprecedented prosperity of that period created pressures to reopen the doors. Full employment made employers desperate for workers. It also removed the fear that had inhibited workers from collective action, and so unions expanded and became more militant. Governments were themselves the main employer in the country, and so directly faced a labor shortage, but they also suffered the backlash of strikes and wage inflation that accompanied union militancy. In the race for growth, bringing in workers from countries with much lower living standards looked to be an astute move. The political Left needed to recruit for the expansion of public services and infrastructure; the political Right needed immigrants who would go precisely to the bottleneck areas, thereby accelerating growth and curbing militancy. So governments loosened immigration restrictions and indeed actively sought to attract foreign workers. Germany targeted Turks, France North Africans, Britain those from the Caribbean, and the United States Latin Americans; for example, America radically eased immigration through the 1965 Immigration Act.

In opening the door they could be confident that people would wish to come through it. The wide income gap gave people in poor countries a powerful economic incentive to move to rich ones. But despite the wide gap, the initial flow of migrants was a trickle, not a flood. As I will discuss in chapter 6, there are many daunting impediments to international migration over and above any legal restrictions.

Economists have only recently been able to model migration with the full array of techniques available to the discipline. The obstacle has always been that data on international migration has been hopelessly inadequate: economists could build theories, but we could not test them. Big data sets are the public capital goods of applied economics: the prolonged effort required to put them together discourages individual researchers from doing so, and so the task falls to the international economic organizations that have sustained resources and public interest mandates. In the last few years such data sets have been trickling out, but only in 2012 did the World Bank release a major one that will likely prove to be a vital resource for analysis. Our factual knowledge has advanced more in the past five years than in the previous fifty, but even so much of our data still stops at 2000.

With this caveat, we now know three big things about what drives international migration. One is that migration is an economic response to the gap in income: other things being equal, the wider the gap in income, the stronger the pressure to migrate. The second is that there are a myriad of impediments to migration, economic, legal, and social, that are cumulatively important, so that migration is an investment: costs must be borne before benefits can be reaped. Since poor people are least able to meet the costs of investment, this generates an offset to the pressure coming from a wide gap in income. If the gap is wide because people in the country of origin are desperately poor, their desire to migrate is likely to be frustrated. The third big thing we know is that the costs of migration are greatly eased by the presence in the host country of a diaspora from the country of origin.[9] The costs of migration fall as the size of the network of immigrants who are already settled increases.[10] So the rate of migration is determined by the width of the gap, the level of income in countries of origin, and the size of the diaspora. The relationship is not additive but multiplicative: a wide gap but a small diaspora, and a small gap and a large diaspora, will both only generate a trickle of migration. Big flows depend upon a wide gap interacting with a large diaspora and an adequate level of income in countries of origin.

By the 1970s the gap between the rich world and the poor was horrendous, but then the Golden Thirty Years came to an end and growth rates in the rich world slowed. Gradually, the baton of fast growth was picked up by developing countries, starting with East Asia. By the 1980s China and India, home to a third of mankind, were accelerating, in the 1990s Latin America started growing, and since the millennium Africa has been growing. But if the gap in income is initially wide enough, even if poorer countries grow more rapidly than rich ones there is a prolonged period during which the absolute gap widens. Suppose that per capita income is $30,000 in a rich country and $2,000 in a poor one, but that the poor country grows at 10 percent and the rich one at only 2 percent. Measured in ratios the two countries are converging at a rapid rate, but the absolute gap in income increases from $28,000 to $28,400 in a year. Measured in the dollar return on an investment in migration, migration is becoming *more* attractive, not less. Further, rising incomes in the countries of origin imply that the initial investment costs of migration are more affordable. Compound growth rates will eventually work their magic. If the poor country keeps on growing more rapidly than the rich one, at some stage the absolute gap in incomes will start to narrow again and the additional income will make little further difference to whether migration is affordable. But starting from a wide gap, the lag between growth rates and the narrowing of the income gap is very long. China is at last reaching the stage at which its absolute income gap with the rich countries is likely to narrow. But the absolute gap between the low-income countries and the rich ones will continue to widen for decades. Further, in the low-income countries, income remains so low that the costs of migration still matter: rising incomes will finance investment in migration. So although there are good prospects that poor countries will gradually catch up, for several decades the income gap will be wide enough to constitute a strong incentive to migration, and one that is actually increasing.

Migration produces diasporas, and diasporas produce migration: which is the chicken and which is the egg? For once, there is no conundrum. The prolonged period during the twentieth century in which the borders of rich countries were closed to migrants from poor countries implied that as of around 1960 there were no significant diasporas. Starting from 1960, migration preceded the buildup of diasporas. Because diasporas were initially negligible, despite the wide income gap, even once borders were opened, there was only modest migration. In the absence of a diaspora to receive migrants, the costs of migration were too high.

The interaction of the income gap and diaspora creates a striking and straightforward dynamic: the flow of migration depends upon the gap and the previous stock of migrants. As the stock accumulates, the flow increases, so that for a given gap, migration accelerates. Economists always search for equilibrium: a point at which opposing forces balance so that the system is at rest. The system of migration could be at rest in two distinct ways. The rate of migration could stay the same instead of accelerating, or, in a more profound sense of being at rest, the net flow of people between countries might cease. Might this simple process of interaction between an income gap and the diaspora produce either of these equilibria?

Why There Need Be No Equilibrium

For a given income gap, migration would only cease to accelerate if the diaspora stopped growing. Since migration is constantly adding to the diaspora, it will only cease to grow if there is some offsetting process reducing the size of the diaspora. The diaspora is a simple concept to understand, but a tricky concept to measure. Typically, measurements use proxies such as the number of people resident in the country who were not born in it. But the pertinent concept of the diaspora is defined not by birth but by behavior. What matters for the rate of migration is the number of people who are related to new migrants *and who are prepared to help them*. In that sense, the rate of exit from the diaspora depends not upon rates of mortality among immigrants, but upon the transmission of culture and obligations. I am the grandson of an immigrant, but completely useless for any aspiring immigrants to Britain from Ernsbach. Although I once went back to the beautiful village that my grandfather left, I have no connection either with its people or with other descendants of Germans in Britain: I am not part of a diaspora. But some other grandchildren of immigrants do belong to a diaspora so defined.

In most societies the boundaries of the diaspora are blurred: many people have one foot in their migrant past and the other in a mainstream future. But for purposes of analysis it is often useful to create clear categories and stylized processes that approximate to reality. We sacrifice the accuracy of a complete portrayal in return for simplifications that enable us to work out the likely implications of interrelationships. So I will consider a stylized society in which an unabsorbed diaspora gradually merges into mainstream society by a process in which each year a certain percentage of the diaspora switches into the mainstream. The process of switching may take many different forms. An immigrant might simply lose touch with, and interest in, the society that she has left. A child of immigrants might redefine itself as a member of the host society, as did my father. Or, over time, each successive generation of descendants from immigrant families may become more psychologically distant from their country of origin. The proportion of the diaspora that switches each year may be high or low, and I will refer to it as the *absorption rate*. So, for example, if each year two out of every hundred members of the diaspora were absorbed into mainstream society, the absorption rate would be 2 percent.

Absorption rates vary depending on where migrants are from and where they have arrived. They vary according to government policies. I discuss such influences more thoroughly in chapter 3. But at this stage I will introduce only one straightforward influence on the absorption rate: it depends directly upon the size of the diaspora itself.

Size matters because the more interactions that a member of the diaspora has with the indigenous population, the more rapidly she is likely to merge into it. But while some of her interactions will be with the indigenous population, some will be with other members of the diaspora. The larger is the size of the diaspora relative to the indigenous population, the smaller will be the proportion of her interactions with the indigenous. This is because there is a practical limit to the total number of interactions that people can manage. Typically, the total number of genuine person-to-person interactions is limited to around 150.[11] So the larger the diaspora, the fewer social interactions there will be with the indigenous, and therefore the slower the absorption rate will be. I should note that in principle, there is an offsetting effect. The larger the diaspora, the more social interactions the indigenous population has with it, and so indigenes absorb diaspora culture more rapidly. But while ever the diaspora remains a minority, the typical diaspora member will have far more contacts with indigenes than the typical indigene has with the diaspora. So if contact carries the same absorptive punch in each direction, the absorption process will be predominantly through the adaptation of migrants. Although a larger diaspora increases adaptation by indigenes, this is unlikely to offset the reduced rate of adaptation of migrants.[12] The important implication is that the larger the diaspora is, the slower its rate of absorption will be.

Introducing a Workhorse

We now have all three of the building blocks we need to understand the dynamics of migration. The first block is that migration depends upon the size of the diaspora: the larger the diaspora is, the easier migration will be. The second is that migration adds to the diaspora, whereas absorption into mainstream society reduces it. The third is that the rate of absorption depends upon the size of the diaspora: the larger the diaspora is, the slower its absorption. It is time to fit the three blocks together. If you possess intuitive genius you will be able to do this unaided. But most of us need some help, and this is what models are for.

A model is a workhorse. Its advantage is that it can provide clear answers to questions that are sufficiently complex to be beyond the reach of unaided intuitive understanding. Models are not alternatives to such understanding; they provide the scaffolding that enables us to grasp what otherwise we might miss. The simplest way of showing how this particular model works is through a diagram. Diagrams can be clarifying, and this one carries a lot of insight relative to its difficulty. From time to time through the book I will use it to generate new insights, so it is worth a few moments of concentration. All diagrams portray some space: almost everyone is familiar with the typical newspaper diagram in which time is measured along the bottom (the horizontal axis), and some newsworthy number such as the unemployment rate is measured up the side (the vertical axis). The diagram in Figure 2.1 portrays a space in which the rate of migration from Tonga to New Zealand is measured up the side, and the size of the Tongan diaspora in New Zealand—the stock of unabsorbed immigrants and their descendants already in the host country—is measured along the bottom.

Now depict the first building block: how migration depends upon the diaspora. Of course, migration also depends upon other things, notably the income gap. So for the moment keep the income gap constant so that we can take it off the stage, leaving just the diaspora

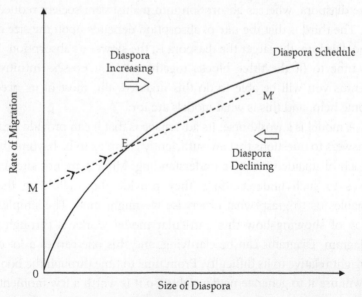

Figure 2.1 The Opening of New Zealand to Migration from Tonga

and migration in focus. For example, we might consider a host country such as New Zealand, and a country of origin such as Tonga, and try to picture how the rate of migration from Tonga to New Zealand varies with the size of the Tongalese diaspora in New Zealand. What you will picture is something like the line M-M' in the figure. Even when there is no diaspora, there is some migration, because the income gap induces some people to relocate. But the larger the Tongalese diaspora is, the faster the migration from Tonga. It will be convenient to have a name for this relationship. Genuflecting to economics, I will call it the *migration function*, but you could equally call it *diasporas support migration* since that is all it is depicting.

Now I turn to the second building block: the flows into and out of the diaspora. What are the combinations of the diaspora and migration at which the inflow from migration equals the outflow from absorption? Evidently, only if the number of new Tongalese immigrants joining the diaspora is matched by the number of past Tongalese migrants and their offspring who cease to be members of the diaspora will the size of the diaspora stay the same. In turn, only if the diaspora is constant will migration stay constant. While the Tongalese diaspora is growing, migration from Tonga is getting easier and so will be accelerating.

Many combinations of migration and the diaspora keep the diaspora the same size. For example, suppose that each year 2 percent of the Tongalese diaspora leave it. If the Tongalese diaspora in New Zealand is 30,000, then each year 600 places become vacant. So the diaspora will be constant if 600 Tongalese immigrants arrive. This link between the absorption rate and the number of immigrants has a simple implication. The Tongalese diaspora will accumulate until it is fifty times the rate of migration.

The combinations of the diaspora and migration that keep the diaspora the same yield the *diaspora schedule*. What does it look like? One point on it is obvious: if there is neither any diaspora nor any migration the diaspora will stay constant at zero. So one point on the schedule is the corner of the diagram.[13] To the left of the *schedule* the diaspora is too small for the number of vacancies generated by absorption to match new immigration. As a result, the diaspora is growing. To the right of the *schedule* the diaspora is shrinking. I show these changes, which economists rather portentously term *dynamics*, by the arrows.

To take stock, we have a picture showing that migration is helped by the diaspora and that the diaspora is fueled by migration and slimmed by absorption. The last building block shows how the rate of absorption depends on the diaspora. The bigger the diaspora is, the more social interactions its members have with each other, and so the slower their rate of absorption into mainstream society will be. The absorption rate is simply the *slope* of the schedule.[14] The slower the absorption, the flatter the schedule will be, so as the diaspora gets larger the schedule gets flatter.

Again, if you are an intuitive genius, then you do not need the model to see how the three different forces play out. But with the model it is straightforward: we can actually predict both where the rate of migration from Tonga to New Zealand will settle down, and the eventual size of the Tongalese diaspora. Of course, our predictions will depend upon our estimate of how Tongalese migration responds to the size of the diaspora and on how the rate of absorption of Tongalese into mainstream society depends upon its size. The model can be no better than the numbers that go into it. But it tells us how these relationships fit together.

From a glance at the diagram you can instantly see where the equilibrium will be: where the lines cross each other. At this point the Tongalese migration induced by the diaspora matches the rate of absorption, which keeps the diaspora the same size. For a given income gap, the rate of migration remains constant and the Tongalese diaspora remains the same size.[15]

Not only is it an equilibrium, but the forces of change inexorably bring the society to it. Until migration commences there is no Tongalese diaspora in New Zealand, so migration starts from point M. As a result, the diaspora grows. But as the diaspora grows, migration becomes easier and so accelerates. Migration and the diaspora fuel each other, marching along the *migration function* together. But rising migration and a growing diaspora do not continue indefinitely. Once migration has accelerated to the point at which it reaches the *diaspora schedule*, no further change occurs. The diaspora has increased until vacancies from absorption match entry from migration. Migration and the diaspora fuel each other in a burst of mutual acceleration, but the fuel eventually burns out and both stabilize.

My depiction of migration from Tonga to New Zealand is entirely hypothetical: I do not know the actual shape of either the *migration function* or the *diaspora schedule* for this pair of countries, and I doubt whether anyone else yet does. In the same spirit of hypothetical analysis I am going to tweak the diagram by taking a pair of countries between which the income gap has been rather wider. We are no longer looking at Tonga and New Zealand in the twenty-first century, but at *The Windrush*, the boat that brought the first migrants from the Caribbean to Britain in 1948. Once the barriers of the Second World War and the 1930s Depression are over, the incentive to migrate is so powerful that this migration is much larger than that from Tonga to New Zealand. Depicting this in Figure 2.2, the migration function has shifted upward: for any given size of the diaspora there is more migration. The change may sound as if it would be of little consequence, but the result is dramatically different. Whereas previously the *migration function* and the *diaspora*

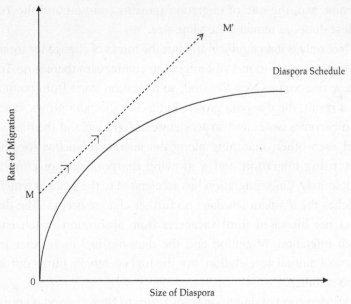

Figure 2.2 The Opening of Britain to Migration from the Caribbean

schedule crossed, now they miss each other. The implication is that there is no equilibrium: migration keeps on accelerating and the diaspora keeps on accumulating.

I should emphasize that I have used Tongalese migration to New Zealand and Caribbean migration to Britain only as stylized examples to illustrate a process. I do not mean to suggest that in actual fact migration from the Caribbean to Britain would not have reached equilibrium. We will never know how unrestricted migration would have played out because in 1968 the British government got sufficiently worried about mounting opposition to accelerating immigration that it imposed restrictions to limit the rate.

But the real value of a model is not that it can illuminate why something happened, it is that it can be used to predict the effects of hypothetical situations, including changes in policies. This model will be our workhorse when the time comes, in chapters 5 and 12, to analyze migration policies. By using it we will be able to show why reactive policies are liable to be damaging and that better alternatives are available.

So much for the first sense of equilibrium: where the rate of migration stabilizes. The other sense, in which the net flow of people ceases, will only occur once the income gap is eliminated. The system I have sketched is a simple interaction of stocks and flows: the stock of past migrants in the diaspora, and the flow of new migrants. Simple stock-flow models are common in all sorts of contexts. In the typical stock-flow systems that are crudely analogous to migration, such as water flowing between two tanks with different initial levels, the flow itself gradually closes the gap: one tank fills up, and the other drains down. This would apply in our present context if migration drove incomes down in host countries and raised incomes in countries of origin. The simple economic models used to predict huge income gains from global migration have just this property. Migrants are the equilibrators: in the absence of impediments to movement, migration continues until incomes are equalized. At this point, migrants themselves may feel a bit like suckers: they have moved for nothing. Those who have remained in countries of origin end up gaining just as much. The indigenous population of host countries loses, but it can comfort itself with the thought that others have gained more than it has lost. As a description of the effects of nineteenth-century migration from Europe to North America, or for that matter from Ernsbach to Bradford, this is not a bad first approximation.[16] As the Midwest was opened up, smallholders who migrated could get larger plots of land than they had farmed back in

Europe. As the Midwest filled up and Europe became less crowded, plot sizes gradually equalized. Eventually, farmer Schmidt in Germany was as well off as farmer Schmidt in Iowa. But as an analysis of migration from a country that has missed out on prosperity and an advanced modern economy, this simple model is worthless. Modern migration is not a quest for land; it is a quest for efficiency.

As you will see in subsequent chapters, the feedback forces from migration onto income in both host countries and countries of origin are weak and ambiguous. Further, even though migration has accelerated, it is tiny relative to the stocks of labor in both the host countries and the countries of origin. So the feedback mechanism depends upon changes that are small and generate responses that are weak. Migration from poor countries to rich ones is not likely to have much impact on closing the income gap.

Facts and Their Implications

We have arrived at some solidly based facts that have powerful implications. The first fact is that the income gap between poor countries and rich ones is grotesquely wide and the global growth process will leave it wide for several decades. The second is that migration will not significantly narrow this gap because the feedback mechanisms are too weak. The third is that as migration continues, diasporas will continue to accumulate for some decades. Thus, the income gap will persist, while the facilitator for migration will increase. The implication is that migration from poor countries to rich is set to accelerate. For the foreseeable future, international migration will not reach equilibrium: *we have been observing the beginnings of disequilibrium of epic proportions*.

The acceleration of migration is apparent from the aggregate data. Overall, the global stock of immigrants increased from

92 million in 1960 to 165 million in 2000. But this increase in the total masks the key change in composition. Migration from the rich world to the poor world shrank to just a few millions. Migration within the rich world flatlined: more movement within Europe being offset by less migration from Europe to the New World. Note that during this period there was a huge increase in both trade and capital flows within the rich world. So much for the inevitability of globalization leading to an increase in migration: within the rich world it didn't. The stock of migrants who had moved from one developing country to another grew modestly from around 60 million to 80 million. What took off, from under 20 million to over 60 million, was migration from poor countries to rich ones. Further, the increase accelerated decade by decade. The largest increase, both absolutely and proportionately was during 1990–2000, at which point the global data currently stops. It is a reasonable presumption that 2000–2010 continued this acceleration.

As migration accelerated, the high-income societies responded by retightening their immigration controls. Primarily this was because the acceleration in migration coincided with deceleration in the growth of the high-income economies: the Golden Thirty Years came to an end. Unemployment rates, which had dropped to around 2 percent by the time immigration controls were loosened, rose to around 8 percent and stuck there. The rise in unemployment was not caused by immigration, but it eliminated the obvious arguments that had been responsible for opening borders, while introducing an apparently obvious argument for closing them again. Variations in policy lags and differences in economic cycles between countries led to some countries tightening almost coincident with others liberalizing. The major American liberalization was in 1965; the first British tightening was in 1968. Australia switched from heavily subsidizing immigration through the 1960s to heavily restricting it by the 1990s.

But just as the initial opening of borders had been based on little more than short-term political opportunism, the subsequent tightening of restrictions was securely based on neither an understanding of the process of migration and its effects nor a thought-through ethical position. Migration policies were furtive and embarrassed. Astonishingly, as migration policy soared up the rankings of the policy priorities of voters, the mainstream political parties dodged the issue. The stance of the political Left, which by this time was largely pro-migration, appeared to be "downplay the issue, have as much immigration as we can get away with, and claim it is pro-growth." The stance of the political Right, which by this time was largely anti-immigration, appeared to be "vaguely oppose migration, but do not be explicit for fear of association with racists, and do nothing that would slow growth." Nature abhors a vacuum, and so do political opportunists. The space left by the mainstream political parties rapidly came to be occupied by a gallery of grotesques: racists, xenophobes, and psychopaths found themselves with an audience of decent, ordinary citizens who were increasingly alarmed by the silence of the mainstream parties. To date, the only thing that has kept extremist parties at bay has been first-past-the-post voting systems. In the United States and Britain, where such voting systems make it hard for third parties to survive, extremist parties have not gained traction. But in virtually all societies with more inclusive voting systems, single-issue anti-immigrant parties now attract a remarkably high share of the vote. Far from forcing sane debate on immigration policy by the mainstream parties, the emergence of extremists has further frightened them away from the issue. Either you regard this outcome as a shocking condemnation of ordinary people, or as a shocking condemnation of the mainstream political parties: I view it as the latter. It is little short of disastrous that in some European countries around a fifth of the indigenous electorate is wasting its vote on pariah parties because the mainstream parties will not properly debate what these voters regard, rightly or wrongly, as the most important issue facing their country.

So what should an honest discussion of migration policy be about? First, it should be based on impartially gathered facts such as the big three I set out above. Of course, there are many more, some of which I will cover in subsequent chapters. Based on these facts, there should then be an open discussion of the ethics of immigration restrictions. If all restrictions are a priori ethically illegitimate, migration will build to rates far in excess of those experienced in recent decades. If they are legitimate, they will be confronting greatly increased pressure of demand, and so the principles and mechanics of controls will become far more important.

PART 2

Host Societies

Welcome or Resentment?

CHAPTER 3

The Social Consequences

IN THIS PART I AM GOING TO ADDRESS the question of how future migration might affect the indigenous populations of host societies. The key word in that sentence is "future." I am not primarily interested in the question "Have the consequences of migration been bad or good?" If pressed for an answer, I would come down on the side of "good," but it is not the pertinent question. Imagine, for a moment, the improbable: a consensus that the right answer is "bad." Even in that eventuality no sane person would advocate that migrants and their descendants should be repatriated. In modern high-income societies mass expulsions are unthinkable. So although "Have the consequences of migration been bad or good?" is concrete and entirely meaningful, it is as irrelevant as asking, "Should you have been born?" The question I am ultimately going to address is hypothetical: if migration were substantially to increase, how would it affect host populations? As I showed in chapter 2, migration accelerates unless subject to effective controls, so although this question is hypothetical, it is pertinent. To orientate your thinking, my approximate answer is going to be that the effects of migration follow an inverse-U shape, with gains from moderate migration and losses from high migration. The important issue is therefore not bad or good but "How much is best?" In turn, I will argue that the answer to "How much?" hinges upon how rapidly migrants merge with the indigenous society.

Since this part is about the effects on host populations, I should admit that some economists think that it is invalid even to pose the question, let alone to try to answer it. The most common ethical framework used in economics is utilitarian—"the greatest happiness of the greatest number." Applied to global issues like migration, it leads to a simple and striking answer: what happens to the indigenous populations of host countries is of no consequence as long as overall there are global gains from migration. Although this moral compass—utilitarian universalist—is standard in economic analysis, it bears little relationship to how most people think. I will turn to this later in the book. Another objection to posing the question, advanced by Michael Clemens, a prominent economic advocate for increased migration, is to say, "Who is 'us'?"[1] He argues that viewed from the perspective of some future century, "us" will be the descendants of both those who are currently indigenous and immigrants. For him the pertinent question is whether immigration produces long-term benefits to these descendants. As you will see, I think that such imagined futures can be helpful. But in this instance the argument smacks of a sleight of hand. To see the limitations of an argument, it sometimes helps to guy it to an extreme. Suppose, entirely hypothetically, that mass immigration led to the exodus of most of the indigenous population, but that the remainder intermarried with immigrants and their joint descendants ended up better off. Knowing this ex ante, the indigenous population might reasonably determine that mass immigration was not in its interest. Whether it would then be legitimate for this perceived self-interest to translate into restrictions on entry would depend upon whether freedom of movement is a global right.

A related argument is that all indigenous populations are themselves mongrels, the result of previous waves of immigration. The extent to which this is the case varies considerably between societies. It is most obviously the case in the countries of nineteenth-century immigration: North America and Australasia. Since Britain is an island, it is evident that all indigenous people are at some point descendants of immigrants, but until the mid-twentieth century the population had been remarkably stable. Recent advances in the study of DNA have enabled genetic descent to be established for each gender: son-father-grandfather and so on back in time; and daughter-mother-grandmother and beyond. Astonishingly, around 70 percent of the current population of Britain are directly descended in this way from the people who inhabited Britain in pre-Neolithic times: earlier than 4,000 B.C.[2] Since then Britain has periodically been enriched by waves of immigration. Neolithic culture and technology were most likely introduced by immigrants. The descendants of Anglo-Saxon and Norman immigrants between them forged the English language, its multicultural origins accounting for its incomparable richness of vocabulary. Huguenot and Jewish immigrants were important stimuli to commerce. But these migrations, stretching over a six-thousand-year period, were in total evidently quite modest. Stability has an implication: over such a long time span, repeated intermarriage results in a pattern in which anyone from the distant past who has descendants alive today is likely to be an ancestor of the entire indigenous population. In this sense the indigenous population literally shares a common history: both the kings and queens and their serfs are our common ancestors. I doubt that Britain is exceptional in this respect. But for the moment the issue is whether the fact that indigenous populations are themselves descended from immigrants in the very distant past erases the right to restrict immigration. Those who have had the good fortune to ascend a ladder should not haul it up after them. But whether this is an appropriate analogy for migration depends upon context. The pre-Neolithic people who came to Britain were settling an unpopulated territory, just as with first settlement elsewhere in the world. They were not taking advantage of an income gap between established societies such as motivates present-day migrants. Indeed, for thousands of years after first settlement Europe was no more prosperous than other parts of the world. The initial settlers were not climbing a ladder, so their descendants cannot be hauling one up.

But for now I ask you to park the issue of whether controls on migration are unethical. Whether or not host populations have the moral right to manage migration in their own interests, they currently have the legal right to do so. Since scarcely any governments claim the legal right to restrict exit, all controls on global migration flows are ultimately set by the perceived interests of host populations. However, although the high-income countries are democracies, their migration policies have often not reflected the views of the indigenous electorate. For example, in Britain 59 percent of the population (which includes immigrants) consider that there are already "too many" immigrants. Nevertheless, in the long term, in a democracy indigenous populations are going to permit migration only to the extent that they perceive themselves to benefit.

So, without more ado, what are the effects of migration on indigenous populations, and how might these effects differ according to its scale? Fortunately, there has been considerable recent research. As an economist I naturally first explored those effects that are economic. However, I came to realize that on this issue the economic effects are unlikely to be decisive. Despite the polemical claims on both sides of the immigration debate, the evidence suggests that the net effects are usually likely to be small. For most societies migration policies should not be determined on the basis of the economic effects. So I am going to put the social effects ahead of the economic effects and then try to assess them in combination.

Mutual Regard

The social consequences of migration depend upon how immigrants relate to their host societies. At one extreme they are treated purely as workers and are not permitted to enter the society on any other basis. A few host societies adopt this approach, and for them the effects are indeed purely economic. But in most countries immigrants become part of the society, as opposed to merely members of its labor force, and so engage with other people in a variety of ways. Migrants increase the diversity of society. In some respects this is beneficial: greater diversity brings greater variety and so brings stimulus and choice. But diversity also brings problems. This is because in a modern economy well-being is greatly enhanced by what might be described as mutual regard.

By mutual regard I mean something stronger than mutual respect. I mean something akin to sympathy or benign fellow-feeling. Mutual *respect* may be fulfilled by everyone keeping a respectful distance from others—the noninterference of the "Don't dis me" society. In contrast, mutual *regard* supports two types of behavior that are fundamental to successful societies.

One is the willingness of the successful to finance transfers to the less successful. Although such transfers have become heavily politicized and dressed up as a conflict between ideologies of libertarianism and socialism, they are more truly rooted in how people regard each other. By this I do not mean how the welfare of other people anywhere on earth should be counted, as in the universalist version of utilitarianism common in economics, but how we regard other members of our own society, and by extension, how we define the limits of what we recognize as the society to which we belong. Mutual regard, or sympathy, gives rise to feelings of loyalty and solidarity for those fellow members of our community who are less fortunate.

The other key way in which mutual regard affects economic outcomes is through cooperation. By cooperating, people are able to provide public goods that would otherwise not be well supplied by a purely market process. Cooperation is enhanced by trust but, to be other than quixotic, trust must be underpinned by a reasonable presumption that it will be reciprocated. The bedrock of rational trust is knowledge that the society is characterized by mutual regard: because people have some sympathy for each other, it is sensible to presume that a cooperative action will be reciprocated.

These cooperative outcomes tend to be fragile. The most popular public institution in Britain is the National Health Service. Ostensibly the NHS requires a willingness to make transfers through taxation rather than cooperation, but in fact it needs both. One unwritten convention has been the willingness to be forbearing in the face of minor errors. This convention has recently eroded so that a growing proportion of the NHS budget is being eaten up by compensation claims. Once claims become common, it would be quixotic for people who suffer mistakes not to seek money in return. But inevitably, this reduces the quality of care that can be financed. A further consequence is that the NHS is now less willing to admit, and therefore learn from, its mistakes. The replacement of forbearance by lawsuits is an instance of the collapse of a fragile cooperative equilibrium.

The trade-off between the benefits of greater variety and the costs of reduced mutual regard has to be navigated by each society. But one principle is reasonably clear. The gains from greater variety are subject to diminishing returns: that is, like most aspects of consumption, each extra unit confers fewer extra benefits. In contrast, beyond some unknowable point the losses from reduced mutual regard are liable to increase sharply as thresholds are crossed at which cooperation becomes unstable. Cooperation games are fragile because if pushed too far they collapse. In fancier language, equilibrium is only *locally* stable. So moderate migration is liable to confer overall social benefits, whereas sustained rapid migration would risk substantial costs. The rest of this chapter substantiates those potential risks.

Mutual Regard: Trust and Cooperation

Through research in experimental economics we now understand what enables cooperative outcomes to persist. In a sense successful cooperation is a minor miracle, because if almost everyone else is cooperating, whatever is the objective will be achieved even if I don't help: so why should I incur the costs of helping? In the vicinity of the fully cooperative outcome, each individual has a strong incentive to free ride, so cooperation should usually be unstable. The persistence of cooperation turns out to depend on more than just widespread benevolence. The vital ingredient is that there should also be sufficient people who go the extra mile. That extra mile is punishing those who do not cooperate. In most modern societies people have become increasingly reluctant to be judgmental about the behavior of others. But the comforting face of benevolence is dependent upon a tough-minded and judgmental minority. Punishment is costly, so people will only be prepared to do it if they have sufficiently internalized not just benevolence, but moral outrage at those who free ride. Cooperative outcomes are fragile because if enough people back away from punishment, then non-cooperation becomes the rational strategy. The role of hero performed by the people who punish noncooperation in turn creates the possibility of ultimate villains. The minor villains are the people who do not cooperate, but the supervillains are people who punish the heroes. Again, since punishment is costly, systematically to get satisfaction from punishing the heroes can only arise if some people feel moral outrage not against the people who undermine cooperation, but against the people who try to enforce it. Why might some people have such dysfunctional moral codes? Conceivably, some people might be ideologically opposed to cooperation, believing that the individual is all, so that those who try to enforce cooperation are enemies of freedom. But the more pertinent possibility is that some people regard being punished as an assault on their honor, even if they are guilty as charged. By extension, some people might feel an overriding personal loyalty to others even if they free ride and then are outraged by those who punish them for doing so.

Trust and cooperation do not arise naturally. They are not primordial attributes of the "noble savage" that get undermined by civilization: Jean-Jacques Rousseau was spectacularly wrong. The evidence suggests precisely the opposite: trust and cooperation beyond the family are acquired as part of the functional attitudes that accumulate in a modern prosperous society. One reason that poor societies are poor is that they lack these attitudes. Two brilliant new studies of Africa illustrate how a lack of trust has been perpetuated. One draws on the painstaking reconstruction of Africa's deep past that historians have achieved over recent decades. Cumulatively, historians have now recorded over eighty violent intergroup conflicts that occurred prior to 1600. Timothy Besley and Marta Reynal-Querol thought to code all these conflicts by their spatial coordinates and investigate whether they were correlated with modern conflicts.[3] The correlation turned out to be remarkably strong: the violence of over four hundred years ago proved to be disturbingly persistent today. So by what mechanism has this persistence occurred? The researchers suggest that the transmission mechanism is the lack of trust created by violence that echoes down the decades. Noncooperation can be reinforced by its own moral code of honor: the vendetta, in which wrongs are repaid with wrongs. Vendettas are a normal aspect of clan-based societies. Historically, clans have been the most common basis for social organization, and in many poor countries they continue to be so.[4] As Steven Pinker shows, vendettas are reinforced because wrongs are systematically exaggerated by victims and minimized by perpetrators, so that the retaliation regarded as justified by victims of the initial wrong creates a fresh wrong in the eyes of the new victims.[5] Vendettas only end once the entire moral code of honor is abandoned. A classic instance of such a transition is the demise of dueling in western Europe during the nineteenth century: it was ended by a cultural revolution that made it look ridiculous.

The other new study of Africa looks at the legacy of the slave trade. Whereas intertribal conflict leads to a collapse of trust *between* groups, the slave trade destroyed trust *within* them: often people sold their own family members to traders. Nathan Nunn and Leonard Wantchekon show how the intensity of the slave trade several centuries ago maps into reduced per capita income today.[6] The transmission route was again the persistence of a lack of trust.

Among the societies with which I am familiar, the one with the lowest level of trust is Nigeria. I find Nigeria exhilarating and vibrant: people are engaged and witty. But Nigerians radically, deeply, do not trust each other. Opportunism is the result of decades, probably centuries, in which trust would have been quixotic, and it is now ingrained in ordinary behavior. Nor is opportunism a reflection of poverty: in Nigeria I typically stay at good hotels where none of the occupants can be poor. My room routinely includes the notice "Honoured guest, before your departure all the contents of this room will be checked against our inventory": the hotel has learned that otherwise its honored guests would run off with the contents. A more serious aspect of the society's opportunism is that it is not possible for Nigerians to get life insurance. This is because, given the opportunism of the relevant professions, a death certificate can be purchased without the inconvenience of dying. For a while this made it very attractive for those Nigerians who valued a large windfall more than a troubled conscience to take out life insurance policies. But as the numbers mounted, the fragile convention on which life insurance rests broke down. Clearly, the root of the problem here was the failure of doctors to internalize professional norms.

If the level of trust differs markedly between societies, the tactics people adopt in games that require cooperation will also differ. This has indeed recently been tested through experimental games.[7] A team of researchers arranged for the same game to be played under standard laboratory conditions by university students in sixteen countries. They found that in some societies supervillains were ruinously numerous. If heroes punished another player for free riding, the outraged response was to punish the heroes. The researchers then investigated whether these differences in behavior were related systematically to observable characteristics of the countries in which the students lived. Directly, the differences in behavior were related to differences in social capital, in other words to trust. But these in turn could be related to differences in the rule of law. In countries where the rule of law was weak, people were opportunistic and so untrusting, and were inclined to be supervillains in cooperation games. I suspect that these differences in the rule of law can be traced yet further back to the difference between moralities based on loyalty to the honor of the clan, and moralities based on the Enlightenment concept of good citizenship. Supervillains should have a bad conscience according to the standards of the Enlightenment, but they are behaving morally according to the precepts of loyalty to the clan. Note that this does not exonerate supervillains. Moral relativism hits the buffers of an economic absolute: trust is conducive to the social cooperation that is valuable for prosperity.

The Cultures of Migrants

So mutual regard, trust, and moral outrage against those who free ride all support an equitable and cooperative society. How does this relate to migration? Migrants bring not only the human capital generated in their own societies; they also bring the moral codes of their own societies. Thus, unsurprisingly, Nigerian immigrants to other societies tend to be untrusting and opportunistic. In a classic study of differences in cultural attitudes, Ray Fisman and Edward Miguel compared the payment of parking fines by diplomats in New York.[8] During the key period, diplomats had legal immunity from fines, and so the only restraint on a refusal to pay was their own ethical standards. Fisman and Miguel found that the behavior of diplomats from different countries varied enormously but was well explained by the corruption level prevailing in the country of the diplomat, as measured by standard surveys. Diplomats brought their culture with them. The study also investigated whether, through exposure to New York, diplomats gradually absorbed local standards of behavior: in this case, the incidence of nonpayment would gradually converge on the very low levels already prevalent among diplomats from the low-corruption countries. Instead, the opposite happened: diplomats from high-corruption countries continued not to pay fines, whereas those from low-corruption countries became less likely to pay. The most reasonable interpretation of these results is that diplomats did not absorb the norms of New Yorkers, but instead began to absorb the norms of the diplomatic community. Not only do attitudes to parking fines reflect the culture of origin, but so do attitudes toward social redistribution. Geert Hofstede has attempted to measure a wide array of cultural differences between countries systematically.[9] His measures correlate with reasonably well-measured differences in observable behavior such as the murder rate. So, uncomfortable as it may be, there are large cultural differences that map into important aspects of social behavior, and migrants bring their culture with them.

People in all societies manage mutual regard for their families, and usually also for their local communities, but the distinctive feature of the high-income societies is that mutual regard embraces a much larger group of people, namely fellow citizens. Thus for example, the French are more willing to cooperate with each other and to make transfers to other citizens than are Nigerians, and this supports a range of institutions and norms that have enabled France to become much richer and more equal than Nigeria. Such differences in mutual regard are not genetic: in the distant past France used to be like Nigeria. But France has benefited from a succession of intellectual revolutions that have gradually reconfigured how people perceive each other.

The effect of immigration then depends partly on its scale and partly on the speed with which immigrants adjust to the trust norms of their host society. Do Nigerian doctors practicing in Britain adopt the norms of indigenous doctors, do they remain a

self-referential group like diplomats, or, in extremis, does a sufficiently large influx of Nigerian doctors retaining Nigerian practices
lead to the decay of coordination games such as life insurance?
I doubt that in any of the high-income societies migration has to
date significantly jeopardized the mosaic of cooperation games. But
I am not assessing past migration: I am trying to infer from relationships observable today the possible consequences of continued
acceleration.

Countries vary in their success in enabling immigrants and their
children to take on the norms of their new society. Among the most
successful is America. Children growing up in America almost
unavoidably assimilate American values. The same is far from true
in Europe. Indeed, there is now mounting evidence that the opposite happens: the children of immigrants are more resistant to
adopting the national culture than are their parents. The children of
some immigrant groups appear to want to self-identify as different
from the prevailing national identity around them. Everyone has
multiple identities, such as worker, family member, and citizen.
Like everyone else, immigrants can take on such multiple identities.
But how they balance these identities affects their behavior. For
example, in a fascinating experiment, researchers tested Asian
American women on mathematics, first emphasizing either their
Asian identity or their female identity. They found that when women
were primed with their Asian identity, they achieved significantly
higher scores than when primed with their female identity.[10] I
have already discussed the economic significance of identity at the
level of the firm.[11] One narrative that, while not unique to immigrants, is atypically common is that of self-improvement. Immigrants are self-selected from among those people who are most
aspirational for themselves and their children. That is why they
choose to uproot themselves. This attitude about opportunities

tends to make them particularly good workers. Thus, migrants and their children may find that preserving a separate identity is no handicap to individual success. This is supported by a new study of second-generation Turkish immigrants to Germany.[12] Germany first treated its Turkish immigrants as temporary guest workers and then adopted a strategy of multiculturalism. Unsurprisingly, neither the first nor the second generation has integrated into mainstream German society. Reflecting this, Chancellor Merkel recently described multiculturalism as "an utter failure." So Germany is clearly at the low absorption end of the spectrum of how rapidly migrants assimilate. The study investigated whether the choice between German and Turkish identity made by the second generation of Turkish migrants mattered for how well they performed in education and for whether they got a job. The approach was to trace back to the first language in which migrants had been raised: German or Turkish. This language choice, made by parents, strongly influenced the identity that their children took on: those reared in Turkish as their first language were much more likely to self-identify as Turkish and less likely to identify as German. However, as long as they subsequently became fluent in German, this made no difference to schooling or jobs. So migrants themselves do not lose out from preserving a separate identity. But as members of society, if immigrants reject national identity, they are indeed choosing to be outsiders. This does not matter in the narrowly defined behavior spaces of school and work, but it may matter in the open behavior space of society at large for the informal nationwide systems of cooperation and political support for redistribution, which distinctively characterize the high-income societies.

The process whereby young people adopt identities is not well understood. Until recently, economics would not even have considered the question well posed: people's preferences were simply givens, and the determinants of behavior were the incentives with which people were faced. However, a central recent insight in social science is that people copy the behavior of others. This appears to have deep neurological foundations: in the mid-1990s it was discovered that the mirror neuron fires both when someone performs an action and when they see someone else perform it.[13] In effect, copying is the neurological default option; behavior that avoids copying an action requires a conscious decision to override the mirror neurons. This does not make us slaves to the actions of others, but experimental psychology is revealing that we are disturbingly suggestible. A subject who observes rude behavior will behave more rudely; a subject who is told to think about the characteristics of the elderly will themselves walk more slowly. The behavior of young people does not follow simply from their genes, their training, and their incentives: it is strongly influenced by what they see around them as pertinent role models. But what, then, are the pertinent role models?

Some role models are much more accessible than others. A concept closely related to that of role model is that of stereotype. They differ in their normative connotations—something described as a role model is usually implied to be good, whereas something described as a stereotype is usually implied to be bad. But what they have in common is the idea that they are ready-made identities. Try to strip the concept of a stereotype of its negative connotations because it has a different characteristic that is important. A role model is usually some individual person: a father can be a role model for a son. But a stereotype is the product of a culture: it is not an individual, who can only be known within a personal circle of acquaintance, but a generalized role model accessible to anyone who is part of a culture. The idea of a "good plumber" is in this sense a stereotype. We do not need to specify all the aspects of behavior that constitute a good plumber; that has already been done for us in any society that has the concept. Betwixt and between role models and stereotypes are celebrities. Celebrities are individual people and so can be role models, but they are also part of a culture and so readily available to anyone within the culture. Typically, the culture will portray a celebrity not as "the man in full" but as a caricature in which certain features are emphasized: in effect, a celebrity is a role model who can function as a stereotype.

Popular culture is a menu of readily downloadable stereotypes. Some young people will be impervious to popular culture and grow up as their own eccentric selves. But many will download some ready-made identity and live it out, probably periodically changing it. If this is a reasonable depiction of how behavior gets shaped, then public policy can influence behavior in two distinct ways. The conventional approach of the past century has been through incentives: for example, we tax behaviors that are socially damaging, such as smoking, and subsidize behavior that is socially useful, such as raising children. But the scope to influence behavior through incentives has often proved to be quite limited: once someone has downloaded the identity of a criminal, incentives may have little power to deter socially costly behavior. The other way of shaping behavior is to alter the menu of downloadable stereotypes. This is, of course, controversial, but to take an example, there is ample evidence that repeated exposure to violence through the media reduces inhibitions to violent behavior.

How might this relate to migration? We now have three seemingly unrelated sets of propositions. One is about mutual regard: mutual regard is valuable for the trust that supports cooperation and the empathy that supports redistribution. The habits of trust and empathy among very large groups of people are not natural but have grown as part of the process of achieving prosperity; immigrants from poor countries are likely to arrive with less of a presupposition to trust and empathize with others in their new society. The second is about identity: the identity that people adopt matters for their behavior; many people adopt some of their identity by downloading stereotypical behavior from their culture. The third concerns the identity adopted by immigrants. In an important new study, a team of researchers investigated variations in the willingness of Hispanic immigrants to America to cooperate for public goods. The variations were designed to pick up differences in how immigrants perceived both their identity and their degree of exclusion from the society around them. An innovation of their research was that in addition to the conventional laboratory games designed to tease out attitudes to others, it included real neighborhood public goods, such as local health and education facilities. They found powerful evidence that how migrants see themselves influences their willingness to cooperate and contribute to public goods. The more migrants self-identified as Latino as opposed to American, the less they contributed. One practical insight of the research was that fluency in English mattered: the more that English was the language used at home, the stronger was a sense of American identity.[14] This study is new and I am not aware of an equivalent one for Europe. However, in America immigrants absorb national identity more readily than they do in Europe, where if anything resistance to taking on national identity appears to be increasing. A reasonable speculation is that in Europe immigrants absorb prevailing levels of trust more slowly than in America.

Immigration, Trust, and Cooperation

A growing group of people with low levels of trust can be destabilizing. If the number of people playing opportunistic rather than cooperative strategies accumulates, it may no longer be sensible for other people to continue to play cooperative strategies. The vital ingredient of successful cooperation is that enough people should be willing to punish those who do not cooperate. But if those who adopt opportunistic rather than cooperative strategies are disproportionately immigrants, punishment may become misconstrued as discrimination, making people more reluctant to punish. Further, other members of the immigrant group might misconstrue punishment of opportunism as discrimination against their group and themselves punish those who punish to enforce cooperation: recall that these are the "supervillains" in cooperation games who most effectively cause cooperation to collapse.

Unfortunately, there is evidence that these concerns are not merely hypothetical. Robert Putnam is a leading social scientist at Harvard and the world's foremost scholar of the concept of "social capital." Using a large American sample, Putnam investigated the effect of immigration on trust.[15] One of his findings, though disturbing, was standard: the greater the proportion of immigrants in a community, the lower were mutual levels of trust between immigrants and the indigenous population. In other words, far from proximity leading to greater mutual understanding, it leads to heightened mutual suspicion. This relationship has been widely studied, and Putnam's results are in line with the majority of other such research.

However, Putnam went on to a completely new result that is far more troubling. The higher the level of immigration in a community, the lower the trust was not just between groups *but within them*. A high level of immigration was associated with a lower level of trust of each other purely among the indigenous people in the community. As would be expected from the importance of trust in fostering cooperation, the lower level of trust manifested itself in many different forms of reduced cooperation. Putnam refers to this effect as "hunkering down": indigenous people living in a high-immigrant community retreat into themselves, trusting less and taking less part in social activities, having fewer friends, and watching more television. I have described Putnam's results as if they were merely simple correlations between the level of immigration in a community and the level of trust. Were this the case his work would be open to a myriad of statistical objections. But Putnam is a highly professional researcher who has carefully investigated and controlled for a wide range of spurious possible explanations for his results. All social science is open to challenge, and given that Putnam's results were politically anathema for many social scientists, it was inevitable that his results would be contested. While they may turn out to be misleading, they should not be dismissed. Despite Putnam's evident discomfort with the results, as he says, "it would be unfortunate if a politically correct progressivism were to deny the reality of the challenge to social solidarity posed by diversity."[16]

The big limitation of Putnam's analysis, which he recognizes, is that it is based on a snapshot: it does not track changes over time. This does not invalidate the results, but the data cannot be used to analyze what might make immigration less damaging to cooperation. What we are left with is a robust result that immigration reduces the social capital of the indigenous population. Unfortunately, at least in America, the effect is quite powerful. At the level of individual communities, it becomes more pronounced the larger the proportion of immigrants is. While the result that social capital even within a group is reduced by diversity is new, the more general result that ethnic diversity in a community inhibits cooperation has been found in many different contexts. Evidently, the salient feature of ethnicity is not genetic but cultural: distinct ethnicities stand proxy for distinct cultural identities. An important example of this research, which ultimately demonstrates the irrelevance of genetic differences, is a study by Edward Miguel of Berkeley that investigated the provision of a basic public good—the maintenance of a village well—in rural Kenya.[17] Kenya has around fifty different ethnic groups, and so villages differ considerably in their degree of ethnic diversity. Miguel found that those villages that were more diverse were less able to cooperate to maintain a well. I will return to this result in chapter 11 because there is an important twist to it.

Putnam and I are not suggesting that the present levels of migration-generated diversity have seriously endangered cooperation. The point is not to castigate past migration but to recognize the potential risks from further large increases in diversity. Paradoxically, the high mutual regard societies of Europe may be more at risk than the lower mutual regard evident in the United States. Unsurprisingly given their very different histories of migration, European countries are more cohesive than the United States, and their norms reflect this greater cohesion. Putnam's results apply only to the United States; to my knowledge there is no equivalent analysis yet for Europe. However, two factors are not encouraging. One is that America has been more successful than Europe in integrating immigrants. This is hardly surprising: unlike Europe, "American identity is rooted not in nationhood but rather in the welcoming of strangers."[18] The other is that America's recent immigrants are largely Hispanics, as in the study discussed above: people from Latin America. Diversity depends not just upon numbers but on cultural distance between immigrants and indigenous populations. The cultural gap between Hispanics and other Americans looks to be smaller than that between immigrants to Europe from poor countries and indigenous Europeans. But would such a judgment of cultural difference merely be prejudice?

An ingenious objective way of measuring cultural distance is by a language tree. Modern linguistics has constructed a global language tree, showing how many branches separate any two distinct languages. But while this provides an objective measure of the distance between languages, does the resulting measure have any traction as a proxy for the distance between cultures? Montalvo and Reynal-Querol have recently investigated whether language distance proxies cultural distance by using it in an analysis of intergroup violence within countries.[19] Does the language gap between two ethnic groups in the same country significantly affect proneness to violent conflict between them? They find that the greater the distance between languages, the greater the proneness to intergroup violence. Their analysis is global, but since intergroup violence in the high-income societies is very limited, the important observations are from other societies. Hence, the result should not be misinterpreted as implying that the immigration of linguistically distant groups makes a high-income society significantly more prone to violence. Modern developed societies have built so many defenses against intergroup violence that it is not a significant issue: the specter of "rivers of blood" flowing from violence between immigrants and the indigenous, which was first raised by Enoch Powell and has haunted liberal intellectuals ever since, is deluded melodrama regardless of the scale of migration.

I am concerned with trust within groups, not with violence between them. But if, in those societies where intergroup violence is not unthinkable, language distance increases it, there is a reasonable presumption that language distance also proxies the more general difficulties associated with forging mutual regard. Mutual antipathy and mutual regard are the endpoints on a common spectrum. Measured by language steps, the cultural gap between immigrant groups and indigenous populations in Europe is indeed usually wider than between Hispanics and the host population of America. Hence, although Putnam's results are for America, Europeans would be cavalier to dismiss their pertinence to Europe simply on the grounds that Europe is different. Here are a couple of recent instances from Britain that may reflect just such a process of the undermining of social capital within the indigenous population that Putnam is analyzing.

Some Illustrative Anecdotes

I have headed this section "Some Illustrative Anecdotes," and that heading is important. The purpose of the following stories is to help the reader see how the rather academic-sounding discussion of trust and cooperation might actually play out in a real context. Since the social theory is about how immigration can weaken trust within the indigenous population, the illustrations necessarily illustrate just that. But whereas theories can only be read with what Daniel Kahneman terms "slow" thinking, stories trigger "fast" thinking reactions: in other words, intellectual effort is replaced by visceral emotions. For the writer this poses a problem: without illustrations the ideas remain too dry to have meaning; with illustrations they risk becoming explosive. To lessen that risk, let me be clear that the following stories are not analyses: the interpretations that I place on these stories might well not be correct. But that they could be correct should help you to grasp the more abstract proposition that migration can have social costs and that on a sufficient scale, the social costs of migration could become substantial.

One of the most remarkable achievements of British culture has been the convention of an unarmed police force. Within Britain this seems so natural that it has largely been taken for granted—there is no right to bear arms in Britain; on the contrary, it is a serious criminal offense. By international and historical standards this state of affairs is highly unusual—a triumph of the civilized society.

The convention is evidently fragile, depending as it does upon a tacit agreement between police and criminals that guns will not be used. Given that the police are unarmed, any one individual criminal would gain an advantage from being armed, yet if criminals routinely carried guns, the police would also do so. This creates a coordination problem *within the criminal community*. Somehow, over the decades, British criminals managed to enforce a code of not carrying guns. In the 1960s one criminal spectacularly breached this code, shooting dead three policemen. What happened next was remarkable: the criminal tried to go to ground within his London social network, but could not do so. Finding himself ostracized, he fled to remote moorland, where he was caught living in a tent. Recall that game theory tells us that such willingness of other players to punish transgressors of cooperation is essential to preserve good outcomes. Now roll on to 2011: two policemen arrest a known criminal with previous convictions. In the car taking him to the police station the criminal pulls a gun; the police are also armed and shoot him dead. What then ensues is in stark contrast to the 1960s. The social network of the criminal rushes to the police station and mounts a protest, several hundred strong, against the police. The criminal, Mark Duggan, is posthumously turned into a community hero. Of course, the two instances of armed criminality are not identical: in the former the criminal fired his gun, in the second, while the criminal pulled his gun, he did not get a chance to fire it. Further, in the decades between the two incidents trust in the police had considerably eroded. But the opposing responses of the criminals' social networks are nevertheless striking. That of the 1960s reinforced the convention that it is impermissible for criminals to resort to guns, whereas that of 2011 undermined it. A salient difference is that Duggan was Afro-Caribbean and that the crowd of protesters that assembled outside the police station was also

Afro-Caribbean. The bonds between Afro-Caribbean people living in the locality were evidently stronger than any sense that in possessing a gun he had breached a taboo. Over a long period relations between the Afro-Caribbean community and the police have revealed a mutual lack of trust, and there is evidence of racism within the police force. Members of Duggan's social network responded to the news by presuming that the police had shot him unnecessarily, rather than, what is perhaps a more likely interpretation of events, that the police officer reacted to an immediate situation of extreme fear. As a result, far from ostracizing him, his network came out in solidarity, aiming to punish the police. This is precisely the role of the "supervillains" whose behavior is ruinous in cooperation games. Such responses clearly threaten to undermine the fragile convention that neither criminals nor the police should carry guns.

The fact that the police were indeed in this instance armed tells us that the convention had already considerably eroded. In part, this erosion was a reflection of a much more generalized acceptance of violence in Western cultures that, as Steven Pinker has shown, began in the 1960s, reversing a centuries-long gradual reduction.[20] But it may also have been accentuated by a highly specific difference between the culture of Afro-Caribbean immigrants and that of the indigenous population. While there are variations within the Caribbean, Jamaican culture is among the most violent in the world. For example, murder rates are *fifty times* higher than in Britain. Guns are normal, so it is unsurprising that Jamaican immigrants brought their gun culture with them; indeed, the gun culture of the Afro-Caribbean community is now a specific concern of British crime policy. That culture is perhaps why Duggan carried a gun: his uncle had been a gun-toting gang leader in Manchester, and he did not recognize it as breaking a taboo. Manchester itself is struggling to live down its description as "Gunchester." In 2012 it was the scene of a tragedy in which, for the first time in Britain, two police-women were shot dead. The shooting has initiated a serious public discussion as to whether British police should be armed: the convention is revealed as fragile. The perpetrator in the Manchester shooting was indigenous. Evidently, over the years, the norms of indigenous criminals have changed. Quite possibly this would have happened without any immigration. But it is also possible that the immigration of a substantial group of people whose social convention was to carry guns had destabilized a benevolent social equilibrium.

Recall that the key prediction of Putnam's work is that the decline in cooperation induced by immigration extends to the internal behavior of the indigenous community. The key damaging effect is not that immigrants and the indigenous population do not trust each other; it is that indigenous people lose trust *in each other* and so resort to opportunistic behavior. What happened in the aftermath of the Duggan incident may illustrate this breakdown in the restraints on opportunism within the indigenous population. The Duggan protests metastasized into looting that spread across the country, conducted by many thousands of teenagers from the indigenous population. The behavior was, as far as we can tell, utterly apolitical. Indeed, public buildings were ignored. The targets were shopping centers, where teenagers smashed windows and gleefully stole the standard accoutrements of teenage life. The behavior was also unrelated to ethnicity: essentially, indigenous teenagers looted from indigenous shops. Such behavior by indigenous teenagers was without precedent. In part, it was accounted for not by cultural change but by technological advance: teenagers, being particularly IT-savvy, were able to coordinate looting on their mobile phones, thereby achieving the safety of numbers. The police response also came in for criticism: having been accused of being too aggressive in the Duggan case, in the riots they were accused of being too passive. But police response to criminal behavior is less revealing than the behavior itself. The looting can reasonably be seen as reflecting a decline in social capital within the indigenous population.

Here is a further possible instance of social capital being undermined by "supervillains." It comes from community responses to the deaths of British soldiers fighting in Afghanistan. Their bodies are flown to an airbase in Britain, and a tradition has developed whereby as the coffins are driven through the local town people line the streets to pay their respects. This is itself a reflection of a much broader socially important convention in which heroism in public service is honored. The British soldiers fighting in Afghanistan reflect the multiethnic composition of British society, and so one of the soldiers killed was a British Muslim. A member of his family was interviewed on television to speak of the soldier's courage and their pride in his sense of duty. But the speaker was too fearful of reprisals from a small but violent minority of other British Muslims to reveal either his name or face: he was interviewed in silhouette. This was a fear of "supervillains." Of course, the fear may well have been misplaced, but one reason that "supervillains" are so destructive of social capital is that there do not need to be many of them to alter behavior.

Anecdotes are not analysis: they merely illustrate what analysis is trying to show. Working merely from anecdotes we can stack up counterexamples where immigrants have clearly contributed to the social capital of the indigenous population. One major such example is the Notting Hill Carnival, which has become the largest annual street party in Europe. The carnival was created by the Afro-Caribbean community, drawing on its pre-immigration traditions, and huge numbers of people from the indigenous population now also take part in it. Street parties are paradigmatic of the social capital that Putnam sees as so valuable.

So, working from anecdote, we could stack up whatever apparent support for whatever story we find appealing. For this reason, it is not a valid means of analysis: rather, it is the stuff of opinionated advocacy. The anti-immigration lobby will use one set of stories and the pro-immigration lobby a counter-set. The purpose of the above anecdotes in which immigration appears to have undermined social capital is decidedly not to strengthen an argument. Their role is purely to help the reader see what in practice both Putnam and the game-theory analysts of fragile cooperation are getting at.

Mutual Regard and Equity

So far I have focused on mutual regard as a source of trust, in turn supporting cooperation. But mutual regard is also important for an equal society. Without public transfers, the distribution of income is likely to become grossly unequal. Indeed, in recent decades technological pressures toward inequality have probably been compounded by social pressures.[21] The growth of the information economy has probably increased the returns to exceptional mental abilities. This new elite of the highly educated tend to cluster together not just at work but socially. They intermarry and their offspring have powerful educational advantages. As a result, social mobility is reduced: a trend that has been most marked in the United States and Britain, where countervailing government policies have been least active. It is not necessary to be on the political left to regard rapidly widening social inequality as undesirable. Wide differences in incomes can make a society less livable. Raghuram Rajan, a respected and sophisticated conservative economist, suggests that the political gridlock in America over fiscal policy may reflect the underlying divergence of interests between America's rich and America's poor: the population in the middle ground has shrunk.

So a technologically and socially driven process of widening inequality calls for more active redistribution. The objective need not be the traditional rallying cry of the Left, a more equal society, but the more modest and conservative one of preventing rapidly increasing inequality. But, in fact, despite the growing need for redistributive policies, actual policies have shifted in the opposite direction. There has been not only a drift to lower taxation of incomes, but, more subtly, many goods and services that used to be supplied through the government are now supplied through the market. Michael Sandel has brilliantly anatomized this process, which since the 1960s has shrunk the role of the state and thereby contributed to rising inequality.[22] Lower taxation and the expanded role of the market have reflected and contributed to a weakened sense of a shared society.

For redistribution to be politically feasible, sufficient fortunate people must be willing to subsidize the less fortunate. So the regard of the fortunate for the less fortunate would need to be deepened. We are back to the concept of empathy: high earners need to be able to see low earners as themselves minus good fortune. Empathy comes from a shared sense of identity. An important way of building common identity is common membership in a network of reciprocal obligations.

The immigration of culturally distant people who disproportionately occupy low-income slots in the economy weakens this mechanism. Low-income people become less like high-income people. In turn, unless this is offset, it reduces the willingness of high-income people to make transfers to low-income people. Many influences contributed to the policies of reduced taxation and increased reliance on the market, not least that of the economics profession. But the pronounced increase in cultural diversity brought about by immigration may have been one of them. For example, the recent phase of the open door in Britain has coincided with a collapse in willingness to fund redistribution. In 1991 a substantial majority of Britons—58 percent—agreed that government should spend more on welfare benefits even if it led to higher taxes; by 2012 this had fallen to an inconsequential minority—28 percent. The argument that cultural diversity reduces the willingness to redistribute income has been formalized and investigated by two highly distinguished Harvard professors, Alberto Alesina and Edward Glaeser.[23] They posed the question of why there has been so much greater willingness to accept redistribution in Europe than in the United States. Their explanation was that the distinctive attitudes of the typical European country were grounded in its greater cultural homogeneity. There is also some evidence that what erodes the willingness to redistribute is the rate at which diversity increases rather than simply its level. However, the importance of the level of diversity is supported by a wide array of evidence.[24] As predicted by the theory, the greater the level of cultural diversity, the worse the provision of redistributive public goods.

As with diversity and cooperation, particular cases merely have the status of illustrative anecdotes: with that caveat, exhibit A is California. Due to the conjunction of geography and opportunity, California has the highest incidence of immigrants of all American states. All these immigrants have arrived in the past fifty years, because until the 1960s America had a closed door. Most of California's immigrants cluster in the lower range of the income distribution. So, according to the theory, California has precisely the preconditions for a growing reluctance on the part of high-income groups to pay for redistribution. California is an immensely rich state: it can certainly afford redistribution. For example, it is home to Silicon Valley. But its most distinctive feature in recent decades has been the collapse of its public services. The schooling system in California has plummeted down the American league tables and is now comparable to Alabama, at the very bottom. The public universities, once world-class institutions, have been starved of funding. In part, the collapse in public services is a consequence of a change in spending priorities away from redistribution toward prisons. California used to educate its poor, whereas now it jails them. But the core of the problem is not the composition of spending but the lack of revenue. Despite its prosperity, California is acutely short of revenue because of a tax strike by higher income groups who succeeded in placing a cap on property taxes. Given the scale of the problem in California, it would be foolish to attribute it to any one cause. However, a plausible contributing factor is that mass immigration has undermined the empathy of fortunate indigenes for poor people. Perhaps in previous times those Californians who were well off saw the less well off as people like themselves who had had less good fortune, whereas now they see them as a distinct group to which neither they nor their children belong.

Just as the indigenous can fail to recognize immigrants as members of a common society, so immigrants can fail to recognize the indigenous. It is time for another anecdote: exhibit B is a grim British court case of 2012 in which a group of middle-aged Asian men ran a sex ring abusing indigenous children. Commentaries on the case tended to polarize into anti-immigrant arguments that such behavior typified Asian culture and politically correct comments that the case had nothing to do with immigration but showed that all middle-aged men are pigs given the chance. But such behavior is far from normal in Asian societies. Indeed, none of the abused children were Asian, and Asian families are noted for the sexual protection of their young people. Nor is it credible to dismiss the immigrant aspect of the case: middle-aged men are not pigs. These men were evidently applying radically different standards of conduct toward children according to their ethnicity: the children of the indigenous were "the other" and of less account.

So mutual regard is valuable in a society both for cooperation and for equity. It is challenged by the introduction of culturally distant groups. Immigrants from very different cultures are likely to arrive with less sense of trust in others. Their societies of origin are not immoral, but the basis of morality is different, reflecting the honor of a clan or family. As Mark Weiner shows in *The Rule of the Clan* (2011), honor codes used to be the global norm. They are remarkably persistent, and breaking them has been one of the triumphs of Western societies. On arrival, immigrants from honor societies may be seen by the indigenous population as "the other" and to see that population as "the other." If these behaviors persist, then the society will become less cooperative and less equal. So the key issue becomes whether they persist or erode: do immigrants absorb the norm of trust, and do both immigrants and the indigenous come to see each other as members of a common society?

The Absorption Rate of Diasporas

The rate at which diasporas are absorbed into society has powerful repercussions, and so the forces that determine it are themselves of interest. In chapter 2 I introduced one important influence: as the size of the diaspora increases, the additional interaction within the group crowds out interaction with the indigenous population, and so absorption slows down. I now introduce three other influences: the composition of the diaspora, the attitudes of migrants, and the attitudes and policies of host countries.

Absorption and the Composition of the Diaspora

For a given size of the diaspora, its composition is likely to affect how rapidly its members merge into the indigenous mainstream culture. Cultural distance is a meaningful concept: you may remember that we can measure it objectively by the number of steps of separation between the languages of two cultures as shown by a language tree. What is more, so measured, cultural distance has significant consequences. A reasonable presumption is that the wider the cultural distance is between migrants and the indigenous population, the slower the rate of absorption will be. I do not propose this as an iron law, but rather as a tendency. Recall that absorption can occur both by migrants adopting aspects of indigenous culture and by the indigenous population adopting aspects of the culture of migrants. But by either means, for a given set of policies, the wider the gap initially separating cultures is, the longer it is likely to take before they merge.

This innocuous-sounding presumption is going to have a surprising implication. As before, if you are an intuitive genius you will leap to it in one bound, but for the rest of us the workhorse model provides a helpful bit of scaffolding. To remind you, the *diaspora schedule* shows the combinations of the diaspora and migration at which the inflow into the diaspora from migration equals the outflow from the diaspora due to the merger into mainstream society. The rate at which the diaspora merges with the indigenous population is depicted by the slope of the schedule. The slower the rate of absorption, the smaller the increase in migration needed to sustain a given increase in the diaspora, so that slow absorption implies a flat schedule. In Figure 3.1, I compare two diasporas that are at different cultural distances from the indigenous population. For purposes of illustration I have chosen Poles and Bangladeshis in Britain, but it could equally

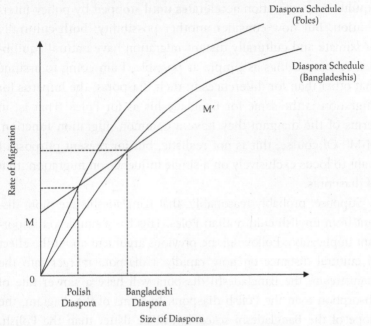

Figure 3.1 Diasporas and Migration in Equilibrium: Poles and Bangladeshis in Britain

have been Mexicans and Eritreans in the United States, or Algerians and Chinese in France. For any given common size, the one that is more distant will have the flatter sloping schedule.

The natural equilibrium for these two inflows is where their *diaspora schedules* cross the *migration function*. This shows what would happen in the absence of any policy interventions such as migration restrictions or strategies for changing the absorption rate of particular groups. As I discussed in chapter 2, the two lines may not cross, in which case there is no equilibrium and the natural rate of migration keeps increasing. So one possibility is that the culturally more distant migration process has no natural equilibrium: migration accelerates until stopped by policy intervention. But now consider another possibility: both culturally proximate and culturally distant migration have natural equilibria. To keep things as simple as possible, I am going to assume that other than for differences in their diasporas, the impetus for migration is the same for Bangladeshis as for Poles. That is, in terms of the diagram they have a common migration function, M-M'. Of course, this is not realistic, but for present purposes I want to focus exclusively on a single influence on migration: that of diasporas.

Suppose, probably reasonably, that Bangladeshis are more distant from English culture than Poles. This has a simple yet important implication. Following the previous argument about the effect of cultural distance on how rapidly a diaspora merges into the mainstream, the Bangladeshi diaspora will have a slower rate of absorption than the Polish diaspora. In terms of the diagram, the slope of the Bangladeshi *schedule* will be flatter than the Polish. Now the value of the diagram comes into its own, because the punch line leaps off the page. In equilibrium, the culturally more distant group, Bangladeshis, will have a larger diaspora. This much is unsurprising: being culturally more distant, Bangladeshis will merge less rapidly and so, for a common rate of migration, the stock of people who identify as Bangladeshi will end up larger than that of people who identify as Poles. But the more remarkable difference between the Bangladeshi and the Polish equilibria is that the rate of migration will end up permanently higher for Bangladeshis than for Poles.

While the first implication is intuitively obvious, this second one—that the rate of migration of the culturally more distant group will be permanently higher—is decidedly not obvious. Indeed, the opposite might have been the intuitive expectation. The model shows why intuition is wrong. So we get the paradoxical result that for a given income gap between countries of origin and a host country, *the sustained migration rate will be greater the more culturally distant is the country of origin from the host country*. As far as I can tell, this result has not previously been known. If that is so, then it vindicates why a model is valuable. Recall that the purpose of a good model is not to do our thinking for us, but to provide supporting scaffolding that enables our understanding to reach further than we could achieve by unaided reasoning.

So, armed with a new understanding that the greater cultural distance of a group increases its equilibrium rate of migration, think how this in turn feeds back onto the composition of the diasporas that build up in a host society. Over time, those migrants that are culturally proximate to the indigenous population absorb into it, while those that are culturally distant remain in the diaspora. As a result, as diasporas accumulate, on average they become more culturally distant. This in turn has consequences for the rate of absorption. Because a larger diaspora is on average more culturally distant from the indigenous population, the average rate at which it is absorbed slows down. Suppose, for example, that there are two countries of origin: one culturally proximate—"AlmostUsLand"— and the other distant—"Mars." Migrants from AlmostUsLand are absorbed more rapidly than those from Mars. As the diaspora builds up, a higher proportion of it is from Mars and so the average rate of absorption declines. This then is a further reason that the overall schedule—representing the sum of all the individual diasporas— becomes flatter as the diaspora increases. Later in this chapter we will see why such a flattening might have important consequences.

The effects discovered by Robert Putnam and others suggest that for a given rate of migration the social costs in terms of reduced trust within groups and increased tensions between them are higher the wider the cultural distance is. Hence, we have arrived at a paradox. The economics of migration is driven by the individual maximizing decisions of migrants and their families. Diasporas reduce the costs of migration, and so the larger the diaspora from a country of origin, the higher will be the rate of migration from it. But the social costs of migration are driven by the externalities that these privately maximizing decisions happen to generate. The paradox is that the economic logic of private maximizing decisions, which by definition reap the maximum economic benefit for decision takers themselves, appears also to increase the social costs.

Absorption and Attitudes of Migrants: Emigrants or Settlers

For a given size of diaspora, the psychology of migrants is also likely to affect the rate of absorption. I have suggested that popular cultures can be thought of as menus of downloadable stereotypes. The attitudes that migrants adopt may be shaped not just by the conventional individual economic variables such as income and skill, but by the stereotypes they adopt. Stereotypes of migration are not set in stone; they change, sometimes quite rapidly.

Just such a change in how migrants define themselves occurred following the end of the Napoleonic Wars in 1815. Thanks partly to the fall in shipping costs and the pent-up demand after a long war, mass emigration from Britain and Ireland to North America took off. There was a solid economic rationale for migration: the fertile lands of North America were available for settlement. But migration at this time was still a momentous decision: North America was not paradise—conditions were harsh. The economic historian of this migration, James Belich, recently spotted something fascinating about how migration was conceptualized.[25] By carefully counting the words used in hundreds of newspaper articles year by year he discovered that between 1810 and 1830 a subtle change occurred in the language used to describe migrants. Around 1810 the term most frequently used in newspapers was "emigrants." But by 1830, "emigrants" had given way to a new term, "settlers." I think that this change was not innocuous; the two terms imply radically different narratives. Emigrants are, essentially, leaving their society of origin behind them to join a new one. Settlers, in contrast, are bringing their society of origin with them. Does this distinction matter?

The most celebrated research paper on economic development of recent years, by the trio of Harvard- and MIT-based scholars Daron Acemoglu, Simon Johnson, and James Robinson, argues that migrants were historically valuable precisely because they were settlers.[26] What they brought with them, on this argument, was their institutions such as the rule of law and the sanctity of contract. By bringing these institutions, settlers enabled the countries to which they migrated to escape the poverty that had until then been the lot of mankind. But while settlers are undoubtedly good for settlers, they also frequently come with some major negatives for the indigenous population. No one can credibly argue that the settlers to North America were good for the indigenous inhabitants of the continent; that settlers to Australia were good for aborigines; or that settlers to New Zealand were good for Maoris. Settlers may, in the long term, prove to have been good for black South Africans, but this did not begin until power shifted to a government intent on ensuring benefits for blacks by transferring income from the settler population. Currently, the most high-profile settlers are Jewish Israelis: while the rights of Jewish settlement of the Occupied Territories are hotly disputed—and entirely outside the scope of this book—no one attempts to justify Jewish settlement on the grounds that it is beneficial for indigenous Palestinians.

In the post-Napoleonic period, when mass migration to North America took off, the group with the greatest appetite to become settlers was the Protestant community in the north of Ireland (emigration by Catholics from southern Ireland did not take off until after the potato famine of the 1840s). The most likely explanation for this propensity is that the Protestants in the north of Ireland were already settlers, brought in from Scotland and England by successive British governments to establish a loyalist population in the unruly colony. That early influx of settlers, now more than four centuries old, is still playing out in bitter divisions, and it is indeed unfortunately still just about meaningful to speak of a "settler" population and an "indigenous" population. Were the "indigenous Irish" to be polled on whether they were glad in retrospect that settlement had taken place from Scotland, it is doubtful that a majority would be positive.[27]

Settlers not only bring their own agendas, but they also bring their own culture. History is replete with instances of settler minorities diffusing their culture onto indigenous populations: an obvious example is missionary activity, which unsurprisingly can be shown to have left a permanent legacy of altered religious affiliation.[28] Sometimes the process of cultural diffusion is straightforwardly brutal. In Latin America the ubiquity of Spanish reflects past settler cultural power. In Angola the ubiquity of Portuguese names among the indigenous population reflects past cultural dominance by settlers. But sometimes sweeping cultural diffusion occurs through a decentralized process rather than a gun barrel.

The most complete such cultural takeover by a settler minority that I have come across occurred in Britain. The settlers were Anglo-Saxons and the period was roughly A.D. 400–600. Before 400 there were few Anglo-Saxons in Britain and at no time did they constitute more than around 10 percent of the population. Nor, as far as we can tell, did they violently conquer and subjugate the indigenous Britons: there is little trace of local violence in the archaeological record.[29] Yet the extent of Anglo-Saxon cultural takeover is apparent from language and religion. Before 400 the languages spoken were probably Celtic, approximately like modern Welsh, and Latin. By 600 the language was English. This new language contained no trace of the original Celtic language; instead it was an amalgam of settler dialects, influenced most heavily by Friesian. Similarly, the Christian religion, which in the early fifth century was the official religion of the country, had almost completely disappeared by the end of the sixth century. Christianity had to be reintroduced from Ireland and Rome. As far as we can tell from the inevitably scanty evidence, in the face of Anglo-Saxon settlement the indigenous Britons suffered a cultural collapse. Quite why the Britons suffered such an extreme loss of indigenous culture is unknown, but something evidently made it cool to imitate the Anglo-Saxons.

Whether we should lament the loss of an indigenous culture is debatable. If it happens, it is after all voluntary. But a culture is, par excellence, a public good: something that everyone values but no one in particular is rewarded for sustaining. At the global level we value the existence of other cultures even if we do not personally experience them: like many things we do not personally experience, they have existence value. At the individual level, parents usually want to pass on their culture to their children, but whether this is feasible depends not just on parental decisions but upon the choices of those around them. Thus, even if when viewed ex post, cultural change is welcomed by later generations, viewed ex ante, indigenous populations may reasonably be wary of the cultural challenge posed by settlers. The message that their grandchildren will take delight in having adopted someone else's culture is not, necessarily, reassuring. Of course, cultural change driven by settlers is only one among many forces for change; but unlike many of the others, it is optional. If indigenous populations do not want it, they need not accept settlers.

Settler migration from rich countries to poor is thus a two-edged sword for the indigenous: settlers bring institutions that are desirable, but cultures that are unwelcome. Now consider, hypothetically, the same process but from poor countries to rich ones. Imagine that poor settlers were to arrive in a rich society, intent on maintaining and spreading their culture. The social models they would bring with them would not be beneficial: poor countries are poor because their social models are dysfunctional. Prosperous societies would therefore have reason to be wary of such settlers.

Of course, poor countries do not send settlers to rich ones. Some modern migrants from poor countries to rich ones may wish they could behave like the former settlers, but they lack any semblance of the political power, based on superior violence, that settlers were able to wield. But perhaps the modern distinction between cultural assimilation and cultural separateness is somewhat analogous to that earlier distinction between emigrants and settlers. Emigrants leave their society of origin behind them and join a new one, making it easier for them to accept the need to assimilate. Settlers have no intention of assimilating: they expect to retain their values and culture in their society of arrival.

Two Meanings of Multiculturalism

Like everything about migration, the cultural narrative appropriate for migrants is highly politicized. At one end of the spectrum is assimilation: migrants intermarry with the indigenous population and adopt the ways of that population. I am the product of assimilative migration. So is Boris Johnson, the mayor of London, whose grandfather was a Turkish immigrant. At the other end of the spectrum is permanent cultural isolation of migrants in a hermetic community where schooling and language are separate and marriage outside the group is punished by expulsion. While such people can be citizens in the legal sense, they are only meaningfully part of society if it is seen as radically multicultural.

Multiculturalism began as a reaction to the narrative of assimilation. Perhaps the main impetus for it was a recognition that many migrants were not keen to assimilate: they preferred to congregate together in clusters that protected their culture of origin. Criticism of migrants for reluctance to assimilate might be seen as implying the superiority of the indigenous culture, which in turn might border on racism. But gradually multiculturalism was framed more positively by liberal elites as desirable in itself: such a society provided more variety and stimulus than a society with a single culture. In this form multiculturalism embraces the permanent coexistence of distinct cultures in the same country. The nation is reconceived to be a geopolitical space in which separate cultural communities peaceably coexist with equal legal and social status. The indigenous community may or may not remain a majority, but it has no special status. An alternative meaning of multiculturalism, perhaps closer to the original idea, is that rather than migrants being assimilated into the indigenous population, there is a cultural fusion between migrants and the indigenous. Unlike assimilation, fusion does not imply that the indigenous culture is either superior or privileged to that of the migrant.

So we have four competing narratives for migrants. They could arrive as traditional immigrants, accepting and aspiring to assimilation with indigenous culture. They could arrive with the intention of cultural fusion, bringing something distinctive to the common table from which all eat. They could arrive as cultural separatists, intent on isolating themselves from indigenous society while participating in the economy: in effect being guest workers. Or they could arrive as settlers, intent on spreading their culture among the indigenous. How do these four narratives stack up, both ethically and practically?

Assimilation and Fusion

Despite having fallen out of fashion, assimilation has some major advantages, not just for the indigenous but for everyone. Ethically, it is consistent with the golden rule of treating others as you would wish to be treated. Most notably, immigrants from poor societies can only ethically demand one of the other narratives if they have themselves supported that narrative back in their country of origin. Yet few poor societies have yet made a success of cultural separatism: this is indeed why Montalvo and Reynal-Querol find that cultural distinctness in poor countries increases the incidence of intergroup violence.[30] The most extreme advocates of cultural separateness speak of assimilation as "cultural genocide," but this is an inexcusable appropriation of a terminology whose emotive force should be reserved for the terrible situations when it is genuinely needed. The initial cultures of immigrants live on as dynamic processes in their countries of origin. There is no ethical reason that, as part of the deal in being admitted to a country, a migrant should not be expected to absorb the indigenous culture. In concrete terms, should migrants be expected to learn the local language? Having a common language is manifestly highly convenient: without a common language it is hard to have a common politics. More than that, it matters for mutual regard: remember that study of Mexican immigrants to America which found that those who learned to speak English were more willing to cooperate in public goods provision. So migrants who are unwilling to learn the local language are free riding on the public goods that a common language has helped to foster. Further, they are liable to be in breach of the golden rule: do they accept that immigrants to their own country of origin should not have to learn the local language either?

Not only is assimilation ethically well based, but its practical consequences are benign. Trust remains at a high level because migrants absorb the attitudes of the indigenous. Migrants and the indigenous learn to have the same mutual regard that already prevails within the indigenous community. Having common cultural behavior, the indigenous and immigrants come to recognize each other as the same people. This is gradually reinforced through intermarriage, which yields common descendants. The prospect of intermarriage is potentially important for the perception of identity. After a prolonged period without migration, such as most European countries experienced until the 1950s, the indigenous population can truly imagine itself as one people: most British people have been British since before Neolithic times. But migrants who expect to assimilate can participate in this same story. Not only will their offspring belong to a common people, but their offspring will themselves be directly descended from the same stock as the indigenous. An immigrant from Sierra Leone to Britain is unlikely to be descended from King Alfred, but through intermarriage her grandchildren are likely to be. If she herself recognizes that link through the future to the past, it may help her to embrace a new identity.

Multiculturalism as fusion is also ethically well based. Unlike assimilation, it readily affords equal dignity to the migrant as she is and to the indigenous. There is no hierarchy of cultures but rather the excitement and creativity of cultural blending. Fusion places demands upon both migrants and the indigenous to be curious about other cultures and to adapt to them. Given the numerical preponderance of the indigenous, there is some presumption that the new blended culture will be predominantly indigenous, and so migrants should be willing to accept larger cultural adaptation than the indigenous. However, such an expectation is merely a practical matter, not an ethical requirement. In Britain chicken tikka has become the most popular national dish, replacing the indigenous fish-and-chips. Chicken tikka is not literally the import of an immigrant culture; rather it is an innovation in Britain by an immigrant who rose to the challenge of fusing his own cultural expertise with an indigenous demand for fast food. In practical terms, fusion has consequences similar to assimilation. The only difference is the potential risk that the social model will become blended in such a way that damagingly dilutes its functionality: remember that in economic terms, not all cultures are equal.

Separatism and Settlers

In Europe, until recently the dominant tendency among political elites has been to espouse multiculturalism interpreted as the right to persistent cultural separatism. This orthodoxy and its supporting policies responded to, and legitimized, a preference for cultural separatism on the part of major groups of immigrants. One objective manifestation of separatism is the spatial pattern of immigrant residence. In the absence of policies to the contrary, immigrants tend to cluster. This is unsurprising: established immigrants are the obvious source of information and assistance for new arrivals. In some countries, such as Canada, governments have actively sought to counter this by requiring immigrants to settle in particular locations. Britain briefly attempted such a policy, dispatching a few Somali immigrants to Glasgow. Within weeks one of them was murdered in a racist attack and the policy was understandably abandoned. But in the absence of policy to the contrary, immigrants to Britain have become steadily more concentrated over time in a few English cities, most especially London. The 2011 census revealed that the indigenous British had become a minority in their own capital. Even within cities there is considerable concentration. According to an index of segregation, Bangladeshis in Bradford are the most spatially concentrated migrant population among thirty-six migrant clusters in Europe. In London migrants have clustered in the inner districts, while the indigenous have moved to the outer districts—the so-called doughnut pattern. Even within Inner London there is a further high degree of concentration. For example, the British census of 2011 revealed that over the past decade the fastest growing borough in the country has been Tower Hamlets, a borough of Inner London, the population of which grew by 26 percent. This growth was largely driven by immigrants from Bangladesh: nearly half of all the Bangladeshis in London live in this one borough, and conversely, over half of the children in the borough are now Bangladeshi.

Separatism also shows up, albeit in a less measurable form, in cultural practices. This is far from universal across immigrant groups and may have more to do with the rise of Islamic fundamentalism than with the policies of host countries. For example, French second-generation Muslim immigrants are less willing than their parents to let their children eat in school canteens.[31] British Bangladeshi women are increasingly adopting the full veil, whereas in Bangladesh itself the veil is not worn: in this case it is clear that immigrants are not hanging on to practices in their society of origin but are differentiating themselves from the indigenous population. In Britain this cultural separatism has led to the suggestion—by none less than the archbishop of Canterbury—that Parliament may need to introduce a parallel legal system based on sharia law. This would be a precise instance of migrants bringing their institutions with them.

One step on from legal separatism is political separatism: spatial and cultural separatism combine to facilitate it. One manifestation is when the political organizations of countries of origin re-form in host countries. For example, the local government of Tower Hamlets is apparently beset by feuding between the two dominant political parties of Bangladesh: the Awami League and the Bangladesh National Party. While the continued functioning of these Bangladeshi political parties within British politics is kept low profile, a more overt instance is that in 2005 British Muslims created their own political party, Respect. It has so far won two parliamentary by-elections, one in Tower Hamlets, the other in Bradford, both constituencies with very high concentrations of Muslim immigrants. Respect is an overtly Muslim and Asian party, appealing to voters on the grounds of their identity. It is also highly oppositional to the mainstream political parties. In Britain voters can register their vote either in person or by post. In Bradford the Respect Party gained three-quarters of the postal votes. Postal voting, somewhat like an unarmed police force, is a useful appurtenance of civilized society, but one that depends upon unspoken conventions. Postal voting has the potential to breach the principle of the secrecy of the ballot. In family structures in which the head of the family has considerable authority over other members, voting forms filled in at home may be subject to undue influence. Of course, this criticism applies to those indigenous households that are hierarchical; however, this is currently a clear cultural difference between many immigrant households and the indigenous norm.

The local government of Tower Hamlets is currently seeking to upgrade its political status from a borough to a city, which would give it considerably greater powers. Given the spatial concentration of immigrants, a continued trend toward political separatism would presumably produce cities ruled by immigrant-dominant political parties. This would approximate to the transfer of institutions, at the city level, from poor societies to rich. Somewhat ironically, precisely the opposite proposal is being made by the eminent economist of the growth process, Paul Romer. He shares the analysis that institutions are fundamental to the difference between poverty and prosperity, but adds a simple-sounding solution: *charter cities*.[32] A charter city would be created on territory that the government of a poor country would cede on a long-term lease to be governed under the laws of some developed country. Bangladesh might cede a patch of land to be ruled under the jurisdiction of Singapore, or for that matter of Britain. With the rule of law so secured, Romer predicts that both investors and people would flood in. An irony of Romer-in-reverse—the transfer of institutions from the societies of origin to the host societies—is that, if Romer is correct, what migrants are escaping from, though they may not realize it, is the dysfunctional institutions that as settlers they appear to want to bring with them.

Despite the momentary successes of the Respect Party in Britain, most immigrants do not separate themselves from the indigenous political organizations. Nevertheless, their political affiliations are often highly distinctive. At the 2010 British national election the indigenous electorate voted in favor of the Conservatives by a little more than four to three versus the incumbent Labour Party. In contrast, ethnic minorities voted by nearly one to five in favor of the Labour Party.[33] The voting pattern of immigrants is also distinctive across Europe. In America it is much less distinctive but still proved decisive in the 2012 election. Mitt Romney's somewhat menacing policy of "voluntary repatriation" unsurprisingly alienated many Hispanic voters.

A reasonable criterion for the political integration of immigrants is that their allegiance should broadly mirror that of the indigenous population. Not only is this an indicator of integration, but it is also the least threatening to an established democratic process. Democracy depends upon an alternation of power between parties, so that the overall vote should be roughly equally distributed between the major parties. If, at the other extreme, immigrants all support one particular party and become a substantial voting bloc, the only way in which the balance of power between political parties can be preserved is if the indigenous population votes disproportionately against the party that attracts immigrant support. This has two undesirable consequences.

One is that the inevitably aggressive and abusive rhetoric of political contest is likely to contaminate the issue of immigration: one party, being dependent upon the immigrant vote, will become perceived as pro-immigrant, while the other party, attracting overwhelmingly indigenous votes, will be seen as anti-immigrant. The other is that the alternation of power between parties involves periods in which immigrants are effectively unrepresented in government, and periods in which the party that has won a majority of the indigenous vote loses power because of the distinctive political affiliation of immigrants. Such situations are not hypothetical: in the elections for mayor of London precisely this pattern of allegiance has emerged: the strategies of the political parties reflect the doughnut-shaped distribution of the immigrant and indigenous populations. The distinctive distribution of the immigrant vote is not an inevitable feature of migration, nor is it anybody's "fault," but it is evidently undesirable. Because highly skewed immigrant political support has such undesirable consequences, there is a strong case that political parties should not differentiate themselves on immigration policies. This is one of the policy areas in which a common approach based upon a shared, evidence-based analysis is preferable. A common approach does not, of course, imply that the mainstream parties should ignore the issue.

Absorption and Attitudes of the Indigenous Population toward Migrants

Migrants from low-income countries are seldom made welcome in high-income host societies. They have to contend with racism and job discrimination, behaviors that demean their hosts and that can be countered by government policies. Here my focus is on the rate of absorption—the rate at which migrants merge into the indigenous population—and it is evident that such attitudes are liable to be an impediment. Social exclusion encourages separate identity.

Beyond the obvious point that xenophobia on the part of the indigenous is scarcely conducive to absorption, what has social science to contribute? One potentially important recent research result is that a more general attitude of the indigenous population matters, namely the level of trust.[34] The higher the level of trust is on the part of the indigenous population, not just regarding migrants but each other, the easier it is for migrants to integrate. This is scarcely surprising: immigrants are better able to form attachments to their new society—Putnam's "bridging capital"—if the indigenous population is trusting.

But if this is correct, then it introduces a further feedback mechanism into our model. Putnam finds that diversity reduces trust among the indigenous population: people hunker down. Translated into our framework, the larger the unabsorbed diaspora, the lower its trust. But now we must add the feedback effect of this reduction in trust onto the rate at which the diaspora is absorbed. The effect implies that the larger the diaspora is, the slower the rate of absorption. Absorption is reflected in the slope of the *diaspora schedule*; the slower the absorption is, the flatter it is. Building in this effect twists the schedule clockwise. I show the possible implications in Figure 3.2.

In the first panel the implication is a larger diaspora and a faster rate of migration. In the second, there is no longer a natural equilibrium: without migration controls, the diaspora and the rate of migration keep increasing. In the final panel the feedback effects of the diaspora on trust and back from trust onto absorption are sufficiently strong that beyond a certain size of diaspora, the number of people absorbed from it actually falls. If this happens, then there is a ceiling to the rate of migration. If migration controls exceed this ceiling, the diaspora keeps on expanding indefinitely.

Absorption and Host-Government Policies

The policies adopted by the host country government can, to an extent, affect the attitudes of both the indigenous population and migrants. Where multiculturalism defined as the maintenance of distinct migrant cultures is official policy, culturally specific social networks among immigrants are accepted and encouraged. Diasporas can become concentrated in a few cities, and some of the schools in these cities may have an overwhelmingly diasporic intake. The

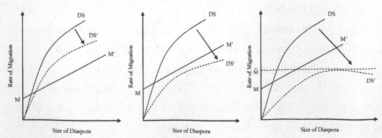

Figure 3.2 Trust and the Absorption of the Diaspora

encouragement of single-ethnicity immigrant schools would have been viewed with a horrified incredulity by the progressives who promoted busing policies for American schoolchildren in the 1960s.

However, while multicultural policies permit and encourage immigrant groups to preserve their cultural and social distinctiveness, policy toward the indigenous population is necessarily different. Well-founded fears of the potential and reality of anti-immigrant discrimination require government strongly to oppose the equivalent networks among the indigenous population. Prior to immigration, the social networks that exist in a country are, inevitably, exclusively indigenous. Antidiscrimination policy essentially forbids such networks: quite properly, they have to become inclusive.

Recent research by Ruud Koopmans finds that the rate of integration is indeed affected by these policy choices.[35] Integration is slower with multicultural policies. Multicultural policies have measurable effects such as a reduced aptitude of migrants in the national language, which we know reduces willingness to cooperate in public goods provision, and increased spatial segregation. Koopmans also finds that generous welfare systems slow integration by tempting migrants into remaining at the bottom of the social ladder. Of course, they also tempt the indigenous population, but they appear to be more tempting for migrants because they are accustomed to radically lower living standards. Even the modest income provided by welfare systems appears attractive, and so the incentive to get a yet higher income by getting a job is weaker. Between them, multiculturalism and generous welfare systems slow integration at home and at work. On Koopmans's figures, both their effects are substantial.

It is easier to build social networks within groups—what Robert Putnam calls "bonding" social capital—than between them—"bridging" social capital. It is also easier to build social networks in small groups than in large. Hence, the conjunction of multiculturalism and antidiscrimination laws can inadvertently give rise to a paradox: immigrants may be better placed to build bonding social capital than the indigenous population. Immigrants are permitted and encouraged to form tightly knit communities that sustain their culture of origin. Indeed, the term "community" becomes routinely affixed to any people who have emigrated from the same country of origin: as in "Bangladeshi community" or "Somali community." In contrast, by force of law all indigenous social networks are required to convert from bonding social capital to bridging. As a result, despite suffering the wrenching social upheaval of migration, the typical immigrant belongs to a denser . social network than the typical indigene. Perhaps this is why Putnam finds that the indigenous population fragments. People are less bonded into social networks—they "hunker down," in his phrase. The conjunction of policies of multicultural separatism applied to migrants, and antidiscrimination laws applied to the indigenous population, breaches the golden rule. One group receives treatment that cannot be conceded to the other. But quite evidently, the indigenous population cannot be permitted to maintain exclusive networks: here the integrationist agenda is essential.

The contrast between French and British policies toward immigrant cultural practices as exemplified by veil wearing illustrates the lack of coherence. Veil wearing quite literally destroys mutual regard. In France this was widely recognized as being incompatible with fraternity and so veil wearing was banned. The ban was supported by both communists and the mainstream Right. In Britain, while some politicians across the political spectrum lamented the increase in veil wearing, all parties defined it as an issue of liberty from government interference. But, as the French decision indicates, the liberty to destroy fraternity need not be considered a

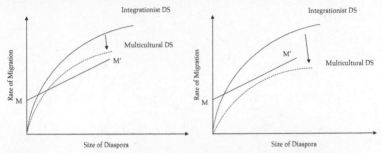

Figure 3.3 Integrationist versus Multicultural Policies in Equilibrium

human right. A consequence of these differences in policy choices is that although Britain has a much smaller Muslim population than France, veil wearing is increasingly common, whereas in France it is nonexistent.

Once again our model can be used to investigate how the choice between integrationist and multicultural policies eventually plays out if migration is allowed to accelerate. Their effect is to alter the absorption rate: integrationist policies raise it; multicultural policies lower it. The slower the rate of absorption, the flatter the diaspora schedule. Slower absorption can play out in two different ways: I show them in Figure 3.3. In the left-hand panel, by slowing absorption, multicultural policies eventually increase both the diaspora and the rate of migration. The right-hand panel depicts another possibility: slower absorption removes the possibility of equilibrium. In the absence of controls, the diaspora and migration both keep increasing.

You may be starting to see the scope for policy blunders. But first it is time to turn to the economic consequences of migration for host populations.

CHAPTER 4

The Economic Consequences

ECONOMICS PROVIDES TWO CLEAR PREDICTIONS about the effects of immigration on host populations. Inevitably, these predictions turn out to be too simplistic and sometimes utterly wrong, but before we get complicated it is well to start simple.

The economic well-being of indigenous households comes partly from private income and partly from government services. As to income, from the first principles of economics, the immigration of workers would be expected to reduce wages and increase the returns on capital. As a result, indigenous workers would be worse off and indigenous wealth owners would be better off. As to government-provided services, the existing stock of public capital—schools, hospitals, roads—would be shared among more people and so per capita provision would deteriorate. Poorer people receive more of their income from work and less from wealth and more of their overall well-being from government-provided services. Hence, the prediction from first principles of economics is that immigration benefits those indigenous people who are wealthy but makes poorer indigenous people worse off. In parody, this already oversimple analysis amounts to the assessment that the middle classes benefit from the archetypal immigrant staff such as cleaners and nannies, but that the working classes lose from competition with workers willing to accept lower pay and competition with immigrant families using social services.

Effects on Wages

It is time to turn to some evidence. Fortunately there is a highly credible new study of the effect of immigration on wages in Britain covering the phase of high immigration.[1] The study investigated not just the average effect on wages, but the changes along the entire spectrum from high to low. It found that at the bottom of the wage spectrum immigration indeed reduces wages, as predicted by the elementary principles of economics. However, along the rest of the spectrum it increased them. Further, the increases were larger and more extensive than the reduction: most indigenous workers gained from migration. While the decrease in wages at the bottom of the spectrum is consistent with elementary economics, the increase higher up the range can only be explained by introducing effects that simple analysis ignores. The researchers themselves speculate that the fluidity introduced by immigrant workers improved the efficiency of the labor market—immigrants concentrated in the cities and niches with the greatest potential for new jobs—in other words the expanding service economy of South East England. The greater ease of expansion enabled by immigration helped entrepreneurs to increase productivity and so pay higher wages.

Another new study of the effects of immigration on the labor market looks at evidence across Europe.[2] It also finds that immigration increases the wages of indigenous workers. However, the mechanism whereby this happens is itself revealing: on average in Europe, immigrants are more skilled than indigenous workers, although part of this is simply the churning of skilled workers around Europe. Skilled workers complement unskilled workers rather than compete with them and so raise the productivity of the unskilled. Of course, this effect depends upon immigration being sufficiently selective to raise overall skill levels.

A standard question economists pose when there are both winners and losers is whether the winners could afford fully to compensate the losers and still be better off. In respect of the impact on wages the better-off indigenous households gain much more than the poorest lose and so could afford to compensate them. However, what actually matters is not just whether compensation could be afforded but whether it actually happens. This returns us to our previous discussion of mutual regard and the willingness of the fortunate to help the less fortunate. While migration increases the need for such transfers, it may reduce the willingness to make them.

So the most likely effects of past migration on wages are that most indigenous workers end up gaining, while the poorest end up losing. While these effects are supportive of migration, they are all quite modest. The effects of migration on the wages of indigenous workers are trivial relative to the fuss that has been made about them. However, the empirical studies can only analyze the effects of migration within the observed range of variation. They tell us little about what would happen if migration continued to accelerate. For that, we would be safer to retreat to the economic first principles with which I started: the wages of most indigenous workers would drop considerably and remain lower for many years.

Effects on Housing

In high-income countries housing is the single most important asset, accounting for around a half of the entire stock of tangible assets. So in addition to the effect of migration on the flow of income from work, its effect on access to housing is potentially important for the economic well-being of the indigenous population. Evidently, through various routes, migrants increase the pressure on the housing stock.

Potentially the most important effect is that those migrants who arrive poor and have families compete with the indigenous poor for social housing. Because migrants tend to be poorer and have larger families than the indigenous population, they have atypically high needs for social housing, but meeting these needs inevitably crowds out the indigenous poor. While the effects on the wages of low-income indigenous workers are tiny, competition for social housing has been much more substantial: migrants are not only poor but they concentrate in a few poor neighborhoods. Even past levels of migration are likely to have had significant crowding-out effects. A continued acceleration would potentially seriously reduce the access of the indigenous poor to social housing.

Whether migrants should have distinctive rights to social housing is an active area of policy debate and an ethically tangled issue. While migrants are needy relative to the indigenous population of their host society, they have already benefited from a massive windfall relative to how their needs would have been met in their society of origin. Meeting the additional tranche of needs provided by social housing requires a transfer from indigenous people who are themselves needy relative to the standards of the host society. Social housing is not the only such rationed public good: a particularly acute conflict is in the classroom. The children of those immigrants who do not speak the indigenous language need extra attention, but so also do the underperforming children of the indigenous poor. Assiduous targeting of budgets could to an extent address this concern, but in practice teachers will be faced by hard choices as to which need takes priority. Universalist utilitarians will nevertheless conclude that since migrants are needier than the indigenous people whom they displace, overall global well-being has been enhanced. But others may conclude that since migrants were already fortunate to have gained a windfall in their private income, there is little reason to transfer a disproportionate share of social housing to them.

The principle of equal treatment of migrants and the indigenous can be applied either to groups or to individuals. If a certain percentage of the indigenous population is provided with rationed access to social housing, then equality of treatment of groups implies that migrants should be entitled to the same percentage, overriding differences in individual characteristics. This has indeed evolved to be the practice in some localities. The impetus has in part been a sense of fairness as perceived by the local indigenous population, and in part a practical concern for integration.

The ethical case against equal rights for groups is that to avoid second-class status each individual immigrant should have precisely the same rights as an individual indigenous person. If migrants are needier than the indigenous, then needs-based criteria should indeed grant greater access to excludable social housing. However, the second-class-citizen argument applied at the individual level itself has limits. As I discussed in chapter 3, the provision of public goods such as social housing depends upon the maintenance of a myriad of cooperative games. Although citizenship is a legal concept, to have moral force it must be grounded in some deeper notion of mutual regard. Citizenship is neither primarily about entitlements to government benefits nor about obligations to respect the law: it is about attitudes toward others. The continued provision of public goods depends upon both migrants and the indigenous population adopting the same attitude of mutual regard as the indigenous population has toward its own members. If the preservation of cultural difference is regarded as an individual right despite its potential threat to public goods, there is a tension between this right to difference and an individual right to the social housing that the indigenous culture has made possible. Whether this principle of group-based rights is seen as ethically reasonable turns out to be a matter of considerable moment, and I return to it in chapter 6.

In addition to competition for social housing, as migrants become established they will compete in the private housing markets, driving up rents and house prices. A recent estimate for Britain by the Office of Budgetary Responsibility is that house prices are around 10 percent higher due to migration. Again this effect via housing looks to be much larger than the effects on wages. Since the housing stock is disproportionately owned by older and richer people, the appreciation in house prices due to migration has implied a large regressive transfer from lower-income groups. Further, since the migration has been spatially highly concentrated, it will have affected regions very differently. The 10 percent increase in national house prices due to migration breaks down into a negligible effect in much of the country, and very sizable price increases in London, the South East, and a few other pockets of high immigration. Paradoxically, by severely widening the north-south divide in house prices, this has made it more difficult to move from the other regions of Britain to the South East. Immigration has increased the ability of firms in growth areas to recruit workers, but it has inadvertently reduced the internal mobility of the indigenous workforce. This introduces a further mechanism of income loss for indigenous workers: they are crowded out of moving to better-paying jobs in growth areas.

If this is the sum total of the economic effects of migration on the indigenous population, it is surely difficult to understand why there is an overwhelming consensus among economists that migration has been such a good thing. Perhaps we are missing some important effects? I now turn to some that have been suggested and some others that I think have as yet been unjustifiably neglected.

The Effects of Immigrant Exceptionalism

An argument often invoked in favor of migration is that big benefits accrue in the long term. The proposition is that migrants are disproportionately innovative, or at least sufficiently different that they think out of the box, and so accelerate the overall pace of innovation. A commonly cited figure is that in the United States immigrants and their children account for a disproportionate number of patented inventions. In short, immigrants tend to be exceptional. This is an important argument: immigration of the innovative may increase the rate of growth out of proportion to immigrant numbers. However, the American experience may be due more to the exceptional nature of America, as a magnet for innovative entrepreneurs, than to the exceptional nature of migrants globally. Further, even if migrants are self-selected to be exceptional, then the gains for high-income countries are offset by losses for poor countries of origin. A talent transfer from poor societies to rich ones is not necessarily something that should be cause for global celebration. For completeness, it is just possible that even if migrants are disproportionately innovative, it is not because innovative people are more likely to migrate, but because the very experience of immigration makes people more innovative. For example, there is some evidence that the challenge of bilingualism raises intelligence.[3]

The long-term growth effects of immigration are difficult to measure. Immigrant exceptionalism is itself likely to persist only for the medium term: in the long term the descendants of migrants merge into the general population. So the one clear long-term effect of migration is that the population is larger. At high income levels there is virtually no relationship between the size of a country's population and its income, so we should not expect much of a long-term economic effect from migration one way or the other. Luxembourg, Singapore, Norway, and Denmark all have small populations yet provide among the highest incomes in the world for their citizens. Hence, whether a larger population is a benefit or a cost depends primarily upon whether the country was under- or overpopulated relative to its usable geographic area. A likely contender for underpopulation is Australia, an entire continent with only 30 million people. Max Corden, the distinguished Australian economist, sets out a convincing case that Australia would benefit from a substantially larger population.[4] At the other end of the spectrum, England and the Netherlands are the most densely populated countries in Europe and, indeed, among the most densely populated in the world. At such high densities open space is scarce. As population rises, not only does that space become yet more heavily used, it contracts absolutely due to the extra need for housing and infrastructure, so substantial net migration is unlikely to deliver net long-run benefits and is ultimately unsustainable.[5]

The tendency of immigrants to succeed helps, in the medium term, to drive the economy forward, and this is a gain for the indigenous. But as with migration more generally, at sufficient scale even the disproportionate success of immigrants can become a problem. Among the least successful part of the indigenous population the success of immigrants can demoralize, rather than inspire. In America, the children of immigrants on average have higher education and wages than the children of the indigenous population.[6] In Britain the overarching perennial social problem has been the low aspirations of children from the working class—a trait precisely opposite to that of immigrants. Both traits tend to be self-fulfilling. Faced by decades of frustration of hopes, the dominant narrative of the indigenous underclass has evolved as fatalism: avoid disappointment by not trying. Being overtaken by immigrants can deepen a sense of the inevitability of failure. Even those children of immigrants whose home language is not English now outperform the children of the bottom half of the indigenous working class. Demoralization may be compounded by competition: those working-class children who buck the social pressure to conform to expectations of failure are, in effect, competing for space on the escalators—colleges and training programs—with the children of aspiring migrants. Further, the problems faced by the children of immigrants—language and discrimination—are concrete and addressable by sufficiently active policy, and so they indeed get addressed. Yet this can tend to crowd out the more nebulous and difficult-to-address problems of low aspirations by sections of the indigenous population.

Even toward the top of the spectrum of achievement, the hyper-success of immigrants can cause problems. Famously, East Asian "tiger mothers" drive their children to attain outstanding accomplishments. Their methods are controversial because some consider them to sacrifice the normal pleasures of childhood—daydreaming and play. So the immigration of East Asians into a society with less effective childrearing practices has the predictable result that the cream of selective educational places will be taken by this particular segment of immigrants. For example, in Sydney, the main city of Australia, the school that has traditionally been considered the best in the city is now around 90 percent East Asian. In New York the premier publicly funded schools, such as Stuyvesant and Bronx

Science, are similarly around 70 percent Asian. The smart children of the indigenous population have been displaced. Of course, the rising generation of Australians and Americans is likely to be even smarter than it would have been without this competition from motivated immigrants. In some meaningful sense, Australians and Americans will benefit overall from this brilliance. Yet it is also meaningful to say that fewer children of the indigenous population will achieve the "glittering prizes" of outstanding success. Whether the indigenous population regards this as a net gain or a net loss is in principle an open question. One below-the-radar response of many North American universities has been to impose de facto quotas on East Asians. Some British private schools appear to be racially discriminatory in the opposite direction: such is the competition to excel in exam league tables that admitting a high proportion of East Asians is a temptingly easy route to success. Decentralized surreptitious discrimination by universities and schools is surely unethical, though it is a natural response to a vacuum in government policy. In turn, this vacuum is a consequence of the taboo on public discussion.

The same process is occurring in Canada but on a larger scale, and scale can matter. East Asians now occupy around half of the university places for subjects such as law. So, quite probably, in the next generation around half of Canadian judges will be of East Asian origin. Whether such a composition of the judiciary is a matter of concern for the host population depends upon how well East Asians integrate into Canadian society. At one end of the spectrum, East Asians simply become Canadians: that half the judges are of East Asian origin is of no more consequence than if half of them were left-handed. But at the other end of the spectrum, suppose that encouraged by multiculturalism, East Asians were to form into a hermetic community, clustered together, with endogamous marriage, and a distinct culture of values and beliefs. It might then quite reasonably be troubling to the host population that such a high proportion of court cases were being judged by a group that had remained culturally distinct.

A further respect in which immigrants tend to be exceptional is their assets. While most migrants from poor countries come with fewer assets than the indigenous population and hence compete for social housing, wealth has become one of the rationing criteria for the right of entry. As a result, the wealth distribution of migrants is skewed relative to the indigenous at both ends: not only more poor, but also more rich. The popular rationale for the policy of admitting the wealthy is that the extra capital they bring will raise productivity and wages. Economists should be skeptical of this argument. Capital flows easily between the high-income countries, so that the additional capital brought by migrants is likely to be offset by an outflow that restores equilibrium in financial markets. But because the direct inflows of wealth are highly visible, whereas the offsetting outflows are unnoticed, politicians have increasingly used wealth as an entry criterion. The immigration of the wealthy does, however, have consequences for the housing market: wealthy people buy expensive properties. For example, in London around 70 percent of elite housing is now being bought by migrants. This might rebound on society. Fred Hirsch coined the concept of "positional goods": those goods that confer social prestige but are in fixed supply.[7] He was concerned that rising prosperity would breed frustration as people found themselves priced out of such goods despite higher incomes. If Hirsch was right, then even the apparently benign, albeit demeaning, national mission statement "Give me your rich" might be questionable.

While the immigration of the superrich may be less benign that it seems, the anti-migration lobby makes play with another respect in which migrants tend to be exceptional, namely their criminality. The data on migrant criminality is surprisingly limited, but a measurable proxy is the representation of foreigners in the prison population. Across Europe, for a variety of reasons, foreigners tend to be heavily overrepresented in the prison population. France is fairly typical, with foreigners constituting around 6 percent of the overall population and 21 percent of the prison population. This tendency is not general beyond Europe: in America migrants have significantly *lower* rates of criminality than the indigenous population. I discussed this evidence with the chief scientific officer of the British Home Office, and there seem to be four distinct influences. One is the culture that migrants bring with them from their society of origin.[8] Professor Sampson, a sociologist at Harvard, explains the below-average criminality of migrants to the United States by some salient social characteristics of Mexicans. He likens their strong family structures, work ethic, and religious commitment, all of which tend to reduce criminality, to the American culture of the 1950s. Since cultures vary enormously between different immigrant groups, this influence is determined by the composition of migration rather than by its scale. A second influence is the legitimate opportunities that migrants face in their host country. If they have few skills and face discrimination in the job market they are more likely to opt for criminality. Whether this influence produces a strong link between migration and criminality thus depends on both the skill composition of migration and labor market policies. A third influence is demographic: most crime is committed by young men, so if immigration rules disproportionately favor those who are young and male, migrants will be overrepresented in the prison population. A fourth influence is social bonds to other people in the society. Being antisocial, criminality is easier to reconcile with self-respect: the weaker the attachment is to potential victims, the weaker the mutual regard will be.

Pulling together the effects on the incomes of the indigenous over different time horizons, the short-term effects depend upon who you are. There seems to be reasonable evidence that at the bottom of the income spectrum indigenous workers face slightly lower wages, reduced mobility, and larger losses on social housing, but most workers gain. In the medium term the tendency of immigrants to succeed raises incomes but may squeeze indigenes out of glittering prizes. In the long term any economic effects are trivial. The one clear long-term effect is that there is less open space per person.

Are Immigrants Needed to Offset an Aging Population?

A further common argument in favor of migration, especially in Europe, is demographic.[9] This is the notion that "We need immigrants because we're aging." A few societies have contrived, as a result of grossly incompetent social policies, to have peculiar demographic profiles for their indigenous population. One of the most extreme is Russia, where the post-Soviet catastrophe of mismanaged economic transition led to a collapse in the birthrate and higher mortality. The Russian population has been declining and is now just starting to recover. An implication is that there will be a phase during which the dependency ratio—the number of dependents per person of working age—rises quite sharply. One way for Russia to correct this imbalance would be to encourage the immigration of young workers. Less dramatically, Italy and China have the same problem. Immigration, if permanent, is a rather drastic way to correct a temporary demographic imbalance. There are several alternatives, such as emigration of some of the elderly: for example, many Norwegians now retire to southern Europe. Or the society can spend some of its assets, just as individual people do once they retire. By spending assets the society would be able to import more goods than it exported. In turn, this would release workers who could instead cater for the needs of the elderly. Such a rundown of assets would be feasible for Russia, which has huge foreign exchange reserves and vast natural resources.

However, the mere fact that a society is aging is not a reason to need extra workers. One of the most encouraging achievements of the interplay between science and public policy is the rapid increase in global life expectancy, by about two years each decade. Born four decades after my father, I have a life expectancy around eight years longer. Given the tendency of the media to pessimism, this is sometimes reported as though it were a problem: a looming liability of the aged infirm. But actually, years of active life are expanding about as rapidly as years of total life. The only reason that aging might give rise to a problem is because of policy ineptitude. When legal retirement ages and pensions were introduced, typically around the mid-twentieth century, politicians lazily fixed the age of retirement at a specific number such as sixty-five or sixty, rather than relative to average life expectancy. Each decade two more years are added to life expectancy and all of this, by default, is added to the period of retirement. As a result, societies go into a frenzy of angry disappointment on the rare occasions when politicians muster the gumption to raise the age to offset some of the increase in life expectancy. With life expectancy rising so rapidly, assigning the entire increase to longer retirement is unaffordable. As a society gets richer, it can gradually afford to reduce the retirement age relative to life expectancy, but the default option should not be set at a particular age.

Given the ineptitude of governments in fixing the retirement age, why not bail ourselves out by some youthful immigration? Why not: because such a strategy would be unsustainable. An influx of immigrants of working age gives a society only a temporary fiscal windfall, whereas increased life expectancy is a continuing process. Economics has developed an unambiguous analysis of how a temporary windfall should be handled: it should be saved. For example, the government could use a temporary increase in revenues from youthful immigration to reduce the public debt. What it should categorically not do is use them to incur new, ongoing obligations for spending, such as pensions. Yet that is what the argument "We need immigrants to counter an aging population" amounts to.

Further, the demographic argument presupposes that migrants reduce the ratio of dependents to workers: being young, they are in the workforce and so balance the expanding retired indigenous population. But working migrants have both children and parents. One of the distinctive norms of low-income societies is the number of children that women want: until they adjust to high-income norms, migrants from low-income societies tend to have disproportionately large numbers of children. Whether migrants bring their dependent parents to their host country will depend largely upon host-country migration policy. In Britain, by 1997 the desire among migrants from low-income countries to bring in dependent relatives was so considerable that only 12 percent of migrants were coming for work. Taking into account both children and parents, there is no presumption that migrants even temporarily reduce the dependency ratio. A series of recent research papers by Torben Andersen, a Danish professor of economics, investigates the likely effect of immigration on the sustainability of Scandinavian-type generous welfare systems. His conclusion is that far from helping to maintain them, migration may make them unviable because of the combination of the higher dependency ratios and lower skill levels of migrants.[10]

Are Immigrants Needed to Fill Skill Shortages?

Another potential benefit of immigration is to fill skill shortages. From time to time, particular skill niches may become underprovided by the indigenous population and are most readily met by selective immigration. In the 1990s Germany found that it was short of IT workers and tried to encourage temporary immigration of skilled Asians to rectify it. In the 1950s France found itself short of construction workers and brought them in from North Africa. In the 1970s Britain found itself short of nurses and recruited them from the Commonwealth. Over a longer period the British Medical Association, the country's politely named trades union for doctors, has limited the supply of doctors (ostensibly to maintain standards, more plausibly to produce the scarcity that would justify high wages). As a result, British doctors are among the highest paid in Europe. In response, the British health service has recruited immigrant doctors. No society can anticipate all its needs for skills. However, as the case of British doctors illustrates, the immigration safety valve may, over the long term, weaken the incentive to address the root of the problem, which is training.

The effect of immigration on the training of indigenous workers has not, to my knowledge, been adequately investigated. Recall that in Europe indigenous workers have benefited because immigrants are skilled: unskilled indigenes can work along with skilled immigrants. But while this is directly good news for the unskilled, indirectly it may not be. The training of young workers in skills depends upon firms choosing to invest in training. Because training is costly and workers once trained can leave for other firms, the most profitable strategy for an individual firm is to poach those who are already skilled off other firms. Because poaching is a zero-sum game, industry associations sometimes try to organize a common commitment to training, policed by peer pressure. All firms in an industry accept the need to do their share of training. However, all outcomes that are dependent upon coordination are potentially fragile. A shock could break the pattern. An influx of trained immigrants could constitute such a shock, destabilizing industry-wide training. With an influx of trained immigrants, hiring already-trained workers temporarily ceases to be a zero-sum game because they do not have to be poached from other firms. Even if training programs collapse, firms may still in the aggregate gain because they now get trained workers without the costs of training. But young indigenes lose because firms are no longer bothering to invest in training them.

Whether this effect is empirically important has not been researched, but prima facie it may have occurred in Britain. There has been a collapse in firm-based training: most notably, many apprenticeship schemes have been abandoned. The retreat from training youth was broadly coincident with the rise in immigration: during the peak years 80 percent of new jobs were filled by immigrants, but whether it was cause, coincidence, or consequence is an open question. Either way, once lost, industry-wide apprenticeship schemes are difficult to revive because of the costs of coordination.

What is good for business is not necessarily good for indigenous people. The short-term interest of business is for the open door: it is cheaper to recruit already-skilled migrants than to train indigenous youth, and the pool of talent will be wider when the door is more open. It is in the interest of the indigenous population to force firms that want to benefit from the country's social model to train its youth and hire its workers. Germany stands as testimony that such a policy need not drive business abroad. But the divergence of interest between business and citizens should make people skeptical of its pronouncements on migration policy. Most weeks I see letters to newspapers signed by some CEO fulminating against restrictions on migration. If they need skilled workers, why don't they train them? Their portentous pronouncements are but pallid variants of the grandiloquent "What's good for General Motors is good for the country."

Does Immigration Induce Emigration?

British policy toward migration is currently defined in terms of the net movement of people: the target is set as immigration minus emigration. For some long-term purposes this is the right way to define policy. If the objective is to preserve the ratio of open space per inhabitant, then *net* migration should be set to zero or there-abouts, depending upon birthrates. But for other purposes emigration and immigration need to be considered separately. In most high-income countries emigration as such has not been a policy concern. Yet recent evidence suggests that for European countries emigration inflicts serious losses on the remaining population.[11] Emigrants tend to be more skilled than the average population and are attracted to high-wage, fast-growth countries such as the United States and Australia. Is there any reason to think that immigration accelerates emigration?

Within a standard stylized economic model of migration, points systems that determine eligibility for the right to migrate create a direct link between immigration and emigration. Recall that a standard feature of points systems is to privilege relatives of the diaspora. The past history of global migration consequently gives Europeans much easier access to the United States, Canada, Australia, and New Zealand than the citizens of low-wage countries. To see how this plays out, consider a three-country world: I will give the countries real names, for ease of recall, but they are not meant as actual countries: they are constructs with assumed characteristics.

Countries A (America) and B (Britain) are identical, high-wage economies, while country C (Chad) is a low-wage economy. America permits migration by British citizens, but not by those from Chad. Britain now adopts an open-door migration policy for the citizens of Chad. The result is that citizens of Chad move to Britain, in the process driving wages slightly down. The small decline in wages is not sufficient to deter continued migration from Chad: the gains to migration remain massive. But now British citizens have an economic incentive to migrate to America. The mechanism that drives emigration from Britain in this simple model is the decline in wages, and this is something that we know does not happen to any significant extent in actual migration. However, that wages do not decline need not imply that living standards are not reduced. For example, as a city becomes more crowded, gains in wages are offset by rising congestion. Over half of the current population of London is immigrant, yet the population of London today is the same as it was in the 1950s when almost the entire population was indigenous. It is not credible that in the absence of migration the population of London would have halved, so the only reasonable interpretation is that immigration has induced the indigenous population to leave London. Where did these people go? Many of them just moved to the outer suburbs.[12] However, both Britain and the Netherlands are currently experiencing high emigration coincident with high immigration. Whether there is a causal link between the two has not been studied.

A mechanism by which immigration is likely to drive emigration of the indigenous is the cycle of boom and bust. International flows of both capital and labor amplify booms and thereby inadvertently also amplify the busts that follow. In the 1990s capital inflows to East Asia led to the bust of 1998—the East Asian Crisis. Analogously, open-door migration policies amplified the booms of 1997–2007 in the United States, Ireland, Britain, and Spain. At the time, politicians such as Gordon Brown claimed that they had abolished the boom-bust cycle. What they had actually done was to intensify it by enabling booms to run for longer: immigration enabled both public and private overspending to continue without triggering the inflation that had previously compelled governments to rein booms in. The legacy was the superbust of 2008. Immigration did not cause the boom-bust cycle, but just as with international capital flows, it amplified the cycle, thereby deepening the bust. During the bust new hiring collapsed, implying very high unemployment rates for young people entering the labor market. For example, in Spain youth unemployment is currently around 50 percent. There could be no mechanism whereby migrants in employment vacated their jobs in favor of new indigenous workers. Faced with unemployment, the indigenous young might reasonably decide to emigrate. Whether newly unemployed immigrants decide to return to their country of origin depends upon the income gap between it and the host country and the ease of movement. Most of the immigrants to Spain came from Africa, where incomes were far lower, and entry into Spain had often been sufficiently difficult that a decision to return home might prove irreversible. So even being unemployed for some years in Spain might be a better option than leaving. In contrast, most of the immigrants to Ireland during the boom years were from eastern Europe. As a result, the income gap was narrower and migration easier, so that during the Irish bust many migrants returned home, easing the labor market adjustment. Nevertheless, by 2011 Ireland was experiencing its fastest rate of indigenous emigration since the nineteenth century. In Portugal, in response to the bust the problem of indigenous youth unemployment became so severe that the government has actively promoted emigration as an official policy. Immigration in the boom years inadvertently generated emigration of the indigenous in the years of recession.

Even if migration does induce emigration, does it matter? From any individualistic perspective, whether utilitarian or libertarian, such a voluntary relocation of the indigenous population is of no consequence. Indeed, if British citizens receive a capital gain on their houses as a result of immigration and this enables them to move to Spain, everyone has gained. The first best would be to remove all immigration controls, but the second best is to take advantage of national differences, shuffling people around the world according to their legal access to high-wage opportunities. If you feel uncomfortable with that conclusion, it is perhaps because you attach some value to the concept of a nation, beyond seeing it as a vehicle for the provision of individual opportunities. Emigration does not matter, beyond the economic effects noted above, as long as it does not fundamentally alter the composition of the population. But were the immigration-emigration link to become a powerful revolving door that transformed the population, it would surely become a matter of widespread concern. Just as if Chad emptied, there would be a global cultural loss, so too if we imagine that Icelanders moved to Norway as Iceland was repeopled with Chinese. How, within a viable ethical framework, this might reasonably be seen as a loss I will return to in part 5.

The Economics of Guest Workers

We have now run through a substantial array of economic effects of migration. Both the narratives that immigration drives down wages for indigenous workers and that immigration is economically necessary are false. The truth is that moderate migration has economic effects on the indigenous population that in the short and medium term are marginal, and most probably modestly positive. Any long-term effects are negligible. In contrast, sustained rapid migration would most likely lower the living standards of most of the indigenous population, both through wage effects and through the need to share scarce public capital. So while controls on migration are important to protect living standards, moderate migration is modestly advantageous. If however, like the Japanese, the society wants to remain homogeneous, then the economic costs are sufficiently modest that it can afford to keep the door closed. After all, without any immigration Japan remains one of the richest societies in the world. In other words, the economic evidence suggests that economics should not be a very important criterion for determining immigration policy.

If not economics, then what should be the criteria? Evidently, the more uncertain, potentially adverse consequences for economic well-being are likely to come through the social effects discussed in chapter 3. There is only one way in which virtually all social effects can be avoided, leaving only the economic effects. That is if immigrants are prevented from integrating in any way into the society other than as workers: that is, in the German euphemism, "guest workers." A genuine guest-worker program delivers the labor markets effect of migration and nothing else.

Some societies, most notably in the Middle East, have chosen to run very substantial guest-worker programs. Since these societies are small and rich, the attractions of such a migration policy to the indigenous population are substantial: they get others to do the work without the composition of the society being changed. Dubai has become a luxury service economy—only 2 percent of its income is now from oil—by this model. An astonishing 95 percent of the resident population of Dubai are immigrants: you might think that no society on earth could tolerate such an influx, but in Dubai immigrants even in such numbers are unthreatening because they cannot acquire citizenship or even the rights of residency. The stay of guest workers is conditional upon both their employment contract and their behavior. Their wages are unrelated to wage levels set for citizens and simply reflect the prevailing global markets in their level of skill. A visit to Dubai is a stark and unsettling reminder of global inequality precisely because, by design, the business model attracts the world's extremes of income. The superrich come to stay in the luxury hotels and the superpoor come to work in them. However, although Dubai exploits the opportunity created by global inequality, it does not cause that inequality. On the contrary, the jobs that Dubai provides help poor people.

In essence, the enthusiasm of economists for migration is enthusiasm for the guest-worker model. Commonly the espousal of guest-worker programs is implicit, since all the other effects of migration are ignored. But Professor Alan Winters, a distinguished economist who has specialized in migration, has had the intellectual honesty to advocate the guest-worker model explicitly. Specifically, he proposes that all the high-wage countries should encourage the mass temporary immigration of unskilled workers from poor countries.[13] In economic terms it is hard to fault this prescription: it would indeed generate global economic gains and benefit almost everyone involved. The world of upstairs-downstairs could be re-created: servile maids from the bottom billion could be stuffed into the attics of every middle-class home. But what kills the proposition is its tin-eared detachment from a workable ethics. The closed, autocratic societies of the Gulf States can indeed enforce a ruthless policy of a complete separation of the rights and entitlements of the indigenous population from those of immigrants. Similarly, they can enforce expulsion of immigrants upon completion of fixed-term contracts. But the open, liberal societies of the West could not begin to operate such policies. Once immigrants have arrived in a country, they are extremely difficult to expel: indeed, with the exception of America, "difficult" should read "impossible." In America the Obama administration has sustained expulsion rates at around 400,000 per year. In contrast, in Europe expulsion is rare, legally protracted, and controversial. Even the original guest workers who came from Turkey to Germany supposedly temporarily in the 1950s turned out to be permanent. Immigrants to high-wage democracies become not just a part of the labor force, *but a part of society*. It is best to accept this evident fact and weigh its consequences in the overall balance of benefits and costs to the indigenous population.

CHAPTER 5

Getting Migration Policy Wrong

ON THE LONG MARCH THROUGH THE EFFECTS of migration on the indigenous populations of host societies, on those left behind in countries of origin, and on migrants themselves, we have reached a convenient resting stage. Having been through the social and economic effects on host populations, it is time for a preliminary assessment and for a preliminary application to migration policy.

Combining the Economic and the Social Effects

A reasonable assessment of the evidence of the previous chapters, stripped of the near-overwhelming desire to see it in the light best suited to whatever are one's moral prejudices, is that moderate immigration has predominantly favorable economic effects on the indigenous population, and ambiguous social effects. There is a gain from greater cultural variety, offset by the adverse effect of diversity on mutual regard, and the potential weakening of a functional social model by diasporas attached to dysfunctional social models. Sustained rapid migration would be an entirely different matter: both the economic and the social effects would most probably be adverse for host populations. The fundamental economic forces of the simple models would kick in: wages would be bid down and public capital spread more thinly. The social benefits to increased variety are most likely subject to diminishing returns, while the social costs of diversity and dysfunctional social models are likely increasing. To think concretely, consider immigration from a low-income country in which the social model is manifestly highly dysfunctional, namely Somalia. For any host society the first ten thousand Somali immigrants are likely to provide a pleasing gain in cultural variety and little else. But immigration that increases a culturally separate Somali diaspora from one million to two million would bring little additional gain in variety, while weakening mutual regard and giving significant weight to a bad social model.

So some controls are necessary, but their purpose is to prevent migration accelerating rather than to close it down. Since my audience will be split into a pro-migration camp and an anti-migration camp, through this provisional assessment I anticipate that I have already aroused the fundamentalists. Is there, however, any way of bringing these effects together?

The pro-migration camp will, at this stage, respond with the sentiment that it would be outrageous to sacrifice large and solid economic gains together with the pleasures of variety for a few amorphous and disreputable social ripples. Similarly, the anti-migration camp will respond with the sentiment that we should not be prepared to uproot the fabric of our society for the sake of a few ephemeral dollars. But if the effects are opposing, how might their net effect be determined?

One approach is to determine which effect dominates in the long run. If the costs of migration were to predominate in the short run but the benefits were in the long run, then migration could be reconceptualized as an investment. Restrictions on migration would be short-sighted. But do the effects of migration fit this temporal pattern? In the long run the only effect of migration is that the population is bigger. For sparsely populated countries such as Australia and Canada this would probably be beneficial; for densely populated ones, such as the Netherlands and England, it would probably be detrimental. The clearest economic gains are in the short run. There is an influx of young workers that temporarily reduces the dependency ratio, and the economy can be run on full throttle without inflation, as during 1997–2007. There may be some further gains in the medium run accruing from immigrant exceptionalism—a higher rate of innovation—but the evidence for this is not general and may depend upon the specifics of host countries and countries of origin. The potential social costs—the decline in cooperation and generosity consequent upon increased diversity and diasporas attached to dysfunctional social models—are medium run. The habits of sociability are robust in the short run to an increase in diversity. In the long run the population blends and so the initial sociability can be reestablished. Does this pattern enable us to resolve the conflict between economic benefits and social costs? For the sparsely populated countries I think it does: since long-term effects are liable to predominate, for such countries far-sightedness favors migration. But for other countries, the open door may be the short-sighted option: an unsustainable economic boom, followed by complex and prolonged social problems.

The other way of resolving how economic gains compare to social costs is to find a way of combining them by means of a common metric. One of the most promising recent developments in social science has been to recognize that income is not a good metric of the quality of life. Led by scholars such as Richard Layard, some economists are reformulating the objective of public policy as the maximization of happiness. Layard has been appointed an official adviser to British prime minister David Cameron, and the government has introduced an official measure to track changes in happiness as distinct from income. Happiness is not the only objective in life, but it is pretty fundamental. Many of the other objectives you might want to replace it with—dignity, achievement, serenity, respect—are all not so much alternatives to happiness as routes toward it.

Potentially, a measure of happiness can synthesize economic and social effects into a common metric that is meaningful for policy purposes. Fortunately, there is one such study that measures the net impact of migration on the happiness of the indigenous population of host societies, namely that of Robert Putnam. Although the focus of his work was on the effects of migration on trust and social capital, he also measured its effect on happiness.

Although Putnam did not measure the economic effects, we can reasonably infer that they were positive. There is no reason to think that the localities that Putnam chose experienced economic effects of migration other than the usual pattern of large gains for migrants and small gains for most of the indigenous population. But he found that the effects on happiness were dominated by social costs: the higher the concentration of immigrants in a community, the less happy was the indigenous population, controlling for other characteristics. That the adverse social effects should dominate the favorable income effects of immigration would not surprise the scholars of happiness. They find that above a relatively low income threshold, increases in income do not generate significant sustained increases in happiness. Further, the income gains from migration for the indigenous are likely to have been modest. Happiness studies find that social relations are far more important than small changes in income, and "hunkering down" is essentially an erosion of these relations.

Too much should not be made of a single study. Unfortunately, my trawl of the literature has not revealed other rigorous studies that measure the effect of migration on the happiness of the indigenous population. There is a vacuum that research needs to fill. Given the present inadequate state of knowledge, all that is warranted is a note of caution to be sounded against the overwhelming enthusiasm of social scientists for open-door migration policies. The effect of migration to date on the overall well-being of indigenous host populations appears to have been modest and ambiguous. Both the economic and the social effects of migration are positive at moderate rates, but beyond that they are likely to become negative. Quite why economists in particular are such strong supporters of increased migration is at this stage in the analysis a mystery: it cannot be coming from the effects on host populations. We will see the likely basis for it in the next chapter.

The Political Economy of Panic

What migration policies do the governments of host countries adopt, and what are they likely to adopt? Among the policies available to the governments of host countries, the one that is most hotly debated is quantitative limits on the rate of migration. But other policies are potentially more important. One range of policies can affect the composition of migrants in various respects: skill levels, the balance between workers and dependents, and the weightings of the social models to which migrants are accustomed. Policies can also affect the rate of absorption of diasporas into the general population. These, rather than quantitative limits, are the important policies. To see this, I am going to use the model to tell an unfortunate story of how migration and policy are likely to evolve in the absence of good analysis.

The story has four phases and is illustrated in Figure 5.1. In the first phase there are no migration restrictions, so migration increases at its natural rate along the *migration function* as shown by the arrows. The desire to migrate is so strong that the function does not cross the *diaspora schedule*, and so there is no natural equilibrium. The continual acceleration in migration becomes a salient political

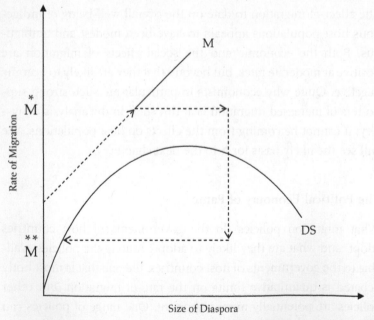

Figure 5.1 The Political Economy of Panic: Quantitative Migration Restrictions

issue, and so I will term this initial period the *anxiety phase*. Eventually, the government imposes a quantitative restriction, freezing the rate at M* to prevent further increases.

As a result we now enter the second phase, which I will term the *panic phase*. While the binding limit on the rate of migration prevents further acceleration in migration, it cannot in itself lead to an equilibrium size of the diaspora. As the size of the diaspora increases, the combination of reduced interaction with the indigenous population, the widening cultural distance in the composition of migrants, and the feedback from reduced trust all reduce the rate of absorption to the extent that beyond some size, the *diaspora schedule* twists back upon itself. In this policy scenario, the rate at which migration happens to be frozen, M*, is not compatible with a stable diaspora. Hence, in the panic phase, although migration is frozen, the unabsorbed diaspora continues to increase: this is shown by the arrows that march along the horizontal line marking the binding migration control. As the unabsorbed diaspora keeps growing, at some point rising social costs, such as the decline in trust within the indigenous population, and competition for social services between the diaspora and the indigenous population, generate renewed political pressure. In this scenario the only policy that the government uses is the quantitative limit on the rate of migration. So the government imposes ever-tightening restrictions.

This takes us into the third phase, which I will call the *ugly phase*. This phase is ugly because until migration is reduced to a level below the *diaspora schedule*, no matter how much it is reduced, the unabsorbed diaspora keeps increasing, and so social costs and political pressure keep mounting. This is depicted by the arrows that trace a path from M* to M**, at which the rate of migration has been so reduced that the diaspora begins to decline.

This takes us to the final phase of *diaspora absorption*. During this phase, which might take many decades, migration is severely restricted while the diaspora is gradually absorbed into the general population and social trust is rebuilt, enabling the fragile equilibria of cooperation to be reestablished.

This story of migration is not especially encouraging. There are very large changes in the rate of migration: it swings from being very high to very low. This is unlikely to be optimal from any perspective. There are also very large changes in the size of the diaspora, with a prolonged period in which it may be so high as to inflict significant social costs on the indigenous population.

While it is not encouraging, it is also not inevitable. In the final chapter I will return to this scenario, starting from precisely the same objective circumstances—the same migration function and the same diaspora schedule—and show how different policies could produce a far superior outcome.

But first, I turn from the interests of the indigenous population of high-income host countries to those of the migrants who come to join them. Other than in the guest-worker approach to migration, migrants become members of their new societies. How does this affect them?

PART 3

Migrants

Grievance or Gratitude?

CHAPTER 6

Migrants

The Winners from Migration

MIGRANTS ARE BOTH THE BIG ECONOMIC WINNERS and the big economic losers from migration. If economic self-interest were the only influence on behavior, the people in poor countries should move heaven and earth to migrate to rich countries, but once there they would vote for the political parties that advocate tightening restrictions on immigration. This conclusion from the economic analysis of how migration affects migrants is sufficiently bizarre that we will take it in stages.

Why Migrants Are the Big Winners from Migration

The first stage is the unsurprising part: migrants are the big winners from migration. The big gains accrue as a result of moving from a country in which workers are paid little to one in which they are paid a lot. The magnitude of the wage differential between rich and poor countries is staggering: it is, indeed, a mirror of the overall gap in income between the rich world of the Organisation for Economic Co-operation and Development and the poor world of the bottom billion. We cannot infer directly from a differential in wages that by moving from a low-wage country to a high-wage country a worker would be able to earn a high wage. Something that every economist takes for granted, but noneconomists find uncomfortable, is that to a first approximation differentials in wages reflect differentials in productivity: people are more or less paid what they are worth. Of course, we are all aware of glaring instances where this is not the case: some people are paid far more than they are worth and others too little. But if employers made large systematic mistakes in matching wages to productivity, they would go bankrupt. So the key issue becomes not *whether* but *why* workers in high-wage countries are so much more productive than workers in low-wage countries.

As a matter of logic there are only two possibilities: the productivity gap is either due to the characteristics of workers or to the characteristics of countries. Economists have studied this issue, and the bulk of the gap is due to differences in the characteristics of countries rather than the people in them. How have they reached this conclusion?

There are a few smart ways of getting at the importance of worker characteristics. One is to compare matched jobs in host countries and countries of origin. Job for job, the wage differentials are massive: for example, in moving from Haiti to the same job in the United States a typical worker would increase his earnings tenfold.[1] Another way is to compare immigrants with indigenous workers in host countries. Immigrants turn out to be almost as productive as indigenous workers. Even this is not quite killer evidence: conceivably, the most productive cream of workers in the country of origin are the ones who choose to migrate. Getting around this possibility requires a degree of ingenuity. The trick has been to find natural experiments in which migration has been randomized. Random migration may sound unlikely, but the literally random allocation process for some visas comes very close to the statistical ideal. For example, the United States conducts an annual lottery for 50,000 visas that attracts around 14 million applicants. So the lucky few who are granted a visa are very likely to take it up and are unlikely to differ from the unlucky majority. New Zealand holds a similar lottery for would-be immigrants from Tonga. Studies that have investigated whether the lucky minority are atypically productive in their home environments have concluded that they are not. Personal characteristics do not account for most of the productivity cliff that migrants climb.[2] A final approach is to explain differences in productivity between countries solely in terms of differences in country characteristics. It reaches the same conclusion: most, though not all, differences in income between rich and poor countries are because of differences in productivity that are due to characteristics of countries rather than of individual workers. This is consistent with the explanation of income gaps that I offered in chapter 2: differences in social models.

Some differences in productivity do remain, even when immigrants and indigenous workers have the same level of education. Typically, immigrants end up taking jobs that are several notches below those ostensibly appropriate for their formal educational attainments. This may reflect sheer discrimination, but it may also reflect underlying differences in skills. However, even if it does, the discount is modest relative to the wage differential between poor countries and rich ones.

That the income gap between the rich world and the bottom billion is predominantly due to the characteristics of countries rather than the characteristics of workers has powerful implications. One tells us what it will take for the bottom billion to catch up with the developed world. Its message is that key characteristics of these societies will need to change. It is not simply a matter of training individuals in skills. As I discussed in chapter 2, the societies of countries of origin will need to change their social models. An uncomfortable corollary is that it is not desirable for migrants from them to bring their social model to their host country. Whether or not migrants realize it, the impetus for their emigration is to escape from those aspects of their countries of origin that have condemned people to low productivity. By the same reasoning, for emigration to have a fundamental impact on countries of origin, it would be through inducing changes in their social models.

Another implication of income differences being due to country characteristics is that migrants will nation-shop. In my research with Anke Hoeffler, we have arranged global migration flows into a large matrix showing all possible host countries for each country of origin. We find that the rate of migration from a country of origin to any particular host country is influenced by not just the income gap between them but the income of the host country relative to other possible host countries.

Nation-shopping is driven not just by differences in average incomes among possible host countries but by where migrants expect to slot in the distribution of income. Those migrants who expect to earn below-average incomes should prefer countries with high redistributive taxation, whereas those who expect to earn above-average incomes should prefer countries that accept greater inequality. Migrants should shop for their preferred tax-cum-welfare system as well as their preferred wage. This was first recognized just as a theoretical possibility: low-skilled migrants would prefer equal countries, and high-skill migrants would prefer unequal ones.[3] But more recently this expected pattern has found some empirical support: the skill profiles of migrants to Europe and

America differ in a way that matches the prediction.[4] Europe is more equitable, with the most generous welfare systems in the world, and it tends to attract migrants with a lower skill profile, although this composition of migration may also be explained by other factors.

The final implication is that simply by shifting a worker from a dysfunctional society to a more functional one, her productivity can increase tenfold. This is an order of magnitude greater than any other process by which productivity can be increased. Globally, the vast edifice of technological research enables productivity to inch forward by a couple of percentage points per year. Over the past two decades China has indeed been an astounding exception: cumulatively it has also achieved around a tenfold increase in productivity. But this is without historical precedent and has required a staggering willingness to postpone consumption: despite China's initial poverty, for the past two decades, half of all income has been saved and invested. Yet simply by getting on a plane, workers can reproduce that hard-won Chinese productivity boost. This is why economists get so excited by enhanced migration: it is the closest the world economy comes to a free lunch.

Who Should Get the Gains from Migration?

Who should eat that free lunch? That is, to whom should the productivity gains from migration accrue? In a market economy the default option is that productivity accrues to the producer: workers are paid according to their productivity. So, in the absence of a policy override, the gains from migration will accrue to migrants. While the economic theory that links income to productivity explains how things *will* be, rather than how they *ought* to be, it does have some moral force. There is clearly some presumption that in large part the fruits of labor should belong to the worker. However, the principle that income can be taxed in order to benefit others is also well established, and so migrants do not have an exclusive claim to the gain in productivity. Of course, like indigenous workers in host countries, they will be subject to the country's tax system, but this is in no sense immigrant-specific. Is there an ethical basis for requiring migrants to contribute more than this, and if so, to whom?

The most prominent such claim has been made on behalf of the societies of origin. Professor Jagdish Bhagwati, a highly distinguished economist at Columbia University and himself an emigrant from India, has long proposed that migrant workers should pay a special supplemental tax, the revenue from which would accrue to their countries of origin. At least superficially, this is ethically very attractive: migrants receive a massive windfall gain that makes them dramatically better off and so able to help their much poorer fellow citizens in the country they have left. From the utilitarian universalist perspective such an income transfer is highly beneficial: since the migrants are much better off than the people left behind, a financial transfer reduces the utility of migrants by much less than it increases the utility of recipients. Of course, within the utilitarian universalist framework the same argument could be used to justify a large tax transfer from the indigenous population of high-income societies.

But if the utilitarian ethical framework leaves you feeling unconvinced, then it becomes somewhat harder to find good reasons to justify a migrant-specific tax. A special tax could be seen as compensation for the education that the migrant received before leaving. But its costs are modest relative to the gains in productivity: they may not justify a significant rate of taxation. Indeed, the migrant might reasonably retort that it is only because elites within her country of origin have mismanaged the society so badly that it is necessary for her to migrate in order to realize the productivity of which she is capable. The elites who control the society should not, therefore, be rewarded by an enforced tax transfer.

The migrant might also plead that she indeed cares sufficiently deeply about her society of origin to send money home, but since she does not trust its elites, she prefers to send it to individuals in her own family. There is plenty of evidence for such behavior: the typical migrant makes remittances of around $1,000 per year to her country of origin. If migrants had to pay a substantial tax to the government of their country of origin, they would probably reduce their remittances: not only would the tax reduce available income, it would provide an alibi for reduced generosity to relatives. Analogously, public provision of welfare reduces private charity.[5]

While the claims of the country of origin for rightful ownership of the productivity windfall from migration are weaker than might at first appear, those of the host country are somewhat stronger. After all, the gain in productivity is due to the superior social model of the host country. This social model is a form of public capital: a productive asset that has been accumulated over a long period, less concrete than a road network but not less important. The accumulation of this public capital has been paid for by the indigenous population. The form of payment might not have been obvious. Inclusive political institutions are now seen by economists as valuable for economic development, but they have usually been produced by political struggle. Modern productivity is built on the back of past street demonstrations and protests that cracked the power of self-serving, extractive elites. So the windfall gains from migration are attributable ultimately to the public capital that has been built by the indigenous population. In a market economy these gains accrue to migrants rather than to the indigenous population.

But that is because they are generated by a *public* good whose provision is not organized in such a way as to capture the benefits. Migrants benefit for free from capital that has been costly to accumulate.

There are, however, very powerful arguments against migrant-specific taxes. All such taxation, whether it accrues to the host country or the country of origin, lowers the net income of immigrants relative to that of the indigenous population in the host society. Were the net incomes of migrants reduced, it would be more difficult for them to match the living standards and life-styles of their host societies. The taxation of migrants would be the surest way of making them second-class citizens, making integration more difficult. Even without migrant-specific taxation, in some host societies immigrants tend to become an underclass due to a combination of less education than the indigenous population, a lack of the tacit knowledge that contributes to productivity, and discrimination. Where this happens it is rightly seen as a social problem to which major resources must be devoted. Imposing a tax on immigrants with one hand while attempting to undo its consequences with the other would be an incoherent policy.

Further, if the revenue from an immigrant tax accrued to the indigenous population, it could have the paradoxical effect of deepening the hostility of the indigenous population toward immigrants. Its true rationale would not be a compensation for losses inflicted on the indigenous population. Rather, it would be a windfall return on public capital. But the political forces that are viscerally hostile to immigrants would surely interpret the tax as recognition by the elite that immigration has been detrimental. The narrative would surely develop that the tax reflected merely a sop by the elite in token recognition of the damage being done to others. In other words, it might inadvertently legitimize the popular misconception that immigration is economically damaging to the indigenous population.

The bottom line is that the free lunch that comes from the windfall productivity gain as migrants move from dysfunctional to functional societies will continue to accrue to migrants. Migrants are *the* beneficiaries of migration.

Migration as an Investment

A corollary is that since these gains are large, people in poor countries should find migration very attractive. Of course, the most direct evidence is from migration itself: as described in chapter 2, migration from poor countries to rich ones has been increasing sharply. Further, few immigrants reveal sufficient signs of regret to decide to return to their countries of origin.

While the fact that someone has migrated is reasonable evidence that he wanted to do so, the fact that someone has not migrated cannot be interpreted as evidence that he does not wish to do so. There are many impediments to migration, both financial and legal.

Many people simply cannot afford to migrate: it is a form of investment. Like all investments, costs have to be incurred up front, while benefits come gradually over time. The costs of migration can be substantial, especially when benchmarked against income levels in poor countries. Typical incomes in the poorest countries are under $2,000 per year, so that even an international airfare would usually require years of savings. But the best time for migration is while the worker is still young. Young people are not so tied down by dependents, and they have longer working lives ahead of them to recoup their investment. But young people face the most acute problems of financing an investment.

Not only does migration have high initial costs and only gradual payback, but that payback is risky. Usually the migrant cannot know whether she will get a job, and if the decision turns out to be a mistake, it is costly to reverse. Not only are there the practical costs of traveling back home and searching for a job, there are psychological costs of publicly admitting to failure in a context where many other migrants are perceived as having succeeded. Imagine being the son who returns home broke to a neighborhood where other families are bragging about how well their sons have succeeded. If the cost of failure is high, then a likely attitude is risk aversion: people avoid taking the risk even if the odds make it a reasonable bet.

In high-income countries investments that are costly and risky do not have to be self-financed: they can be financed from a variety of sources. But in the poorest countries financial institutions do not serve ordinary people. The only source of funding is the family. This gives rise to two important characteristics: selection by income and family decisions.

At first glance it might be imagined that the people most likely to migrate would be the poorest: after all, the driver for migration is income differentials, and the differential between income in the country of origin and the host country is widest for the poorest potential migrants. But while the income differential determines the eventual payoff, the initial level of income determines the ability to finance the investment. In combination, these opposing influences generate a relationship between income and the propensity to migrate shaped like an inverted U. The poorest people would like to migrate but cannot afford it; the richest people could afford it but would get little benefit, while the people in the middle of the income distribution have a substantial incentive to migrate and are also able to finance it. Migration helps people to transform their lives, but these people are not among the poorest. Selection by income is important both in determining who within a country migrates—the middle-income people—and which countries have the highest emigration rates. For example, the Sahel, the world's poorest region, has not had emigration rates commensurate with its extreme poverty. Being so crushingly poor has made it difficult for people to finance the costs, while its being landlocked has made migration particularly expensive. Finance constraints give rise to an apparent paradox: an increase in income in the country of origin can actually increase emigration from it.

Young people are not usually in a position to finance their own migration. Their obvious recourse is the family, but the family is likely to expect something in return. Nor would such an expectation be unreasonable. Parents will have made sacrifices for the education of their children. Few sons give the proverbial response "Mother, you've worked hard for me all your life, now go out and work for yourself"?[6] Further, the loss of a young worker leaves the family with fewer breadwinners. The most obvious potential payback is remittances. The deal: we finance your migration now, but you will send us a share of your earnings later. Such a deal sounds attractive, but it is potentially problematic. It cannot be legally enforced; it is just a promise. Worse, it is a particularly unpromising type of promise—one that economists term "time inconsistent." Economists inhabit a rather chilling world in which people act only on their rational self-interest. Fortunately, our actual world is often more generous-spirited—hence mutual regard—but the implications of brute rational self-interest cannot be lightly dismissed. Unfortunately, while it is rational for the young would-be migrant to promise remittances in order to get his ticket paid, once the ticket has been handed over, it is also rational for him to break his promise. International migration enables the migrant to escape the clutches of the family in the country of origin, and so enforcement is more difficult than is the usual promise. Evidently, what matters is trust. Especially in poor societies where overall trust levels are low, families function as islands of high trust. But even so, those migrants who wish to honor their commitment may wish regularly to signal to their family back home that they are doing their best. This may explain one of the current paradoxes in the analysis of remittances, namely that migrants typically choose to make small regular payments home.[7] From the naive economic perspective, small and regular is stupid. The transactions costs of making remittances include a fixed charge that heavily penalizes small transfers. It would be much cheaper for the migrant to accumulate cash and occasionally send a single large payment. The only big winner from the prevailing pattern of small-and-frequent appears to be the wire agency Western Union. But one unexplored explanation for such behavior is that small and frequent installments signal to the family back home that they are not forgotten. They give the appearance that the migrant is constantly struggling to put together something to send back. In contrast, were the family to receive only infrequent large amounts (albeit with the same total), the behavior could be misinterpreted as indicating that the migrant had done very well but was only fitfully remembering his obligations.

If the family is financing the costs of migration and benefiting from it through subsequent remittances, it is possible that the decision to migrate is not truly a decision of the migrant, but of the migrant's family, and numerous studies of migration support this depiction.[8] In effect, rather than people choosing to change their country, families are choosing to become transnational. Families in poor countries are the mirror image of companies in rich ones. While the multinational companies are predominantly anchored in high-income countries, the multinational families are predominantly anchored in low-income ones. Through companies, households in high-income countries send their surplus capital to poorer countries; meanwhile through families, households in low-income countries send their surplus labor to rich ones.

Please Let Us In

The need to finance the investment in migration is only one of the impediments to it. People might want to migrate and be able to finance it and yet be unable to do so because they face immigration restrictions in their preferred host country. Indeed, as discussed in chapter 2, in response to accelerating immigration, all high-income countries now impose immigration restrictions of some form or another. Faced with restrictions, the potential migrant has three options other than to remain at home. He could try to acquire the characteristics that enable him to satisfy the restrictions. He could try to cheat: getting the permission to migrate despite lacking the necessary characteristics. Most desperately, he could try to evade the physical barriers that impede the immigration of those who do not have permission to migrate. Put yourself in the place of a would-be migrant pondering these options.

The restrictions that host countries impose on migrants vary considerably. Most impose some minimum requirements for education, and some add professional skills. This is because indigenous populations in host countries gain more from a highly educated migrant than from an uneducated one. For one thing, the distributional consequences are also likely to be better, with immigrants less likely to be in open competition with the lowest earning indigenous workers. Australia and Canada pioneered educational entry requirements, probably because they are so obviously immigrant societies that the details of policy toward immigration cannot be dodged by the mainstream political parties. Migration policy has been actively debated and so is coherently designed to be in the interest of the indigenous population. Reflecting this, Australian and Canadian educational requirements are the most demanding. America is next: perhaps again, because immigration is in America's DNA, policy debate has been somewhat more open. Europe has the least educationally demanding entry requirements. This surely reflects the absence of reasoned policy debate on the issue, as discussed in chapter 1. European immigration requirements are now rising, but this may have been driven more by the need for gestures than by a well-reasoned case.

An unintended effect of these restrictions is to increase the demand for education in poor countries: educational attainment is the passport out. Young people may not even know whether they will want to migrate, but education is a form of insurance. This is particularly important for ethnic minorities that might face discrimination in their country of origin: education provides protection. An instance of this behavior is the Indian ethnic minority in Fiji. After a long period of peaceful coexistence, a coup by indigenous army officers led to a period of anti-Indian rhetoric and discrimination that drove many people to leave. Since then, even though the interim government lost power and policy returned to normal, Indians have invested heavily in education so as to be able to gain entry to Australia if necessary. As a result, the Indian ethnic group has become significantly better educated than the rest of the indigenous population. Educational responses to the opportunity to migrate turn out to be important for the effects back in countries of origin, which I will consider in part 4.

While educational restrictions are increasingly common, host countries also impose a wide array of other conditions. The most important of these concern family ties: migrants are allowed to join family members who are citizens of host countries. But family ties are not set in stone: marriage creates them. Indeed, it is a truth universally acknowledged (at least in countries of origin) that an unmarried migrant in a high-wage country is in want of a wife. Especially in the context of arranged marriages, where the selection of the spouse is a family decision, families in countries of origin may decide to overcome entry barriers through marriage. Were the marriage contracted with the intention of it being purely a temporary device by which to gain the right of entry, it would clearly be an abuse of that right. But if families routinely decide on marriage partners on the basis of financial eligibility, then a preference for migrants as spouses is understandable, and indeed inevitable. So two of the predictable consequences of restrictions on migration are that families in the country of origin struggle harder to educate their children and send flattering photographs of their unmarried offspring to established migrants.

The next option for gaining access is to cheat, acquiring the permission for legal migration by illegal means. The most straightforward way of doing this is to bribe a visa official in the local embassy of the host country. Most of these officials are relatively junior, not particularly well paid, and living temporarily in the country of origin where they will inevitably get to know some local people socially. Nor is their job particularly enriched by intrinsic rewards: their role is to keep back a tidal wave of demand while granting a hugely valuable entitlement to a few fortunate applicants who happen to meet a set of byzantine, apparently arbitrary, and rapidly changing rules. In this situation it would not be surprising if some officials accepted payment for favors. There are many ways in which an official might reconcile this behavior with his conscience: the rules are unfair; the needs are acute; the personal payment merely compensates for the danger of punishment. The upshot of the evident difficulties of administering a visa system is that in many instances there is a "going rate" for an illegally acquired visa. Because the gains from migration are so large, the going rate is typically several thousand dollars.[9]

Another way of cheating is by masquerading as a member of a category that is eligible for entry. For example, in the 1980s Sweden initially had a very generous policy of granting citizenship to asylum seekers from Eritrea, then a province of Ethiopia beset by civil war. However, as the numbers grew, the policy became less generous. In response, some of the Eritrean immigrants who had acquired Swedish citizenship lent their passports to similar-looking friends and relatives: in the days before bio-recognition Swedish immigration officials found it difficult to challenge identity just on the basis of a passport photograph. Swedish officials then hit on a nonphotographic way of discriminating: Eritreans who were Swedish citizens had inevitably learned some Swedish, whereas those attempting to misstate their identity had not. But just as would-be immigrants can acquire the education, or the spouse that makes them eligible, so they can learn Swedish: in the midst of civil war and famine desperate Eritreans were learning Swedish in order to masquerade as Swedish citizens. A further version of masquerading is to pose as an asylum seeker. The ugly pattern of repression in many poor countries creates an evident need for asylum. In turn, the willingness to grant asylum creates an opportunity to cheat. Falsely posing as an asylum seeker is doubly reprehensible because it undermines the legitimacy of a vital humanitarian institution, but such ethical considerations may cut no ice with desperate people. The number of asylum seekers is likely to be an order of magnitude greater than legitimately met needs, reflecting the extreme difficulty of refuting claims of abuse at the hands of authority. Further, the standards of governance that are required by the host country courts before a country of origin is considered nonrepressive appear almost insultingly high: for example, only four out of the fifty-four African countries meet the standards required by the British courts for their citizens to be returned involuntarily to them.

The ultimate option is both expensive and risky: it is to travel without permission to enter the host country and try to evade physical restrictions. As barriers have become more sophisticated, their evasion has come to require specialist knowledge, generating a profession of people smugglers. As with crooked visa officials, they can sell places on boats, places hidden in a container truck, or places on a fence-crossing party, for several thousand dollars. But the key difference with illegitimately acquired legal entry is the risks. One evident risk is of detection. People caught attempting to enter Australia illegally are currently held in detention centers off the mainland: they can be stuck there for a long time. Illegal migrants to the United States are deported in very large numbers: in 2011 a remarkable 400,000. The costs of detection are humiliation, a period of restricted living, and the loss of the costs incurred in the attempt. The second risk is of the physical hazards of the enterprise: boats sink and stowaways suffocate or freeze to death. But the final and potentially most troubling risk comes from the people smugglers themselves. By its nature, this is an unregulated industry run by criminals in which the client-enterprise relationship is one-off. Having paid their money up front, would-be migrants have no recourse if the smuggler defaults or underperforms. Cash-strapped illegal migrants may be attracted by offers in which part of the payment is deferred until after successful arrival in the host country. But smugglers who offer such deals must build mechanisms for enforcing the obligation: in effect, illegal immigrants become temporary slaves to their smugglers. Among the limited options for profitable and enforceable slavery, the most obvious is prostitution:

illegal immigrants who dreamed of becoming secretaries end up as sex slaves. Once smugglers have such a mechanism of enforcement, why should they stop merely at recovering the notional debt? Slaves are likely to remain slaves until they escape or perish. Once arrived, even if illegal immigrants escape dependence upon people-smugglers, they have few options. To survive they need an income that they cannot legally earn. So illegal immigrants are either driven into the hands of tax-evading employers or must find extralegal self-employment such as crime. Policies for dealing with the problem of illegal migration have been inept even by the dismal standards of overall policies toward migration. I will suggest better ways of managing it in the final chapter.

The Lifeline

From the perspective of the would-be migrant, the combination of the need to finance migration as a costly investment and the need for a nonrisky means of overcoming legal restrictions has one dominant solution: family members who have already migrated. Diasporas turn out to be overwhelmingly important in determining the pattern and scale of migration. Diasporas facilitate migration through many distinct routes.

Because family ties are privileged in the allocation of visas, diasporas create opportunities for the legal access of subsequent migrants. Unsurprisingly, established migrants come under intense pressure from their family in their country of origin to facilitate the legal process. It is much easier to do this from within the host country, than by visiting its beleaguered embassy in the country of origin. Further, once migrants are citizens, they acquire voting rights and so can lobby their local political representatives to write to officials on their behalf. For example, in high-immigrant constituencies in Britain as many as 95 percent of the surgery visitors to members of Parliament concern the immigration of family members.

Diasporas can also provide local information about opportunities. For example, in a recent experimental study mobile phones were provided to households in Niger to discover whether they affected subsequent migration. Because workers now had better connectivity with relatives and friends in foreign jobs markets, emigration significantly increased.[10] The information provided by relatives abroad may, indeed, inadvertently be somewhat gilded because of the natural tendency of the migrant to exaggerate his own success. Diasporas generate not just information about opportunities but the opportunities themselves: many migrants establish small businesses, a natural consequence of the conjunction of the aspirations associated with migration and the discrimination they often encounter in the jobs market. Their businesses can find temporary room for newly arrived relatives even if they are not very productive, since minimum wage laws can easily be evaded. In addition to information and opportunities, diasporas directly lower the costs of arrival: while searching for work migrants can live with their established relatives.

Perhaps above all, diasporas can facilitate the financial costs of the investment in migration. Often, established migrants will be in the best position to pay for travel tickets: they are earning far more than their relatives in countries of origin. If the money is provided as a loan, they are in a strong position to enforce repayment: they can observe success, and they can make life difficult for defaulters. Deals are less liable to be time-inconsistent. Even if the money is provided by the family remaining in the country of origin, the diaspora social network provides pressure on the new migrant to meet the obligation to remit, and so makes the provision of finance less risky.

All these forces converge to make diasporas critical. As a result immigrants tend to concentrate in a few cities, as I described in chapter 3. Not only do diasporas affect the locations that subsequent immigrants choose, they are the single most important influence that determines the scale of migration. That is what is captured in the workhorse model. The accumulated stock of migrants increases the flow, so that migration tends to accelerate. The first migrant must overcome a far more challenging set of barriers than the millionth migrant. With my colleague Anke Hoeffler, I have tried to estimate the typical effect of diasporas on migration from poor countries to rich ones. Our results, which are only provisional, illustrate why diaspora-fueled migration is liable rapidly to accelerate.[11] Ten extra diasporas at the start of a decade induce seven extra migrants during the decade. In consequence, the next decade begins with seventeen extra diasporas that therefore induce twelve extra migrants during the decade. Following such a process through from 1960 to 2000, an initial addition to the diaspora count of 10 would grow to 83 by 2000.

But the effect of diasporas that is now receiving the most attention from economists is not that they increase the rate of migration; it is that *they change its composition.* From the perspective of indigenous populations it is better to attract highly educated workers than poorly educated workers and people who are dependents. Points systems that ration access are designed to have this effect. But diasporas enable migrants to override points systems. Their effect is so powerful that whenever family connections are deemed to confer entitlements to entry, they will dominate the effect of education and skill-based rationing.[12] This message from recent research gives rise to a sharp potential collision between a perspective based on the individual rights of migrants and one based on the rights and interests of the indigenous population.

Current immigration policies typically reinforce the tendency of migration to accelerate and undermine points-based systems, because through family reunification programs they privilege the relatives of existing immigrants. But does the right to immigrate necessarily confer on the migrant a right to grant others the right to immigrate? If so, do those others in turn have the right to confer the same right? Evidently, if rights are structured in such a way, educational points systems become largely moot: relatives will crowd out the skilled.

We now come to the most important ethical choice in this book. I have already introduced the distinction between group and individual rights in the context of social housing. Since migrants have greater needs than the indigenous, individual-based rights will allocate them a larger share of social housing than the indigenous, whereas group-based rights will allocate them the same share. But social housing pales into insignificance when compared with the right to bring in relatives. Only a small minority of the indigenous population wishes to bring in a foreign spouse or other relative: that is why it became a right. In contrast, a substantial proportion of the diaspora wishes to bring in a foreign relative. So if migrants are granted the same individual rights as the indigenous, then the composition of migration is skewed heavily toward dependents. There is thus a strong practical case, and perhaps a legitimate ethical one, for defining equal treatment at the level of the group: migrants should collectively benefit from excludable public goods such as social housing and the right to bring in a relative to the same degree as the indigenous population.

The allocation of social housing is already sometimes based on group-based equity, depending upon the practices adopted by local authorities. In contrast, the allocation of entry rights for relatives is currently scarcely based on any clear principles. However, the mechanics of operating group-based equity to the entry rights would be straightforward. Some countries already assign some categories of entry rights through quota-bound lotteries. They are an internationally standard way of reconciling fair access with a fixed target. Societies may choose to structure their immigration rules so as to confer unrestricted rights for each individual immigrant to bring in relatives. But while such a policy is generous, it is not the only rule consistent with an ethical approach. Limiting the rights of the diaspora to bring in relatives and prospective relatives is not primarily about controlling the total amount of migration, it is about controlling its composition. Educational points-based systems can only be effective if the individual rights of members of the diaspora are bounded by the objectives set by the system.

A Dramatic Implication

Where we have got to is that migration from poor countries to rich ones generates a massive windfall gain resulting from a productivity gap, and this gain is captured by migrants. There are two major barriers to accessing this gain: financing the initial investment in migration and overcoming a myriad of legal restrictions on entry. Diasporas reduce both of these barriers, so that as migration proceeds and the stock of migrants accumulates, more people are able to realize the gain from migration: the annual flow of migrants will tend to accelerate. Other changes in the world economy are also tending to increase migration: technical progress has substantially reduced the costs of travel, phone charges have fallen massively so that it is much easier for diasporas to remain connected to their country of origin, and rising incomes in very poor countries will enhance the ability to finance migration, while the absolute income gap will remain massive. The big brute fact remains those huge gains in productivity that migrants capture, which are inhibited by sizable barriers.

The barriers to migration lead to a prediction: actual migration should considerably understate desired migration. For evidence on desired migration the standard source is a Gallup Poll that covers a large sample of people from around the world. In total, around 40 percent of the population of poor countries say that they would choose to migrate to rich ones if they could.[13] Even this probably understates what would happen in the absence of financial and legal barriers. Imagine if 40 percent of the population indeed emigrated from a country. The resulting diaspora would be enormous and most likely highly concentrated in a few high-income cities. These cities, with their radically higher income than the capital of the country of origin, would quite possibly become the new cultural locus of the society: for those young people who had stayed behind, life would beckon from elsewhere.

Economists are rightly wary of intentions stated in surveys such as the Gallup Poll. Intentions may not translate into actual decisions. A rare natural experiment in which a relatively low-income society found itself with unrestricted access to a high-income society is therefore of interest. That natural experiment is Turkish Cyprus, which has been in economic terms similar to Turkey and therefore very poor by European standards. However, due to a complex political history, Turkish Cypriots have had privileged migration access to Britain. Did they make use of this access? Recall that the economic theory of migration predicts that for such a case there would be no equilibrium. Since Turkish Cyprus is in the middle-income range that is most conducive to migration, and is relatively close to the host country, clusters of the Turkish Cypriot diaspora would build up rapidly, and this would in turn accelerate until the original population of Turkish Cyprus nearly emptied. This is a very stark prediction that does not take into account many potentially offsetting factors. So how does it stand up when confronted with what actually happened? Unfortunately, British immigration statistics are paltry, but as of 1945 there were probably only around 2,000 Turkish Cypriots in Britain. The current Turkish Cypriot population in Britain is variously estimated at 130,000 to 300,000, the upper figure being the official estimate of the British Home Office. Meanwhile the number of Turkish Cypriots actually resident in Cyprus has declined from 102,000 as of the 1960 census, to around 85,000 as of 2001. So, there are now approximately twice as many Turkish Cypriots in Britain as in Cyprus. While Cyprus did not literally empty, the Gallup survey figure of 40 percent of people wanting to migrate does not appear exaggerated. But Northern Cyprus has not depopulated: instead it has had its own massive influx of immigrants, from Turkey: the indigenous Turkish Cypriots have become a minority in Northern Cyprus.

The evidence that but for the barriers the low-income societies would empty implies that for better or worse the barriers really matter. From the perspective of the indigenous population of potential host countries, the continued existence of some barriers that over time will tend to rise to offset the tendency of migration to accelerate is probably for the better. They are all that prevents massive inflows that would probably drive down wages and endanger mutual regard. From the perspective of the people who would remain in countries of origin, a massive and prolonged exodus would also have major effects, which I will discuss in part 4. But from the utilitarian universalist and libertarian ethical perspectives the barriers are a frustrating disaster. Huge gains in income for several hundred million poor people who would like to earn them are being denied. The utilitarian laments the avoidable reduction in well-being; the libertarian laments the restriction on freedom.

CHAPTER 7

Migrants

The Losers from Migration

NOW IT IS TIME FOR THE SURPRISING STAGE: why are migrants also the big losers from migration? The answer is that those who have already migrated lose, at least in economic terms, from the subsequent migration of others. They lose because the argument that migrants compete with low-wage indigenous labor, which I reviewed and substantially dismissed in chapter 4, contains a grain of truth. Migrants seldom compete head-to-head with indigenous workers, because, through a combination of tacit knowledge, accumulated experience, and discrimination, indigenous workers have a substantial advantage over migrants. Migrants compete head-to-head not with low-skill indigenous workers *but with each other*.

Migrants are not in close competition with indigenous workers, even in respect to those indigenous workers who have a similar level of education.[1] The indigenous advantage may be that they have better command of the language or that their greater tacit knowledge of social conventions makes them more productive.

Or it may be because employers discriminate against immigrant workers. Whatever is the explanation, the upshot is that immigrants form a distinct category of worker. Additional immigrants therefore drive down the earnings of existing immigrants. This is, indeed, the only clearly established *substantial* effect of immigration on wages. As I discussed in chapter 4, the effects of immigration on the wages of indigenous workers vary between being very small losses and modest gains. If immigration policy were to be set by its effects upon wages, the only interest group bothering to campaign for tighter restrictions should be immigrants.

The individual behavior of immigrants evidently belies this interest: immigrants typically devote considerable effort to trying to get visas for their relatives. But these two interests are not inconsistent. An immigrant who enables a relative to join her benefits from the resulting companionship, the kudos, and the peace of mind that her obligations have been fulfilled. The increased competition in the jobs market generated by the extra migrant is suffered by other immigrants. In effect, a tightening of immigration restrictions would be a public good for the existing immigrant community as a whole, whereas assisting the immigration of a relative is in the private interest of each immigrant individually.

There may be further social reasons why the existing stock of immigrants has an interest in tighter restrictions. Social trust may decline as the size of immigrant populations increases. The size of the immigrant stock also affects attitudes of the indigenous population toward immigrants: contrary to the hope that exposure increases tolerance, the opposite appears to happen. The indigenous population is more tolerant of low numbers than of high numbers. Intolerance is a public bad suffered by immigrants as a whole, which is thus inadvertently generated by the individually maximizing migration decisions of each successive migrant. Heightened intolerance is a consequence of these decisions that is not taken into account by individual migrants but may cumulatively severely affect the existing stock of migrants.

Hence, we arrive at the paradox of migration. Individual migrants succeed in capturing the huge productivity gains from migration. But migrants collectively have an interest in precisely what individually is most detrimental: entry barriers.

Migrants capture the lion's share of the large productivity gain from migration, and this handsomely repays the initial investment in the costs of the journey. But are there any continuing costs of being an immigrant in a culturally somewhat alien environment? As with the net effect on host populations, data permitting, we can use happiness as an integrating measure of economic gains and social costs. Whether happiness is a good measure of well-being is currently controversial. Research finds that above a modest income threshold increases in income do not generate sustained increases in happiness, although they do have transient effects: if you win the lottery you feel happier. But the warm glow fades away after a few months. If we apply this to migration, for the typical migrant from a low-income country to a high-income country, the income gain is overkill. Income increases from well below the threshold to well above it. According to the economics of happiness, the first few thousand dollars would increase happiness, but the remainder would be slack. Above the threshold by far the most powerful determinants of happiness appear to be social: marriage, children, and friends are the stuff of happiness, not the size of a paycheck. Migration has clear effects on these social characteristics, but they are negative. Families are separated, and the migrant spends his life in a culturally alien environment. He may tune in to the radio from his home country, surround himself with friends from the diaspora, and return home annually, but day by day the absence from home may tend to make him less happy. If we accept that happiness is a usable proxy for the quality of life, a convenient feature for our purposes is that it subsumes both the effect of higher income and any nonmonetary psychological costs: it gives us the net effect of opposing forces.

However, happiness is not the only alternative to income as a measure of well-being. An approach favored by some economists is the "ladder of life" in which people are asked to imagine on a ten-point scale the worst possible life and the best, and then place themselves on this scale.[2] This produces self-reported estimates of well-being that more consistently increase with the level of income, so we cannot necessarily conclude that migration provides an income gain that is overkill in terms of well-being.

Potentially, both happiness and the ladder of life can be used to address the question of whether migration increases the well-being of migrants. There is already a large academic literature that purports to measure these effects, but unfortunately the methods used are not up to the demanding requirements for reliable results. For example, several studies show that migrants tend to be less happy than the indigenous host population. But a leap of faith is then required to infer from this that migration has made people less happy than they otherwise would have been: there is no reason to expect that prior to migrating they were as happy as the host population. I have found only two studies that deploy methods that get around such pitfalls in research. Both are very recent and as yet unpublished, implying that they have not yet been through the rigors of an academic refereeing process. They are, however, as far as I can determine, all that we have got by way of reasonably reliable international evidence on this intriguing question.

The first study considers migration from Tonga to New Zealand.[3] Its research design takes advantage of an entry scheme introduced by the government of New Zealand entitled the Pacific Access Category. The key feature of this scheme was that it was run as a lottery and so granted and refused access to applicants from Tonga on a random basis. Such natural randomization is hugely convenient for researchers. By combining it with some sophisticated techniques, the researchers were able to overcome the pitfalls that have tripped up other studies. Because winning is random, the lottery winners as a group should not differ much from the lottery losers. Hence, following their migration the lottery winners can be compared with the lottery losers, and any new differences between them can reasonably be attributed to the fact that the winners have migrated. Tonga is fairly representative of many poor countries—income is around $3,700 per head, whereas average income in New Zealand is over $27,000. So the winners of the migration lottery also metaphorically won a financial lottery. Unsurprisingly, this showed up in the data: four years after migrating, the lottery winners had increased their incomes by nearly 400 percent. But the interest of the study is that it carefully measured the effects both on happiness and on the ladder of life. One year after migrating, there were no significant effects on either. After four years there were still no effects on the ladder of life, but people had become significantly *less* happy, by 0.8 points on a five-point scale.[4]

Before considering the implications of this study, let me describe the other one that tracks migrants from villages to cities within India. It, too, investigates how their well-being changed relative to a nearly identical group of people who had stayed behind.[5] This study compared how migrants perceived their current and past well-being with the assessments of other members of the household who had remained in the village. By construction of the sample, they had shared the same life prior to migration. While this research design is strong, since its context is migration within India, it is far from an ideal guide to international migration, where both the income change and the cultural change are much larger. It should, however, provide some indication of what effects are to be expected. As with the migration from Tonga to New Zealand, rural-to-urban migrants in India substantially increased their income. Consumption rose by an average of around 22 percent. This was, of course, very much less than the gain from international migration, but even that 22 percent gain from the low level of rural incomes should raise people's well-being as measured by the ladder of life, which was the researchers' chosen metric. Both types of migration incur a degree of social dislocation, but just as the income gain from moving to a city within a poor country is much less than that from moving from the same village to a city in a high-income country, so is the dislocation. The migrant moving from the village to the city within India suffers the shock of the urban and the separation from family, but not the dislocation of an alien culture. So, without claiming that the context can be extrapolated to international migration, it should constitute a halfway house. As with the Tongan study, this one finds that migrants place themselves no higher on the ladder of life than their siblings who stayed behind. Their higher income comes at the price of cultural dislocation, manifested by strong nostalgia for their former village life. An implication is their migration incurs a substantial hidden cost that offsets the readily apparent gain in income.

That, as far as I can tell, is currently the sum total of rigorous studies of the effect of poor-to-better-off migration on the quality of life. As with the impact of migration on the happiness of host populations, it is breathtakingly inadequate relative to the importance of the question. Manifestly, these studies do not permit us to draw any strong conclusions. Nor, however, do they permit us to dismiss them simply because they are inconvenient for our prejudices. Refer back to the important messages from the work of Jonathan Haidt and Daniel Kahneman: resist the temptation to let your moral tastes override cautious and effortful reasoning.

A tentative inference from these studies is that migrants incur substantial psychological costs that may be broadly commensurate with their large economic gains. The implications of this inference may appear to be far-reaching. The massive productivity gains from migration that so excite economists and that migrants capture appear not to translate into additional well-being. Migration does not deliver the anticipated free lunch, or rather the free lunch comes at the price of indigestion. But these implications themselves need to be qualified. Even if the psychological costs of migration turn out more generally to be consistent with these initial studies, migration might nevertheless eventually raise well-being. In the case of rural-to-urban migration within the same country, a reasonable presumption is that the children of migrants grow up without the nostalgia of their parents: for them the city is home. This second generation and subsequent ones not only have higher incomes than they would have had their parents remained in the village, but, since they themselves do not suffer offsetting psychological costs, they are also happier than they would be had their parents stayed in the village. Rural-urban migration thus conforms to the nineteenth-century narrative that migrants move for the benefit of their children rather than themselves. Urbanization is essential for opening the opportunities that enable the mass escape from poverty. The psychological costs borne by migrants may well be enormous, wiping out the income gains that accrue to them, but they are unavoidable costs of progress and so have the status of investments.

But for international migration from poor to rich countries, both the income gain and the cultural dislocation are an order of magnitude greater than those of rural-urban migration. Whether the psychological costs are for a single generation or persist depends upon whether subsequent generations feel at home or continue to feel dislocated. Whereas the costs of rural-urban migration are highly unlikely to persist beyond the first generation, in some situations the descendants of migrants might continue to feel alien. In the worst-case scenario, continuing psychological costs would offset the gains for several generations: migration would not be an investment, it would be a mistake.

PART 4

Those Left Behind

CHAPTER 8

The Political Consequences

MY WORKING LIFE HAS BEEN FOCUSED ON COUNTRIES that have largely missed out on rising global prosperity: the countries of the bottom billion. My original motivation for writing this book was to try to answer the question of how important migration is for these countries—that is, how it affects not migrants themselves, but the people left behind in their countries of origin. In any calculus of the overall benefits and costs of migration, the impact on the billion people who remain in countries that for decades have offered little hope of escape from poverty should be given a significant weight.

The miracle of economic prosperity is at source about *social models*: the fortuitous combination of institutions, narratives, norms, and organizations that in the eighteenth century began to lift Britain, and subsequently many other countries, out of the poverty that had persisted for millennia. Ultimately, the effect of migration on conditions in the bottom billion depends upon how it affects the social models prevalent in these countries. A critical aspect of the social model, recently emphasized by Acemoglu and Robinson (2011), is the shift in political power from extractive elites to more inclusive government that empowers the productive. So the opening chapter of this part focuses on the effects of migration on the politics of countries of origin, rather than the more conventional concern with brain drain and remittances, which I deal with in the next chapter.

Does Emigration Generate Pressure for Better Governance?

In Fiji emigration has been skewed toward the ethnic minority Indian population. This is one typical political effect: minorities are more likely to emigrate than those from the majority group. This feeds back onto the political economy of the country of origin in distinct ways. If people can escape from discrimination and perse-cution, then such vicious but tempting strategies may become less attractive for repressive governments. By providing minorities with an alternative, the migration option thereby improves their bargain-ing power and makes migration less necessary. However, some governments may actually want their minorities to leave, in which case migration would encourage them to adopt discriminatory policies. Quite aside from the feedback onto government policies toward minorities, the emigration of minorities will gradually change the composition of the society. How this affects those left behind depends upon how well the society copes with diversity. The same migration that increases social diversity in host countries reduces it in countries of origin. So, whatever the implications of the increase in diversity for host societies, the effects are likely to be the opposite in countries of origin.

While the disproportionate emigration of minorities may have political costs or benefits for those left behind, the more important effects are likely to come from the political behavior of diasporas.

Diasporas may be latent assets, yet many governments of countries of origin regard them as latent dangers. Diasporas are breeding grounds for political opposition: dissidents can find a safe haven, money can be raised to support opposition parties, and ideas and examples can become influential.

Many of the governments of countries of origin should indeed be threatened by their diasporas. After all, a key reason that some countries remain very poor is that they have not developed functioning democratic institutions, including accountability to electorates, respect for the rights of minorities and individuals, the rule of law, and checks and balances on arbitrary power. Many polities that have the superficial appurtenances of a proper democracy, such as contested elections and political parties, are in fact a sham. As a result, these countries continue to be misgoverned. Once living in high-income host countries, migrants can see what decent governance looks like, they know that their countries of origin lack it, and they want to pressure for change. To my mind the key issue for migration is whether this pressure is effective. But it is easier to pose this question than to answer it.

A famous early analysis of development by Albert Hirschman captures the essence of the ambiguity. He categorized the options facing those suffering from poor governance as "voice or exit."[1] People can protest, or they can get out. Migration is the ultimate exit option, and so it directly reduces voice—the domestic expression of opposition to poor governance. However, at the same time, an engaged diaspora can make that depleted domestic voice more effective.

A common way of expressing the direct effect of exit is that migration of the talented young provides bad regimes with a safety value: those who remain are self-selected to be more quiescent. Diasporas may kick and scream, but bad regimes may be able safely to ignore them or even turn them into scapegoats. A current likely instance of the safety-valve effect is Zimbabwe: a million Zimbabweans have fled to South Africa because of gross mismanagement by the Mugabe regime. In South Africa they have little influence either on political developments back in Zimbabwe or on the attitude of the South African government and its people toward President Mugabe. Quite possibly, had they remained in Zimbabwe, highly disaffected, vocal, and numerous, the regime's forces of repression would not have been able to contain them.

So improved governance is critical to whether the people left behind achieve prosperity. Migration has both favorable effects on governance and adverse effects, so a reliable estimate of the net effect would be decisive for an overall assessment of the impact of migration on countries of origin. When I turned to the technical economic literature on migration, which is now extensive, I was astonished to discover that this particular issue was virtually terra incognita, so I set to work, trying to get reliable research answers. I must confess that I now understand why this particular question has attracted so little credible research: it verges on being unanswerable given the current availability of data.

Here, in a nutshell, is the nature of the problems. Governance is a somewhat slippery concept. Within reason we know both good and bad governance when we see it, but smallish changes are hard to measure. Although there are now several data sets that purport to measure it in various dimensions, very few provide long time series with comprehensive international coverage. Further, migration can feed back on the governance of countries of origin in a variety of ways with opposing effects, so it is insufficient to investigate only one or two of them; it is their totality that matters. But the most acute difficulty is to sort which is the chicken and which the egg. While migration may affect the quality of governance, the quality of governance most surely affects migration. A badly governed country is likely to experience a lot of emigration: people who cannot vote with a ballot slip vote with their feet. Compounding the potential for confusion, many characteristics of a society are liable to affect both migration and governance. A country is poor so people leave, and also government becomes more difficult. So a simple empirical association between migration and governance cannot be interpreted. Is migration causing governance to deteriorate, is bad governance driving people out, or is poverty causing both? Economics often encounters such situations, and in principle this one has solutions. But a solution to this problem depends upon finding something that clearly affects migration but is independent of governance. Unfortunately, so many things could potentially influence governance that in practice this approach has not yet generated convincing solutions.

Researchers have, however, recently made a beginning. There are two broad ways to proceed: macro and micro. Macroanalysis depends upon looking at country-level data, investigating differences between countries and over time. Microanalysis depends upon building ingenious experiments in which ordinary people take part to investigate particular channels through which migration might have effects. In the end, the questions are macro, but the most reliable approach is currently micro.

The macroanalysis is in its infancy and may remain there. One long-established measure of governance is the degree to which a country is democratic, measured year by year for many countries. The degree of democracy is a very crude metric for the quality of governance: incumbent rulers are often able to manipulate elections so that they meet the appearance of legitimacy without threatening their power. Or politics becomes so corrupted by money that voters face a pointless choice between rival crooks. China, which avoids elections, is better governed than the Democratic Republic of the Congo, which, despite its name and its contested elections, is mired in corrupt and ineffective rule. But nevertheless, other things being equal, more democracy is likely to trump less democracy. The analysis of democracy evidently suffers from the same problems as any other aspect of governance. But according to the best macroanalysis currently available the net effect of migration is ambiguous, depending upon its composition and the scale of the brain drain.[2] The migration of the unskilled unambiguously makes countries somewhat more democratic. However, given the trends in the migration policies of high-income countries, the more pertinent issue is the migration of the skilled. Unfortunately, the emigration of the skilled has two potentially opposing effects on the pressure for democracy. Although migration builds a diaspora that brings external pressure, it may drain the stock of educated people. This matters because the greater the proportion of the population that is educated, the stronger the pressure for democracy. Where the brain drain predominates, which unfortunately is what happens in most of the small, poor countries, although migrants bring external pressure for political reform, they have depleted the resident pressure brought by the educated. Research has as yet been unable to resolve this ambiguity: the macro approach leaves us in the dark.

The microanalysis is also in its infancy but is growing. To my knowledge the first serious experiment was by my colleagues Pedro Vicente and Catia Batista. Pedro works on governance and has chosen to do his fieldwork in two small formerly Portuguese island colonies, Cape Verde and São Tomé. I reported on some of Pedro's ingenious work in *The Plundered Planet*. Meanwhile, his wife, Catia, was working on labor market effects of migration. I suggested that they might extend their marriage to the intellectual domain and try a partnership investigating the effect of migration on governance.

Indeed, Cape Verde would be the perfect location for a field experiment because it had the highest rate of emigration in Africa. Pedro and Catia duly transformed that suggestion into a revealing piece of research.[3] Their idea was to see whether the exposure to democratic ideas provided by migration increases the pressure for political accountability. By presenting people with a chance to lobby for better governance, they show that households with a migrant are more likely to take part. Cape Verde might be dismissed as just an exceptional little island, but the same transfer of political engagement via migrants back to home populations has recently been shown for Mexico.[4] How do migrants influence the political behavior of their families back home? There is nothing very mysterious about this, but researchers are now onto it. During the Senegalese elections of 2012, Senegalese migrants living in the United States and France were surveyed. Through phone calls, daily or weekly, most of these migrants were urging their relatives to register to vote, and nearly half were recommending whom to support.[5]

While Pedro and Catia focused on the influence of migrants who were still abroad, complementary studies investigate the impact of migrants who have returned to their countries of origin. A particularly convincing new study is by my colleagues Lisa Chauvet and Marion Mercier. Their choice of country was Mali.[6] Mali may seem to be the ultimate little country far away, but in 2012 it was thrust onto the front pages on the international press by a succession of increasingly catastrophic political events. In the last days of Colonel Gaddafi, the regime hired mercenaries from the nomads of northern Mali. Libya had accumulated huge stockpiles of sophisticated, money-no-object weapons that these mercenaries were able to loot as the regime collapsed. While as mercenaries they had little interest in fighting for Gaddafi, back home in Mali they had long-standing grievances and aspirations to separatism: fancy weapons were just what they wanted. All that stood between the rebels and power was the Malian army. The army was under democratic control: Mali was an established democracy. Indeed, it was sufficiently democratic that the incumbent president had decided to retire: the rebel invasion coincided with the approach of an election and the withdrawal of the president into lame-duck inactivity. Mali was under the standard donor pressure to minimize its military expenditure, so while the rebels had all the technology that a deluded and oil-enriched military dictator had been able to lay his hands on, the Malian army was threadbare. The army lobbied the president to increase the military budget, but the president prevaricated. Facing defeat in the field, the army mutinied and overthrew the government. Since Mali was promptly ostracized by the international community, this did nothing to improve the military situation, but it did plunge the society into political chaos as refugees flooded south to escape the rebels, and the coup leaders partially handed back power, but to whom? Meanwhile, the rebel movement was infiltrated and overpowered by incoming al-Qaeda fighters who smelled a promising opportunity to create a haven for terrorism. As I write, the French military has dramatically intervened at the request of the Malian regime and is pressing it to return power to civilians. So politics in Mali suddenly matters.

Lisa and Marion investigated whether the political exposure provided by a period of emigration affected political participation and electoral competition once migrants had returned home: specifically, did people turn out to vote? They found three effects in ascending order of practical importance. Least important: returning migrants are significantly more likely to vote than nonmigrants. More remarkable: this behavior gets copied by nonmigrants. Those living in the vicinity of migrants are also more likely to vote. This result is not dependent only upon whether people tell interviewers that they voted. Economists are suspicious of self-reported information because it might be subject to bias. The higher voter turnout was there to see in the election returns. Now for the really remarkable: among nonmigrants, the ones most inclined to copy the behavior of returning migrants were the less educated. This is really encouraging. Not only do return migrants bring back new norms of democratic participation learned in the high-income societies, but they are also catalysts for change among the uneducated, who are otherwise hardest to reach. Is Mali exceptional? A very recent study for Moldova finds the same result.[7] The latest research is also revealing that it matters where migrants have gained their exposure to foreign political norms. The better governed and more democratic the host society is, the more significant the transfer of the norms of democracy: France and the United States are better seedbeds than Russia and Africa.

This recent evidence is a skimpy basis on which to answer what is potentially the most important question on migration. Although migrants themselves do well from migration, it can only be truly significant in addressing hardcore global poverty if it accelerates transformation in countries of origin. In turn, that transformation is at base a political and social, rather than an economic, process. So the potential for migration to affect the political process for those left behind really matters. These studies provide straws in the wind. Political values nest into a larger set of values about relations with other people in society that, as I discussed in part 2, differ markedly between host countries and countries of origin. On average, the social norms of high-income counties are more conducive to prosperity, and so in this restricted but important sense they are superior. After all, it is the prospect of higher income that induces migration. So do functional social norms diffuse back to countries of origin in the same way as norms of democratic political participation? A new study of fertility choices finds precisely this result. Desired family size is one of the stark social differences between rich and poor societies. The experience of living in a high-income society not only reduces the preferred family size of migrants themselves, but feeds back to the attitudes of those back home.[8] Evidently, this benign process of norm transfer depends upon migrants themselves being sufficiently integrated into their host society to absorb the new norms in the first place.

While bad governments in countries of origin may appear to deserve all they get from disaffected diasporas, not all diaspora pressure is for the good. Indeed, diasporas are often regarded by governments as hotbeds of extremist political opposition that fuel conflict. These fears are not entirely fanciful: diasporas are disproportionately drawn from ethnic minorities that have been oppressed in their countries of origin and harbor lingering resentments. At their worst, diasporas are seriously out of touch with present-day realities in their countries of origin but continue to nurse grievances over long-past conditions as badges of differentiated identity within their host society. They finance and otherwise encourage the most extreme elements within their country of origin as symbols of solidarity with their imagined identity. A disastrous instance of this phenomenon is the support provided by the Tamil diaspora in North America and Europe for the Tamil Tiger separatist rebellion in Sri Lanka. This has most surely left Sri Lankan Tamils worse off than had the diaspora been quiescent. Nor is the existence of safe havens from bad governments unambiguously beneficial. The regime of the Russian czars epitomized misgovernance, but the return of Lenin from safe haven in Switzerland frustrated what might otherwise have been a transition to democracy. Similarly, the return of Ayatollah Khomeini to Iran from safe haven in France scarcely ushered in an era of sweetness and light. While in such extreme instances governments are right to fear diasporas, more commonly policies of discouragement appear to be based on little more than resentment at success. For example, Haiti, with its huge latent diaspora asset, has denied migrants the right to dual citizenship. Governments are only slowly waking up to the need to manage this asset as carefully as a conventional sovereign wealth fund. The potential is far greater: while placing substantial financial capital abroad at negligible interest rates makes little sense for a poor country, it will inevitably have a huge stock of human capital abroad and so should plan to use it well.

The diaspora as an asset is of particular importance in postconflict situations following civil wars. Typically, civil wars last many years, during which the educated young get out. Political instability and religious divisions both fuel migration.[9] Wealth also flees, as an alternative to being destroyed. So by the postconflict stage, much of the society's human and financial capital is abroad. The challenge is to get both back, and the two are linked: if people return, they are more likely to bring back their wealth in order to build homes and establish businesses. The severity of the skill shortage in postconflict situations is often alarming. For example, during the brutal rule of Idi Amin in Uganda in which around half a million people were killed, the educated were systematically targeted. One of the priorities postconflict was to restore higher education. A search of the Ugandan diaspora found forty-seven doctorates just in the South Pacific: one was persuaded to return to run the country's first think tank.

As indicated by Uganda, the government of the country of origin has some scope to encourage return. There is also scope for the migration policy of host countries to facilitate postconflict recovery. High-income countries have a manifest interest in the success of postconflict situations: in recent decades the costs of trying to shore them up have been stupendous. Historically, close to half of them have reverted to violence, so if migration policy can be helpful, it is sensible to make it so. However, if restrictions on immigration from the country are tightened once peace has been restored, those who fled during conflict may be less inclined to risk return: will they be able to get back if necessary? The right time to adopt migration policies that would be helpful in postconflict situations is during the conflict. Both from the perspective of the duty of rescue, and to help preserve the country's human capital from violence, during conflict a migration policy needs to be exceptionally generous. The conventional criteria of skills and family need to be overruled by one based on human needs and human rights. However, the right of residence in the host country could be linked to the duration of the conflict. If rights of residence lapsed following the restoration of peace, migrants would be encouraged to be psychologically and socially better prepared for return: for example, they would send more remittances. As rights of residence in host countries expired, they would provide postconflict societies with a substantial influx of skill and money.

Does Emigration Increase the Supply of Good Leaders?

While one route by which migration might affect the quality of governance is through political pressure, another is through the supply of capable and well-motivated people. Small, poor societies hemorrhage educated emigrants.[10] At the apex of public policy the vital talent could be drained away. However, it could instead be enhanced because a few key people come back, having gained vital experience while abroad. By the nature of their chosen path, instances in which people leave their societies who would otherwise have become valued leaders are unknowable. My own favorite plausible case concerns Tidjane Thiam, a former minister of economic development for Côte d'Ivoire who left following a coup. Once in Britain he revealed truly exceptional talents by rising in the highly competitive world of international business to become CEO of the largest insurance company in Europe.

But while such credible cases of serious leadership loss can be found, what is much more striking in small, poor countries is the disproportionate number of competent presidents, finance ministers, and governors of central banks who have had periods living in host countries, whether as students or longer-term residents. President Sirleaf of Liberia, winner of a Nobel Prize; President Condé, the first democratic president of Guinea; President Outtarra, the skilled technocrat who is restoring Côte d'Ivoire, and the highly respected Nigerian finance minister Dr. Okonjo-Iweala, are all current instances of countries of origin calling on valuable experience built up elsewhere. Overall, as of 1990, over two-thirds of the heads of government of developing countries had studied abroad.[11] Given this remarkable overrepresentation of former migrants in the leadership teams of small, poor countries, the net effect is surely positive: as a result of migration, these countries have more educated leaders.

This raises a further question: does education matter for leadership? President Mugabe accumulated several degrees during the liberation struggle, and his cabinet was similarly well educated, but this did not avert misgovernance. However, Zimbabwe turns out to be an outlier. Recent work by Timothy Besley, Jose G. Montalvo, and Marta Reynal-Querol investigated whether education affects leadership performance and found a significant and substantial beneficial effect.[12]

We should therefore expect that whereas the emigration of the already educated has ambiguous political effects, emigration in order to get education should be beneficial. A recent study by Antonio Spilimbergo provides convincing evidence.[13] Using a remarkable global data set compiled by UNESCO on students studying abroad since 1950, he investigated the link between their experience of political regime while studying, and the subsequent political evolution of their country of origin. He found that foreign study has lasting influences wholly disproportionate to the raw number of people involved: evidently, students trained abroad in later life become influential back home. But it is not the training per se that matters: students trained in undemocratic countries do not exert pressure for democracy. The more democratic the host country, the stronger the subsequent influence for democracy. The precise route by which this works remains to be researched, but Spilimbergo suggests that it might be through personal identity. Akerlof and Kranton, whose work I introduced in chapter 2, suggest that just as an effective firm encourages workers to identify with the organization, so education in a democracy may inculcate a sense of common identity with the international democratic community.[14] As part of studying, students have their norms reset to the standards of democratic societies and bring them back home.

If education improves the quality of leadership, and education in high-income democracies inculcates democratic political values in students from poor countries, we should expect that if a future leader gained her education in a high-income democracy, the quality of her leadership would benefit twice over. Not only would she be educated, but she would have absorbed democratic values. This is a precise hypothesis, and in principle it is testable: it just requires painstaking data collection digging out the personal histories of hundreds of leaders. Reassuringly, new research finds the supporting evidence: Marion Mercier has just done it.[15]

So, pulling this together, in the typical country of the bottom billion, although migration depletes the overall stock of educated people, it enables the society to draw upon foreign-educated students and other former migrants for its top public positions, and this in turn significantly improves the quality of governance.

While through a combination of pressure and selection of leadership, migration has beneficial effects on governance, it is only one of many influences, and its importance should not be exaggerated. The presumed importance of a politicized diaspora was one of the crucial misjudgments concerning postinvasion Iraq. Two African societies with the largest diasporas are Cape Verde and Eritrea. Both have had prolonged and massive emigration to the West, particularly to the United States, over decades. In both the diaspora has remained heavily engaged: the government of Cape Verde periodically visits Boston, which probably has the largest cluster of Cape Verdians anywhere in the world, and the Eritreans in Washington, DC, also get regular visits from their government. Yet in respect of governance, Cape Verde and Eritrea are poles apart. On the Mo Ibrahim Index, a comprehensive rating system run by Africans, Cape Verde regularly scores around the top: in 2011 its retiring president won the $5 million Mo Ibrahim leadership prize. Meanwhile, Eritrea routinely scores around the bottom: the regime is highly authoritarian, with power concentrated around the president and its youth desperate to escape the country but conscripted en masse into the army.[16] If such a high common exposure to migration to America can coexist with such diametrically opposed styles of governance, then perhaps migration is not such a powerful force for change.

CHAPTER 9

The Economic Consequences

IN ADDITION TO ITS INDIRECT POLITICAL EFFECTS on those left behind, migration has direct economic effects. The most common phrase used to describe them is "brain drain": emigration draws off the brightest, most ambitious, and most educated people from the society. But we should be wary of the premature use of labels that have such a strong normative force. "Brain drain" preempts the issue of whether the emigration of the most talented is overall adverse for the society.

Is "Brain Drain" the Right Concern?

Superficially, there seems to be no issue: the most talented people are an asset for their society. Although most of the returns to talent accrue to the talented, some of their productivity spills over to others. In the production process, educated people raise the productivity of less-educated people, thereby raising their wages. Further, high-earning people pay higher taxes, and these finance public goods that benefit everyone. So if emigration reduces the number of talented people in a society, it will affect the less talented adversely. While this might appear to close the issue, it hasn't. The key question is whether the emigration of a talented person in fact reduces the stock of talent remaining in the society.

Evidently, in a direct sense if a talented person emigrates, the stock of talented people is indeed reduced by one. But talent is not primarily innate. The talent that produces high productivity is not given by the gene pool; it is built by education and effort. Education, like migration itself, is an investment. Effort is, well, effortful: given the choice, we would all prefer sloth, albeit disguised by a term kinder to our self-esteem. My own motivation for working on the bottom billion was the recognition of the vast untapped potential locked up in mass poverty. My father was a bright man who was taken out of school at age twelve and then faced the Depression of the 1930s: he had no chance in life. I see the frustrated life of my father millions of times over in these countries. The possibility of emigration opens up life chances dramatically, not just for the migrant but for the entire family. Recall that in many cases migration is more a family decision than that of the migrant alone: the migrant is not escaping from the family but rather is part of a larger strategy of enlarging opportunities. From the perspective of other family members, migrants are investments that often pay off handsomely through a prolonged stream of remittances and enhanced access for further migration. But parents know that for their children to stand a reasonable chance of accessing these family-enhancing chances, they must stay in school and do well in it. At low levels of income, schooling is expensive. Roger Thurow gives a moving account of the choices facing a typical Kenyan mother as she decides day by day whether to use the food she has grown to feed her family or sell it so as to meet the school fees without which her children will be excluded. Not only is schooling expensive, but success depends upon effort.[1] Most parents will be familiar with the routine trial of encouraging and coercing children into trying harder, but the prospect of migration starkly raises the stakes.

The better the chance of migrating, the bigger the payoff to education and effort. So instead of having only a single effect of migration on the amount of talent available in the society, we now have two: a direct one that reduces talent and an indirect one that increases it. It might seem that the indirect effect could merely soften the adverse direct one. After all, parents are only more strongly motivated to tap the latent talent of the children if they intend them to migrate. If children do migrate, there is no offsetting replenishment of talent. But the opportunity to migrate is limited by a variety of barriers. Many people will struggle up the educational ladder only to find that despite success at school their hopes of emigration are frustrated. Albeit reluctantly, they will augment the supply of talented people left behind. An analogy is the British savings-cum-gambling scheme known as Premium Bonds. The bonds are secure assets that can be redeemed at par. While they are held, each month they attract the possibility of winning a lottery— the Premium. The prospect of winning this lottery enhances the return on saving, and so many people purchase Premium Bonds. An overwhelming majority of bondholders never win, but they have nevertheless saved. So it is entirely possible that the pool of those lured into educational investment by the prospect of migration, but then not lucky enough to migrate, is sufficiently large that it more than offsets the direct loss of talent.

Within conventional economics, this effect of migration works through a probability: getting an education is like getting a lottery ticket to a better life. But there is also likely to be a different mechanism at work that does not depend upon probabilities: successful migrants become role models for others to emulate. Superficially, this may seem to amount to the same thing, but there is a deep analytic distinction that goes back to Keynes. He suggested that, confronted by unmanageable complexity, people fall back upon narratives that provide rules of thumb. The imitation of role models, which modern psychology now recognizes as a powerful influence on behavior, is just such an application of narratives: a role model is a set of rules for living. A successful migrant can have far-reaching influence, much as a celebrity footballer can have influence. Imitators are not calculating the odds—if they did so, they would usually be dismayed—they are lured by an idea of how to live.

The two mechanisms are not alternatives. Although economists ended up rejecting Keynes's analysis as a description of financial markets, as a description of how ordinary people take such decisions both types of behavior surely coexist.[2] Although migration directly reduces the stock of talented people, indirectly it generates both an incentive and influential role model, augmenting the flow of new talent.

These subtle mechanisms by which the prospect of possible migration increases the flow of talent may be sufficient to counter the direct loss. However, the increased flow of talent works entirely by increasing the *demand* for education. A different mechanism is at work changing the supply. All governments spend money on education, usually by providing it through public schools and universities. The relative importance of public provision varies between countries, but in the poorest countries public provision is often dominant. Emigration changes the incentive of governments to spend on education. Most obviously, it reduces the social benefits of education and so weakens the case for public subsidy. Offsetting this, governments benefit from the remittances generated by emigration. So potentially governments can think of public money spent on education as an investment in future remittances. Nevertheless, the studies that have tried to measure government responses have found that usually education budgets are reduced.

The overall impact of migration on the supply of talent is a combination of the direct loss, the increased demand of parents for the education of their children, and the reduced willingness of government to pay for it. However, the initial effect is always adverse: the stock is first depleted, even if it then recovers. Economists have been able to measure these effects: they are no longer just cute theories.[3] The estimates vary country by country: there are winners and losers. The crucial discovery is that if the initial exodus is large, then it cannot be recovered. A large exodus builds a large diaspora and that gears up migration—as discussed in part 2. Most of the countries that remain very poor are small, and this matters for their rate of emigration: small countries have proportionately much higher emigration rates than large countries. So unless there are strong additional effects to the contrary, large countries will tend to be net gainers and small countries net losers.[4] Further, an early exodus of the skilled feeds back not just onto the wages of those left behind, but onto the capacity of the economy to innovate and adapt new technologies. The poorest countries need to catch up, but emigration drains them of the very people who would enable them to do so.[5]

To take an extreme, Haiti, with a population of around 10 million, has lost around 85 percent of its educated people. Such high emigration of the talented is not surprising: within Haiti the burden of history and prolonged misgovernance have left a legacy of shriveled opportunities, whereas it is offshore from the largest pool of employment opportunities on earth. In turn, the massive Haitian diaspora in North America makes migration both a natural and a realistic aspiration. In order to offset the loss of 85 percent of its talented people, the prospect of migration would need to augment the supply of talented people by around sevenfold. The actual response is much smaller than this, and so emigration indeed drains Haiti of its talent. As of 2000, which is the most recent year for all the empirical work on these effects, Haiti is estimated to have been one of the biggest overall losers: it has around 130,000 fewer educated workers than it would have had without emigration. President Clinton, who has worked passionately for Haiti over many years and especially since the earthquake, has this word-perfect. He describes America as having been blessed by mass immigration from Haiti, but at the same time laments that Haiti has lost too much of its talent. He wants to see an expansion of higher education in Haiti, both to compensate for the loss and to produce educated young people who are more inclined to stay, being less equipped with portable qualifications.

Almost all the small, poor countries have ended up as losers from migration. A sophisticated new study identifies twenty-two such countries in which the self-interested decisions of emigrants are inflicting overall losses on the society.[6] In effect, these countries would benefit from emigration controls, but of course these are neither practicable nor ethical. Many of these countries are in Africa. Those that, like Haiti, have been stagnant for decades have, unsurprisingly, lost talent: Liberia, Sierra Leone, Malawi, Zimbabwe, Zambia, Guinea-Bissau, Mozambique, Afghanistan, and Laos read like a roll call of the bottom billion. But more troubling, even the more successful small developing countries have suffered net losses: Ghana, Uganda, Vietnam, Mauritius, and Jamaica. Doing well is apparently not enough to retain talent: Jamaica is estimated to have had a net loss of 14 percent of its skilled labor. In contrast, the few really big developing countries—China, India, Brazil, Indonesia, Bangladesh, and Egypt—enjoy an overall increase in talent. The prospect of emigration induces more investment in education, while relatively few people actually leave. The beneficial effect on the large countries is *proportionately* much smaller than the adverse effect on the small, but the large dominate: their modest gains more than outweigh the serious losses of the small.

A further way in which the supply of talent can be increased by emigration is through return: some emigrants come back home to work. One stream of returning migrants will be those who have not done as well as they had hoped. After a phase in work, they find themselves unemployed and go back. In the process of working, even these unsuccessful migrants gain experience and skills. They may not be up to the standards required for success in a high-productivity economy, but they may, nevertheless, be productive by local standards in their countries of origin. Another stream of returning migrants has been educated while abroad. The most important such flow of students has been the Chinese: China's rapid absorption of Western technology has been substantially accelerated by the knowledge acquired by its students trained in the West. But the size of this flow depends not just upon how many young people leave from countries of origin for their education, but how many come back. China has benefited so much from migration because a high proportion of its students choose to return. But the needier the country of origin, the less likely that students will want to go back. The spectacular growth of China has made its students abroad confident that in returning home they are not damaging their prospects: they are rejoining the fastest-growing economy on earth. Until very recently, Africans have been far less willing to return, because prospects have been so poor relative to those in the advanced economies. It is indeed hard for the poorest societies to compete with the advanced societies as attractive living places for their talented students abroad. Even if salaries are bid up to competitive levels, implying horrendously wide wage differentials within the society, there is an acute lack of both public goods and many private goods that high-income people learn to enjoy. Nevertheless, many students do return: for example, the academics teaching at African universities mostly have degrees from Western universities; without them African universities would have collapsed. Similarly vital, in presidential offices and ministries of finance key people have been educated abroad.

As with the prospect of emigration on education, the decision to return can be viewed both as a calculation and as copying role models. The difference in the payoffs to returning to China and Africa are clear enough, but this may be reinforced by differences in the narratives. China's spectacular growth readily seeds a narrative that acquiring Western higher education is just a springboard to harnessing opportunities within China: it is the prelude to domestic success. In contrast, for Africans return migration has long been associated with failure to make it in the West. Once established, the role models derived from such narratives may take on a life of their own and drive decisions well beyond the range implied by objective rationality.

For societies that are small and poor it may all sound a bit desperate: those left behind must content themselves with being lured into education induced by prospects that do not materialize, the return of developed economy rejects, and a trickle of returning students. But then, the situation of the bottom billion is pretty desperate. While the diaspora might not itself drive growth, it may be well placed to gear it up once some other factor gets it going. Currently, several African countries have started to grow quite rapidly thanks to resource discoveries. While resource-based growth has often proved to be unsustainable, as I discussed in *The Plundered Planet*, it may be the trigger for attracting back the diaspora. Such a coordinated influx of talented people may be critical in breaking bottlenecks and so improve the chances that growth can be sustained. A large diaspora is a latent asset for a country of origin that can be tapped once the conditions are right. It is a human variant on the sovereign wealth funds that are now fashionable.

Where does this leave the "brain drain" as a concern? For developing countries as a group the concern is clearly misplaced: gains outweigh losses. But the category "developing country" can no longer be taken seriously. China, India, and many other countries are rapidly converging on the high-wage countries. Intractable poverty as a problem that warrants substantial and sustained international attention is becoming concentrated in the small, poor countries that have suffered significant net losses of their scarce skilled population. As their diasporas build up, their rate of emigration is likely to increase. For these societies, "brain drain" unfortunately remains the right concern.

Is There a Motivation Drain?

So far, I have considered only education. While this is important, it is a narrow perspective on the productivity of a worker. In chapter 2 I introduced the idea that productivity depends on whether a worker internalizes the objectives of the organization.[7] If a plumber, does he self-discipline because being a good plumber has become part of his own identity; if a teacher, does she turn up for work and refresh her skills because she identifies herself as a good teacher? More generally, do workers identify themselves as "insiders" or "outsiders" in the organizations for which they work? As with other aspects of behavior, these alternative attitudes to work can be imitated. Migrants will tend to come from among those people who have the most positive attitudes to work: they want to move to jobs in effective organizations where their talents will be harnessed.[8] This feeds back to the remaining population. The conscientious teacher has emigrated; it is the ineffective one who is still in the classroom. It is this ineffective teacher with whom young teachers interact and who sets the norms of what is expected. With fewer "insider" role models to imitate, remaining workers are more likely to choose to self-identify as "outsiders." Nobel laureate George Akerlof and Rachel Kranton have developed a model that predicts just such an effect. As "insiders" selectively emigrate, those left behind face higher costs of becoming insiders themselves: they would stick out like a sore thumb. But as fewer people choose to become insiders, the productivity of those left behind declines.[9]

While their model has yet to be tested in poor countries, there is some supporting evidence. A study of trainee nurses in Ethiopia tracked their motivation both at the time of completing their training and three years later, when they had been placed in government clinics.[10] Unsurprisingly, on the eve of their career as nurses, most of these young people wanted to be Florence Nightingale: they were motivated to heal the sick. Three years later, their attitudes conformed to those prevailing in the clinics to which they had been assigned, with cynicism and corruption being widespread. While this does not tell us about migration, it does support the Akerlof and Kranton mechanism that whether young workers become insiders or outsiders depends on the balance between them in the workplace. But there is one study that is indeed about migration from poor places to rich ones. It is about migration of educated African Americans from the inner cities, which remain predominantly African American, to those parts of America that are predominantly white.[11] It finds that the exodus of the black middle class is a major reason for the persistence of poverty and dysfunction in these neighborhoods. The opportunity for exodus must still be an incentive for education. But even were there to be a brain gain, it is more than offset by the reinforcement of outsider attitudes. Productivity is not directly determined by education, but by what people do with it.

Is the loss of role models for insider attitudes important for poor countries? We simply do not know, but we can split the question into two parts: are outsider attitudes to work an important problem in these societies, and does migration significantly contribute to them? Outsider attitudes are prevalent in the public sectors of many of these countries, and these sectors are large. In many countries it is common for nurses to steal drugs and sell them, for teachers to skip classes, and for government officials to take bribes. In all these organizations there are also insiders, but they stand out as valiant exceptions and often incur the disapproval of their peers. There are now comparable indices of corruption that substantiate concern, but a more graphic way of grasping the severity of the problem is an anecdote from a ministry of health. As before, I offer an anecdote not as evidence, but for understanding. Offered aid to purchase antiretroviral drugs, the ministry's chief official secretly set up his own company to import them. Using his authority, he duly purchased the drugs from his company for his ministry. But onto this abuse of his public office, he added a dramatic twist: in order to cut costs, the drugs he imported were fakes. The chief official in a ministry of health had so failed to internalize the objective of his organization as to find mass mortality an acceptable price for personal gain. With such extreme outsider attitudes at the top, it would be unsurprising were outsiders common throughout many public organizations. While outsiders to the organizations for which they work, such people are not immoral in their own terms: they are insiders to their clan, using their corruptly acquired money to help their extended family. Similarly, a common critique of Haitian society is that people have become mired in outsider attitudes: passive dependence on external aid, and a zero-sum game narrative in which there is an exaggerated fear of being exploited. So let us accept that outsider attitudes are a problem for many poor societies.

What is much less clear is whether migration significantly accentuates this problem, as it appears to do in America's inner cities. Even if insiders self-select into migration, in most occupations the scale of emigration is too modest to have much impact on the balance of attitudes. Where the mechanism may matter is in more senior and skilled positions in dysfunctional organizations. A continuous loss of the few insiders may prevent them from ever accumulating to a tipping point at which insider attitudes are self-sustaining. The issue has not yet been researched.

Remittances

Even if migration from small, poor countries results in a net loss of talented and motivated people, it might nevertheless be beneficial for the people left behind. As discussed in chapter 6, the migration decision is often taken jointly by the migrant and her family; migrants stay very much connected to their families, and a key form that this connection takes is remittances. Many migrants come from rural areas of poor countries. From the perspective of the family back home, whether the migrant has moved a few hundred miles to relatives in Nairobi, or a few thousand miles to relatives in London, may be less important than the size of the remittance that the family receives.

So how generous are migrants? An early study of how much money Nairobi-based migrants sent back home to rural Kenya caused a stir because it seemed so high: 21 percent of earnings went back to the village.[12] Benchmarked against this sort of generosity, how do international migrants compare? The range varies enormously.[13] Mexican migrants to the United States remit an astonishing 31 percent of their earnings. But some migrants are even more generous. Migrants from El Salvador living in Washington remit 38 percent. The Senegalese in Spain remit a world-beating 50 percent of their earnings; the Ghanaians in Italy remit around a quarter; Moroccans in France remit a tenth of their earnings, while Algerians are a bit lower at around 8 percent. Continuing down the league table of generosity, both the Chinese in Australia, and Filipinos in the United States, come in at around 6 percent. Two high-profile migrant groups skulk near the bottom: Turks in Germany and Cubans in America return a measly 2 percent.

In aggregate, all this generosity adds up to enormous sums. Remittances during 2012 from high-wage countries to developing countries total around $400 billion. This is almost four times global aid flows and roughly on a par with foreign direct investment. However, such numbers should not mesmerize because they are highly skewed: they give an exaggerated sense of the importance of remittances to poor countries. Neither generosity, in the sense of the proportion of earnings that the migrant remits, nor how much in total a country gets is the right yardstick for impact. On the absolute amounts the two big winners among countries of origin are India and China with over $50 billion a year each. But while $50 billion is not exactly chickenfeed for China, neither is it that important. The best measure of the importance of remittances for the people left behind is to benchmark them against the income of the country of origin: converted into a more human concept, this shows remittances relative to income for the average household back home. Globally, the remittances of migrants from low-wage countries living in high-wage countries are around 6 percent of the income of countries of origin, the average remittance per migrant per year being around $1,000. However, as with the concept of the brain drain, the averages are of limited use because the underlying concept of "developing countries" has become redundant: variation among those formerly "developing" countries is now the story.

Haiti again provides an example of a high-emigration, impoverished country. Haiti suffers a substantial brain drain: so many educated Haitians leave that, despite the enhanced incentive to get an education, the society suffers a net loss of its talent. But the remittances from this massive pool of skilled emigrants are in consequence substantial at around 15 percent of income. This is not enough to lift Haitians out of poverty, but if you are up to your neck in choppy water, it does make you feel a little safer.

Haiti is one of the major beneficiaries of remittances, but it is not entirely exceptional. Those generous Salvadorans also make a substantial difference to the people left behind: remittances are 16 percent of income. Even for a few of the big poor countries, remittances matter a lot: for both Bangladesh and the Philippines the figure is 12 percent. For Africa as a whole, remittances are much less important. The highest remittance inflow in Africa is for Senegal: the world-beating generosity of those Senegalese migrants shows up in a contribution of 9 percent of income.

So for the typical country of origin remittances add a few percentage points to the income of the people left behind. Of course, had the migrants stayed home they would have earned an income, and this would also have helped their families. Since the typical remittance is only around $1,000, migrants would not have had to be particularly productive in order to match through their work the contribution made by remittances. So it seems doubtful that post-migration income is substantially different from what it would have been without migration: remittances largely offset the loss of output. The difference is that there are now a few less mouths to feed, and so per capita expenditure can be a little higher.[14]

Skepticism about aid does not extend to flows that are person to person: whereas governments are assumed to do no right, self-interested people can apparently do no wrong. But in fact donors face the same problem whether they are a development agency or a migrant. They want their money to be well used, but they do not control how it is spent. Both types of donor face a credibility problem if they throw a tantrum and threaten to suspend further gifts: the recipient knows that this is unlikely. Both can try to limit the choices of the recipient: the aid agency can specify a project that it will finance; the migrant can do likewise. But the recipient can largely circumvent such earmarking. In extremis, he can ignore the earmark and hope to explain away the change as a sudden necessity, but the most straightforward strategy is to persuade the donor to finance something that the recipient secretly intended to produce anyway. The new school is a gift of the American people: see the plaque. Actually the school would have happened anyway: it is the four-wheel drives for bureaucrats that would not otherwise have been bought. Similarly, the new school uniform is a gift of Amer in London: thanks Amer, here's the photo. Actually, that was already budgeted: the remittance money went on Dad's drinking binge. Experimental evidence shows that migrants, just like donor agencies, would like recipients to save more of the money that they are given. When offered the chance, migrants opt for greater control over the money, right up to dual-key systems in which the donor has to coauthorize each item of expenditure from a bank account. Development agencies were once driven to just such a system in Liberia. So the issues surrounding whether remittances are well used are not so different from whether aid is well used.

Not only are the issues similar, but so are the difficulties of measuring the effects. As with aid, there is a macro approach and a micro approach. Ideally, the macro approach would be more decisive, but it is also more problematic. On aid, the most recent serious study finds, fairly convincingly, that it has modestly net favorable effects on growth.[15] On remittances, the results are currently inconclusive: three studies showing positive effects on growth, and three showing zero or negative. Fortunately, the micro approach to remittances is more revealing than the micro approach to aid; unlike aid, it can focus directly on recipient households.

The most ingenious way of teasing out how people use remittances is to find situations in which there is a change in remittances that is unrelated to the circumstances of the recipient. One such natural experiment occurred through the East Asian crisis of 1998, during which the region's currencies collapsed against the dollar by differing amounts. Depending on where a migrant was working, her remittances suddenly changed value substantially in local currency. Dean Yang has used this variation to study the effect of remittances in the Philippines.[16] Some households had migrants working in the United States, and these remittances suddenly became 50 percent more valuable once converted into local currency. Other households had migrants working in Malaysia and Korea, and remittances in their currencies fell in local currency value. Comparing the responses of households with such differently located migrants yields a convincing account of how remittances are used. Was this remittance windfall frittered away unsustainably on consumption, or was it used for investment? The study found a strikingly clear result: all the extra money was spent on investments of various types: the education of children and new businesses. This seems almost too good to be true, and it probably is: this natural experiment involved a remittance shock that was clearly likely to be temporary, resulting from a currency crisis. Economists have long understood that temporary shocks to income are absorbed predominantly by changes in assets rather than consumption. Hence, while ingenious, it is not a good guide to how remittances will be used if they are expected to persist for many years.

So for how long do remittances persist? There is evidence that they are motivated by the desire to protect inheritance rights: if so, young migrants are in it for the long haul.[17] But even if remittances are not used only for investment, in some circumstances even the tough-minded would want recipients to use them for consumption. Poverty is like living up to your neck in choppy water, so at times when the water rises it would be comforting if remittances rose in response. Mobile phones have helped migrants to respond to adverse shocks because they can stay regularly in touch. So do migrants provide such a lifeline? Again, natural experiments can be used to tease out a convincing answer. The ideal shock to study is the weather. Changes in local rainfall produce temporary shocks to household incomes in the country of origin (again, as it happens, the Philippines), and the researchers simply need to observe whether remittances respond. Sure enough, they rise when income falls and fall when income rises. The insurance effect is substantial, with around 60 percent of an adverse shock being offset by extra remittances.[18] Households with migrants were much better able to protect consumption than those in which the entire family had stayed home. Similar effects have been found for hurricanes in the Caribbean, a region with both large shocks and large diasporas. Around a quarter of the damage was offset by additional remittances. The insurance role of remittances matters both because of its direct benefits in keeping heads above water and because of its less obvious consequences. Precisely because living up to your neck in choppy water is scary, people resort to desperate and costly strategies to avoid drowning. They are willing to sacrifice some of the income they could expect on average if this makes the remaining income less volatile: they opt to be poorer but safer. So by being an effective insurance mechanism, migration enables people to take the risks inherent in raising their longer-term level of income.

If remittances are helpful to those left behind, what migration policies of host countries increase their size? Superficially, it might appear that the answer is simple: increase migration. But easing restrictions on migration can have counterintuitive effects on remittances. An ingenious recent study finds that the easier are the restrictions on migration, the *less* willing are migrants to send money back home.[19] The explanation is that in response to easier restrictions migrants bring in more of their relatives, and this reduces their need to send remittances: bringing mother to the host country is an alternative to sending her money. So, paradoxically, remittances to countries of origin can be larger with restrictive than with open migration policies. It might also seem that migrant for migrant, the more educated would remit more than the less educated, so that an educationally selective policy would increase remittances. To an extent this is surely correct: with education earnings rise and so migrants are better able to afford to remit. But beyond a certain level, further education actually reduces remittances. The migrant is less likely to wish to return, his relatives back home are themselves likely to be successful and so less in need of remittances, and the migrant may be able to afford to bring his relatives in, rather than send them money.

In teasing out such effects, somewhat surprisingly the key gap in the evidence turns out to be data on the policies of host countries. There is as yet no comprehensive quantitatively usable version of the myriad of complex changes in rules and practices, country by country. As a result, testing a theory of how policy affects remittances has to use proxies for policy. For example, one proxy for the restrictiveness of migration policy is whether the country has a formal guest-worker program, since guest workers have no right to bring in relatives. Another is the sex ratio of migrants, since this is likely to reflect whether wives and mothers can be brought in. With these caveats, there is solid evidence that remittances to most countries would be increased were the migration policies of host countries somewhat more restrictive, in the sense of not letting in the relatives of migrants. The effect is quite powerful: not being able to bring in mother makes educated migrants considerably more generous in their remittances. The educational selectivity of migration policies is somewhat easier to proxy, through whether a country operates a points system. Such systems strongly reduce remittances, suggesting that most countries are beyond the peak of the inverted U that describes the relationship between remittances and education. These results are important because they provide nuance to apparent conflicts of interest between poor people in countries of origin and the indigenous poor of host countries.

While at the margin some forms of migration are likely to reduce remittances, overall the remittances generated by migration have been beneficial and substantial for the people left behind in some of the poorest countries of origin. Like other forms of aid they are not game-changers, but they have helped to relieve poverty.

Does Emigration Ease Overpopulation?

Among the emails I receive from readers of *The Bottom Billion*, the most common criticism is that I neglected to discuss population growth as a cause of poverty. If population growth is harmful to the poorest countries, then migration should be helpful: there are fewer people among whom to share the national cake. So are fewer people a good thing for poor societies? The clearest beneficial effect should be in the labor market: with fewer workers competing for jobs, the earnings of those who stay at home should be higher. The effect of emigration on the earnings of those left behind has only recently been well investigated. One such study, by one of my students, Dan Brown, is for Jamaica. He has estimated how wages have changed as a result of emigration. For example, if 10 percent of the skilled labor of a particular age cohort migrates, by how many percent does the wage for remaining workers rise? His results were typical of such studies, being in the vicinity of 4 percent.

This suggests that the effect of emigration on the wages of people left behind is benign but rather modest. Further, this effect is only within a skill category. If educated workers become scarcer, this also has implications for the wages of uneducated workers. Skilled workers enhance the productivity of unskilled workers, so that a loss of skilled workers reduces the wages of the unskilled. Indeed, you may recognize this as the obverse of the effect of immigration on host populations: skilled immigrants boost the earnings of unskilled workers. So as the skilled emigrate from countries of origin, they become scarcer and increase the wage premium for skill, while the unskilled have fewer skilled people with whom to work and so are less productive. Transferring fairy godmothers from poor societies to rich ones may be nice for the fairy godmothers and for the people they help in rich societies, but it is a stretch to present it as a triumph of social justice.

The greater inequality resulting in poor countries from the deepened scarcity of the skilled is compounded by an elite layer of returned highly skilled migrants who command international salaries. Because wages at the bottom are so low, the extent of social inequality generated by these differences in productivity is staggering; greater even than the wildest excesses of corporate America.

More generally, I did not discuss population growth as one of the problems for the bottom billion because I do not believe that it is inevitably a serious problem. Other than in a few cases such as Bangladesh, these countries are not intrinsically overpopulated. Often, on the contrary, they still have rather low population densities so that public goods are spread very thin. A natural experiment in addressing overpopulation by emigration is nineteenth-century Ireland. The population of Ireland rocketed up with the introduction of the potato, until 1845 when the potato crop was disastrously blighted. Over the next century Ireland lost half its population to emigration but remained chronically poor by European standards. Any favorable labor market effects of this massive emigration, far in excess of anything that could be conceived from countries of origin nowadays, were evidently pretty modest. Eventually, the huge diaspora generated by 150 years of mass emigration has become a substantial asset for Ireland. For example, the Irish American lobby in the US Congress has ensured that American companies that invest in Ireland get especially favorably treated by the US tax system. But 150 years is quite a long time to wait.

So emigration as a counter to overpopulation is not an important way in which those left behind can benefit. The scale of population loss is trivial, it draws off precisely those people who are most needed, and the effects on the productivity of the remaining workforce are ambiguous.

The most important counter to the Malthusian pressures of overpopulation is not migration from increasingly land-scarce rural regions to the cities of the developed economies but migration to cities *within* the country. A particularly convincing study of the benefits of such movements tracked migrants from rural area of Tanzania over the period 1991–2004, recording the incomes of both the migrants and the people who stayed put.[20] The gains from migration to Tanzanian towns and cities were dramatic, averaging an increase in consumption of thirty-six percentage points. Overall, migration accounted for around half of the entire reduction in rural poverty. Cities work by reaping scale economies that make ordinary people more productive than is possible if they remain dispersed.[21] Whereas in agriculture high population density results in poverty, in cities high density is the handmaiden of prosperity. Paradoxically, the same people who are most supportive of migration from poor countries to rich ones are often most hostile to migration of the rural poor to cities within their own country. It is as if peasants should be preserved in aspic in their rural idylls. Mass emigration from impoverished rural areas is essential if the remaining population is to achieve prosperity: the amount of land per person has to be substantially increased. So it is vital that cities perform their function of raising the productivity of the rural migrants who arrive in them.

Some of the conditions that determine whether cities succeed in this function are determined at the level of the nation, but others are determined by the city itself. Some cities provide much more effective ladders for migrants than others. Issues of zoning and local transport can make a major difference.[22] Although Paris is a high-productivity city, the suburbs in which migrants from rural areas of poor countries were encouraged to congregate have been dysfunctional. They are zoned so as to permit only residential uses yet have very poor transport connectivity to centers of employment. In contrast, cities such as Istanbul have attracted migrants to districts in which high-density residence and enterprise are intermingled. The same intermingling occurs in the typical African city, but there settlement has been so informal that people have not invested in multistory housing. As a result, although African shanty towns appear stiflingly crowded, they are not in fact high density. This diffusion spills over into fewer opportunities for enterprise: density breeds prosperity by concentrating demand and thereby enabling specialist firms to find a market. So migration is indeed decisive for countering overpopulation in the bottom billion but not for migration to high-income countries.

CHAPTER 10

Left Behind?

WE HAVE NOW REVIEWED all the various channels by which migration is likely to affect those left behind in poor countries. What does it add up to? The political effects of migration appear to be modestly beneficial, although the evidence is only just starting to flow in. The economic effects are dominated by the brain drain and remittances. Globally, brain drain is a misleading label: the possibility of migration stimulates the supply of talent rather than draining away a fixed stock. But for the countries around the bottom of the world economy, that draining away is a reality. For these same countries, however, earnings from work abroad provide a lifeline: remittances cushion desperately difficult living conditions. For most countries, the benefits of remittances are likely to outweigh the loss of talent, so the net economic effects are also modestly beneficial.

We can therefore safely conclude that migration is good for those left behind. But in fact, that conclusion is an answer to the wrong question. The pertinent question is not whether migration harms or benefits countries of origin, but whether *faster* migration would harm or benefit them. The practical policy issue is whether the continuing acceleration of migration from poor countries would be better for them than were the governments of host countries to introduce effective controls. It is this that needs to be evaluated from the perspective of those left behind, not the overall effects of migration. If you are thinking that this distinction is a pedantic quibble, then flip back through part 4 and think again. The distinction I am making, which is fundamental to much economic analysis, is between the *total* effect of migration and its *marginal* effect. That the total effect is positive tells us precisely *nothing* about the marginal effect.

However, from the *path* of the total effect we can deduce the marginal effect. In Figure 10.1 the solid line shows the path of the brain gain/drain for different rates of migration. We know, for example, that China and India, with low rates of migration, get a large brain gain, whereas Haiti, with a far higher rate of migration, suffers a brain drain. The dashed line deduces the marginal contribution of migration. As a matter of simple logic, when the gain is at its peak, a small change in migration makes no difference: expressed more fancily, the marginal effect is zero. Once the gain is declining, extra migration must be making things worse, so the marginal effect is negative. Clearly, the ideal migration rate from the perspective of those left behind is when the brain gain is at its peak. Haiti is evidently way beyond that peak: we can safely conclude that on the criterion of the brain gain/drain, its actual rate of migration has been far in excess of its ideal rate. With a much lower rate of migration Haiti would have turned a brain drain into a brain gain, like China and India.

The total and marginal effects of migration on remittances can be analyzed in the same way and are illustrated in Figure 10.2.

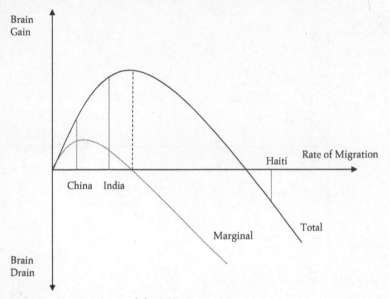

Figure 10.1 Migration and the Brain Drain/Gain

Clearly, unlike the brain drain/gain, except in rare instances remittances have positive total effects. The only case I have come across in which migration has reached the point at which remittances are taking money out from those left behind instead of bringing it in is South Sudan. During the war, skilled people left with their families. Postconflict, they are highly reluctant to return and can only be induced if the government pays high wages for the skills it needs. Even then, those who come back to work leave their families abroad and so send remittances back to them. Hence the paradox that one of the poorest countries in the world is making net remittances to some of the richest.

However, although remittances are normally substantial, they also have a peak beyond which further migration becomes counterproductive. If the door is opened too wide, migrants bring their relatives through it rather than sending remittances to them. A similar peak

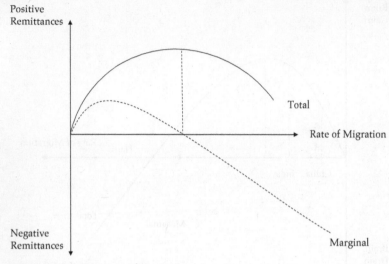

Figure 10.2 Migration and Remittances

applies to the skill level of migrants. Further, there is solid empirical evidence that most poor countries of origin are firmly beyond the point at which remittances are at their peak. While without migration there would obviously have been no remittances, at the margin these countries would get even more remittances were migration more restrictive, most especially in limiting the rights of educated migrants to bring in their families.

So the implication is that while migration is helping those left behind, it would help them even more if there was less of it. But countries of origin cannot control emigration themselves: the rate is determined by the policies of host countries. The polemical debate, migration is good versus migration is bad, makes it much harder to frame an ideal policy: not a door that is open or closed, but one that is ajar.

Lifelines keep people going, but they do not transform lives. Migration from overpopulated rural areas is, ultimately, the big engine of development. But the decisive flows of migration are not to the cities of the high-income countries, but to the cities of the low-income countries themselves. A country such as Turkey, which has lifted itself out of poverty over the last half-century, has done so not by sending two million Turks to Germany: relative to the ninety million people remaining in Turkey this was trivial, and you may recall that those German Turks are among the least generous remitters in the world. Turkey's economic miracle has been driven by the migration of its rural poor to Istanbul, in turn attracted by the growth of opportunities.

The most likely role of international migration as a catalyst is as a transmission channel for ideas. Having a diaspora exposed to societies where the social model is more functional might fast-track the absorption of the ideas that make a difference. But there is little evidence to suggest that resident diasporas, as opposed to temporary student migrants, are important. While ideas matter, in each of the major instances of transformation discussed in chapter 2—eastern Europe, southern Europe, and the Arab Spring—diasporas were incidental to their transmission. Indeed, although diasporas are often politically engaged, they tend to be backward-looking, massaging old sectarian grievances as a way of preserving their distinctive identities in the host society, rather than being the ambassadors for the characteristics that, ultimately, have induced them to migrate. Further, institutions cannot be transferred lock, stock, and barrel. Societies are highly idiosyncratic, and so to be functional, institutions need to be organic. Even the superficially similar "Anglo-Saxon" societies—the United States, Britain, Australia, and New Zealand—have substantial differences in their political and economic institutions. Successful institutions come to fit with a society, albeit bearing a family resemblance to an international model, rather than being transplanted: transplants tend to be rejected. So the resident population of a society may be better placed than the diaspora to absorb and apply ideas. It is able to download the international models it learns of through the Internet and through a spell of education abroad, but it has its finger on the pulse of how its own society is evolving and so can develop viable domestic institutions. In contrast, a diaspora is at once too close to the host society to distill the big picture and too distant from its society of origin, which it recalls in nostalgic fantasies.

Even where diasporas are forward-looking rather than mired in the past, they have increasingly become redundant as vehicles for ideas. Technology has shrunk distance without the need for physical movement: young people in Egypt downloaded material from YouTube and Google and communicated with each other by mobile phone and Facebook. As Niall Ferguson has succinctly argued, the West got ahead by inventing a series of "killer apps" such as competition that reorganized their societies, but now these apps are readily downloadable and are being downloaded around the world.[1]

Potentially, emigration of the talented from the countries of the bottom billion creates a sense that "life is elsewhere." Indeed, such a sense is fundamental to the incentive and role model effects on talent that offset the brain drain. At its worse, a sense that life is elsewhere is debilitating, captured by Chekhov in the poignant refrain "Moscow, Moscow!" But for a small society that has long been stagnant and impoverished, life, in the sense of opportunity, really is elsewhere, and its young people are fully aware of it. Even without emigration, technology and globalized youth culture expose them to an inviting world just beyond their reach. Given the technology, the portals of this world are merely basic literacy, which is why the cultural backlash from radical Islam is so scared of education: the Boko Haram terrorist movement in Nigeria translates as

"Western education is sinful." But like all terrorism, Boko Haram is a strategy doomed to failure. Even were migration to be curtailed, exposure would continue unabated: the success and vibrancy of life elsewhere cannot be erased or hidden. The prospect of migration and connections with relatives abroad are as likely to soften the frustration of exclusion as to intensify it.

"Life is elsewhere" is potentially debilitating, but it can be countered. A triumph of postmodern culture has been to decenter: excitement is increasingly distributed, and there is no longer a unique pecking order. A challenge for great leadership in the societies of the bottom billion is to promote a credible vision of the excitement of catching up, joining the increasingly diverse group of societies where life is here and now. This is surely the spirit that has embraced modern China and, to varying degrees, Africa. It has little to do with international migration.

So emigration from the bottom billion is neither a menace nor a catalyst for the people left behind. It is a lifeline: a decentralized aid program. Like other aid programs it will not be decisive, but it most surely makes life better for millions of people living in conditions that are radically inappropriate in our globalized and prosperous century. But like the aid debate itself, the key issue regarding migration is not whether it is good or bad, but how best, at the margin, it can be improved. There is reasonable evidence that for the bottom billion, migration has been beneficial overall. But at the margin it is detrimental, draining talent and reducing remittances.

Migration as Aid

Virtually all host countries have aid programs for the bottom billion: addressing poverty in these countries is rightly seen as a global public good. Aid programs are an expression of the character of a society, an act of generosity toward societies that are desperately in need. Whether or not they are very effective, they exercise our humanity and thereby deepen it. Just as individual acts of kindness cumulatively come to define not just how we appear to others but how we are to ourselves, so collective acts of kindness come not just to reflect a society but to shape it.

The ethical basis for aid looms particularly large at present. The severe and prolonged recession across the developed economies is leading to deep fiscal retrenchment. Where in the priorities for spending should the aid budget be positioned? All aid budgets are tiny relative to overall government spending, and so whether they are cut deeply or fully protected makes only a trivial difference to the alarming fiscal challenge. But a time of budget cuts wonderfully concentrates the mind: it is a time for hard choices, publicly debated. What priority do the poorest societies have relative to the needs of our own society? Conversely, periods of fiscal laxity reveal little about a society's true priorities: if money is easy, all sorts of nice-to-have spending takes place. As I write, each rich society is revealing something about its true priorities, and what is revealed is starkly different country by country. Nor are priorities well predicted according to the crude characterizations of the political spectrum. In Britain a government of the Right is fully protecting the aid budget; in America a government of the Left is slashing it. Nor are these merely eccentric deviations of public policy from democratic pressures. The British public appears to be quite relaxed about revealed priorities. Recently, the right-wing magazine *The Spectator*, itself virulently antiaid, held a public debate on whether Britain should cut its aid budget. I was enlisted to speak at the event and went along with some trepidation: if there was any audience in Britain likely to favor cutting the aid budget, this was surely going to be it. But we won the debate by a large majority. My own argument was not that aid is supereffective, for I doubt that it is, but rather that our decision about aid would inevitably reflect the sort of society we aspired to be. In the election both parties of the ruling coalition had committed to protect, and indeed increase, the aid budget, and we should honor our commitments to the world's poor. I feel rather proud to belong to a country that, at a time of adversity, reaffirms its sense of generosity. I doubt that Americans as people are any the less generous spirited. After all, at the time of the earthquake in Haiti, half of all American households made individual donations to the earthquake appeals, an astounding proportion. Perhaps the American reluctance to provide aid reflects the heightened suspicion of government that currently characterizes much American public debate: public aid is government squared, as money passes through first the US government and then that of the recipient country.

As part of policy coherence, where different policies affect the same goal, governments should try to reinforce their achievement of the goal by coordinating the policies. At a minimum, governments should avoid striving to achieve a goal with one policy instrument while undermining it with another. So the migration policy adopted by a host country will have effects on a country of origin that either complement or undermine its aid policy depending upon the effects of out-migration. Since the net effect of emigration on countries of origin is beneficial to those left behind, and rich societies see it as ethically right to have aid programs to help the poorest countries, migration policies should be viewed, in part, as adjuncts to aid programs. Of course, migration has other effects that the governments of host countries will also legitimately want to take into account, but the effect on those left behind should be a consideration.

The two big economic transfers between the rich countries and the poorest generated by migration are remittances and the brain drain. Remittances are a hidden form of aid from the rich to the poor, whereas the brain drain is a hidden form of aid from the poor to the rich. Let me try to bring them out of hiding.

Directly, remittances are financed out of the posttax income of migrants, and so they as individuals are the donors. But ultimately, the high productivity that enables migrants to earn the incomes that finance remittances is not predominantly attributable to migrants themselves. After all, in their home societies these same people would be radically less productive. In moving to high-wage countries they are the beneficiaries of the public capital in its many forms that collectively make the rich societies rich. That public capital has been accumulated by the indigenous population of the host country. As I discussed in part 2, while there is an ethical case for the indigenous population to claim this productivity premium, as a practical matter it would be ill advised since it would relegate migrants to second-class status. Nevertheless, it is entirely reasonable for the indigenous population to claim joint credit with migrants for the remittances that benefit those left behind in countries of origin. Migration enables the indigenous population to make a substantial financial contribution to these poor countries: it is an aid program administered by migrants. And of course, an attractive feature of this particular aid program is that it costs the indigenous population nothing: it is financed out of the windfall productivity gain that migration generates.

The brain drain is financed by the education spending of the governments of countries of origin. Their investment in the education of children who then migrate to high-income countries is an inadvertent aid program to host countries. The host societies are receiving in taxes on the income of immigrants, a flow of revenue that is a return on education that the host society has not itself financed. No reasonable person could justify such a transfer, so there is a case for compensation. The governments of host countries should make payments to the governments of countries of origin reflecting those tax receipts that are a return on the investment in education. An approximate benchmark for compensation is the share of education in the budget of the host-country government. For example, if education accounts for 10 percent of public spending, then a tenth of the tax receipts from immigrants might be deemed to be just compensation for the fact that the host society had received an influx of educated labor that some other society had paid for. Suppose that tax revenues account for 40 percent of national income in the host country, that immigrants constitute 10 percent of the population, and that they pay a share of tax that is proportionate to their share of the population. In this case the appropriate compensation for tax revenues generated by the windfall supply of educated workers would be 0.4 percent of national income. Of course, the numbers I have used are meant to be merely illustrative. However, if the numbers indicate orders of magnitude, they have an interesting implication. The United Nations target contribution for aid budgets is 0.7 percent of national income. So a substantial proportion of this target might be accounted for merely to offset the implicit aid provided by countries of origin to host countries. In fact, most high-income countries provide far less than 0.7 percent, typically around half of that target. So conceivably the left hand is providing aid while the right hand is receiving it: aid is not a donation but a repayment.

Rethinking Migration Policies

CHAPTER 11

Nations and Nationalism

England for the English?

Somewhere in England an elderly man reverts to the behavior of disaffected teenagers and daubs a slogan on a wall. He writes "England for the English." The perpetrator is tracked down by the police and rightly prosecuted and convicted: the sentiment is clearly intended as racial abuse. More generally, in much of the high-income world the concept of the nation-state has become unfashionable both with educated elites and with the young. Modernity strings identity between one pillar of individualism and another of globalism: many young people see themselves both as fiercely individual outsiders in their surrounding society, and as citizens of the world.

Modern individualism has deep roots. Around the time of the birth of the modern concept of the individual, Descartes was deriving our knowledge of the existence of the world from his undeniable experience of his own thoughts: *cogito, ergo sum.* Many modern philosophers now think that Descartes got things back-to-front. We cannot have knowledge of ourselves except in the context of an awareness of a society of which we are a part.

Hence, right at the foundations of philosophy, there is a tension between people as individuals and people as members of society. These different perspectives permeate through politics and social science. Politically, there is a spectrum from socialism through to individual libertarianism—politicians such as Margaret Thatcher with her brilliantly focused remark "There's no such thing as society," and thinkers such as Ayn Rand, who regarded social organization as a conspiracy of the slothful majority against the exceptional minority. In social science the individual-maximizing perspective of economics has long been pitted against the group analysis of sociology and anthropology. People are both individuals and members of a society. An adequate theory of human behavior has to incorporate both aspects of our nature, much as progress in physics depended upon the realization that at the subatomic level matter behaves both as particles and waves.

The balance between people as particles and people as waves can shape how we see a country. At the particle end of the spectrum, a country is an arbitrary geographic-legal entity inhabited at any one time by some particles. At the wave end of the spectrum, a country is a people, sharing a common identity and bound together by mutual regard. The country-as-people end of the spectrum involves two distinct steps: the notion that community rather than just individual is important, and the notion that a country is a key unit of organization for community. A potential source of confusion is that the former is an idea usually associated with the political Left, while the latter is an idea usually associated with the political Right.

Community or Individual?

First consider the notion that the community rather than just the individual is important. Recent developments in philosophy, psychology, and economics have pushed back from the individual as all. In philosophy, Michael Sandel has shown how over the last generation the individualist assumptions built into economic analysis have shifted key goods from collective provision to being met by the market.[1] The march of the market has had substantial distributional repercussions, with an unprecedented increase in social inequality. Some philosophers now question free will, the bedrock of individualism. Their critique is based on the new evidence from social psychology of the power of imitation.[2] People adopt role models of behavior from a limited range of available choices, and thereafter their responses to situations are set by their role model: personal responsibility is not eliminated, but it is weakened when seen from such a perspective.

In psychology, Jonathan Haidt and Steven Pinker have shown how attitudes and beliefs that affect behavior toward others evolve over time and have major consequences for well-being. Haidt argues that a sense of community is one of the six fundamental moral tastes that are virtually universal.[3] Pinker attributes the dramatic decline in violence in Western society since the eighteenth century to an increased sense of empathy: especially through the growth of literacy and the popular novel, people became better able to put themselves in the position of others and imagine themselves as the victims of the violence done to others. Even psychoanalysis, traditionally the ultimate self-regarding mode of analysis, now roots personal problems in relational attitudes such as shame.

Economics has long been the bastion of selfish, maximizing individualism. Its foundations were laid by Adam Smith in *The Wealth of Nations*, where he famously demonstrated that such behavior generates social benefits. But Smith also wrote *The Theory of Moral Sentiments*, about the foundations of mutual regard. Belatedly, that work is receiving its due recognition.[4] It is being expanded by the new subdiscipline of neuroeconomics, in which the regard for others is neurologically grounded.[5] Experimental economics has found that a propensity to trust is both valuable and varies between societies. Studies of happiness find that what really matters is social, not material: how we relate to others, and how we are regarded by others. But even judged by the narrow metric of income, a group within which there is high regard and trust for others will be better off than one of selfish individualists. A controversy is currently raging as to whether sociobiology could explain the genetic emergence of a predisposition toward trust. While the competition between individuals cannot explain trust, both competition between genes and competition between groups may be able to do so: mutual regard within groups may be hardwired.[6]

For all these scholars, behavior is in part derived from a sense of community and the attitudes shared by the community. People have a predisposition for mutual regard within a group; but these sentiments can be undermined by individual selfishness, as they were over the past generation with the encroaching domain of the market.

Is a Nation a Community?

Community is important, as a primary value for most people, as a key determinant of happiness, and as a source of material benefits. So what units of organization are most important for community: family, clan, locality, ethnic group, religion, profession, region, nation, or world? People are perfectly capable of multiple identities, and many of these are noncompeting. How important is the nation in this array of possible clubs?

Nationalism was condemned by Einstein as "measles," and it has become fashionable in Europe to suggest that the nation has been superseded. Nations are challenged from below by regional identities: Spain is currently threatened with the secession of Catalonia, and Britain with the secession of Scotland. Nations are challenged from above both formally by the transfer of power to larger entities such as the European Union and culturally by the emergence of globalized educated elites that mock at national identity. Yet that identity is enormously important as a force for equity.

Nations are overwhelmingly the most important institutions for taxation. Only if people feel a strong common identity at this level are they willing to accept that taxation can be used for the redistributions that partially offset the vagaries of divergent fortunes. Take that Catalonian desire to exit from Spain. Catalonia is Spain's richest region, and exit is being driven by reluctance to continue transferring 9 percent of Catalan income to other regions. A stronger sense of Spanish nationalism would be highly unlikely to trigger warlike intensions against Portugal but would, perhaps, reconcile Catalans to helping their poorer neighbors. In other words, modern nationalism is less like a mass infection of measles than a mass injection of oxytocin.[7]

Of course, it would be even nicer if a sense of shared identity could be built at a yet higher level than the nation, but nationalism and internationalism need not be alternatives. The key word in "Charity begins at home" is *begins*. Compassion is like a muscle: by exercising it toward fellow citizens we can develop feelings of regard for those who are not. Further, we now know that building a shared identity beyond the level of the nation is extremely difficult. Over the past half-century by far the world's most successful supranational experiment has been the European Union. Yet even after that half-century, and the memory of when nationalism was more like anthrax than measles, the European Union redistributes far less than 1 percent of European income between countries. The travails of the euro, and the fierce opposition of Germans to the notion of a "transfer union"—read "paying for the Greeks"—is testament to the limits of refashioning identity. Fifty years of the European Community have demonstrated that people cannot muster enough common identity even as Europeans to support any significant redistribution. Within Europe, around forty times as much revenue is dispensed by national governments as by the European Commission. By the time we get to the global level, the mechanism for redistributive taxation—aid—is even weaker. The international system has struggled and failed for the past four decades even to reach a tax rate of 0.7 percent of income. From the perspective of cooperation between people, nations are not selfish impediments to global citizenship; they are virtually our only systems for providing public goods.

Not only does the redistribution provided by a nation utterly dominate redistributions by any higher-level systems of cooperation, it also dominates lower-level systems. Subnational governments almost invariably handle a much smaller share of revenue than the national government. The exceptions, notably Belgium and Canada, are precisely where a sense of identity is largely subnational, reflecting language divisions. For example, Canada is unusual in assigning the ownership of natural resources to the regional level rather than the nation. While this is a necessary concession in the face of a weak sense of nationhood, it is otherwise undesirable: it is more equitable if valuable natural resources are owned nationally rather than benefiting only those lucky enough to be living in the region where they are found. It is not as if Albertans put the oil in

Alberta, they just happen to be sitting a bit nearer to it than other Canadians. Even the ultimate decentralized system of redistribution, the family, is but a pale reflection of the state. Indeed, charity does not, literally, begin at *home*; it begins in ministries of finance and is modestly supplemented by family generosity. The state is even heavily involved in the transfer of resources from parents to young children: in the absence of state-financed and state-required education, many children would be left uneducated, as was my father.

Nations function as systems of redistributive taxation because, from the emotional perspective, identifying with a nation has proved to be an extremely powerful way in which people bond. A shared sense of nationhood need not imply aggression; rather it is a practical means of establishing fraternity. There is a good reason that the French revolutionaries who ushered in modernity bundled in fraternity with liberty and equality: *fraternity is the emotion that reconciles liberty with equality*. Only if we see others as members of the same community do we accept that the redistributive taxation needed for equity does not infringe our liberty.

In many ways the most challenging people to socialize are young men: as teenagers they appear to be genetically programmed to be antisocially violent and contrary. Yet national identity has proved capable of drawing in wild young men, indeed, all too capable. Think of those hordes of young men in August 1914 demonstrating in each national capital in favor of the war that subsequently slaughtered many of them. The prevailing wariness of nationality as identity is not usually because of its inefficacy but because of its historic propensity to warfare.

Not only are nations good at raising and redistributing tax revenue, from the technical perspective they are the level at which many collective activities are best undertaken. Collective provision reaps economies of scale but sacrifices variety.[8] In the trade-off between scale economies and variety, very few activities appear to be worth organizing at the global level. But national-level provision has proved to be the norm. To an unknowable extent, the concentration of public goods provision at the national level is because nations have proved to be powerful units of collective identity, rather than because identities have been shaped by the logic of the gains from cooperation. But matching identities to collective action has been valuable.

National identity may also be helpful in motivating the workforce in the public sector. Recall the key distinction between insiders and outsiders: whether workers internalize the objectives of the organization. One criterion for assigning an activity to the public sector rather than the private market is where motivation by financial incentives is problematic. It may not be easy to link performance to pay because outputs are too amorphous to be well approximated by quantitative measures or because performance depends heavily upon teamwork. Conversely, many activities commonly assigned to the public sector, such as teaching and caring for the sick, lend themselves readily to internalization. It is easier to get intrinsic satisfaction from teaching children to read than from selling perfume. But in building worker commitment in public organizations symbols of nationalism are manifestly useful. In Britain the public health organization is called the *National* Health Service, and the insider nursing union the *Royal* College of Nurses. The ultimate public organizations in which reliance is placed upon commitment rather than incentives are the armed forces, and they are festooned in the symbolism of the nation. Indeed, the one illustration in *Identity Economics*, the book by Akerlof and Kranton, is of recruitment into the American military.

Just as Michael Sandel laments the transfer of provision of many goods from the public sector to the private market, so, within the public sector, there has been a corresponding shift from commitment to incentives. As with the more general trend, much of this has been driven by an exaggerated belief in the efficacy of money. But it may have been compounded by a growing reluctance to use national identity as a motivator and by its reduced efficacy, given that migrants often make up a substantial proportion of the public sector workforce.

Africa provides a potent example of what happens when identities and collective organization are mismatched. Nations were patched together on maps by foreigners, whereas identities had been forged through thousands of years of settlement patterns. Only in a handful of countries have leaders got round to building a sense of common citizenship: in most, identities are predominantly subnational, and cooperation among different identities is difficult because of a lack of trust. Yet in most of Africa public provision is heavily centralized at the level of the nation: this is where revenues accrue. The outcome is that public provision works very badly. A standard characterization of African political economy is that each clan regards the public purse as a common pool resource to be looted on behalf of the clan. It is regarded as ethical to cooperate within the clan to loot, rather than to cooperate at the level of the nation to deliver public goods. Founding president Julius Nyerere of Tanzania was a notable exception to the failure of African leaders to build a sense of common national identity. In chapter 3 I described how Kenya's fifty different ethnic groups impede village-level cooperation in maintaining wells. However, the same study compared not only Kenyan villages with different degrees of diversity but also Tanzanian villages just across the border. Because the border was an arbitrary nineteenth-century construct, the underlying ethnic mix on both sides of the border was the same; the key difference was leadership efforts at nation building. Whereas

President Nyerere had emphasized nation over ethnic identity, his counterpart in Kenya, President Kenyatta, had played on ethnicity as a means of building a loyal following, and his successors had continued the strategy. These distinctive approaches to national identity turned out to have consequences. Whereas the different ethnic groups found cooperation difficult in Kenyan villages, they found it normal in Tanzanian villages. In fact, in Tanzania the degree of diversity made no difference to cooperation. National identity has its uses.

Between the individualists who belittle the need for social cooperation, and the universalists who are fearful of nationalism, nations as solutions to the problem of collective action have fallen out of favor. But while the need for cooperation is real, the fears of nationalism are outdated. As Steven Pinker argues, warfare between developed countries is now unthinkable. Germany currently faces difficult choices over support for Greece: without financial support Greece will have to withdraw from the euro, jeopardizing its continued existence, whereas with financial support the incentive for Greece to implement economic reforms will be diminished. Chancellor Merkel has committed Germany to maintaining the euro at all costs, arguing that its collapse would revive the specter of war between the European powers. But this fear, though a heartfelt reflection of Germany's past, is blatantly ridiculous as a prospect for its future. European peace is not built on the euro or even on the European Community. We can test whether Chancellor Merkel is right in her fears, by comparing prospective German relations with Poland and Norway. During the Second World War, Germany invaded and occupied both of them. But now, whereas Poland has adopted the euro and is a member of the European Community, Norway has done neither. Yet is Germany one whit more likely to invade Norway than Poland? Quite evidently, Germany will never again invade either of these countries. What underpins European peace is not a currency and a Brussels bureaucracy, but a profound change in sensibilities. A century on from 1914, no European crowd is going to cheer for violence.

The more reasonable fear of nationalism is not that it will unleash war with other nations but that it will not be inclusive: nationalism will be a front for racism. Instead of defining the nation by the people who live in it, it might be defined by the majority ethnic group. The British Nationalist Party really means the Indigenous English Party; the True Finns really means ethnic majority Finns, and so forth. But allowing racist groups to hijack the potent symbol and effective organizational unit of the nation is itself dangerous. If, by default, other politicians underplay a sense of national identity, it hands a potent political tool to evil. There need be no tension between being nationalist and yet antiracist. A superb example of just such a stance happened by a peculiar collective chemistry during the London Olympic Games in 2012. Britain, to its own amazement, won gold after gold. Those gold medals were won by a racial rainbow that was itself a part of national pride. Identities are forged by symbols: the British reaction to the Olympics was both an expression of something already forged, and that forging in process: a multiracial nation. Analogously, the phrase "England for the English" should be as anodyne as "Nigeria for the Nigerians." Mainstream politicians should have defined English identity in the same way as the Scottish Nationalist Party has defined "Scottish" as "those who live in Scotland." National identity should not have been allowed to become the presumptive property of racists. Nations have not become obsolete. Reducing nationality to a mere legalism—a set of rights and obligations— would be the collective equivalent of autism: life lived with rules but without empathy.

Is National Identity Consistent with Rapid Migration?

National identity is valuable and it is also permissible. So is it threatened by immigration? No glib answer is warranted: a sense of shared identity is not necessarily perturbed by immigration, but it may be.

The assimilation and fusion approaches to migration are clearly potentially consistent with the maintenance of a strong common national identity. The narrative of assimilation assigns to the indigenous population the role of being proselytizers for their nation. Migrants are to be welcomed and inculcated with the culture. This role is not only consistent with pride in self-identity, it is reinforcing. For most of American history this was the country's migration model: Americans have been proud of their nation, and immigration reinforced a common self-image of American exceptionalism. Similarly, the French have for over a century been proselytizers for their national culture, and substantial migration has been compatible with a continuing sense of pride.

The problems with assimilation and fusion are practical. As I set out in chapter 3, the lower the rate of absorption the more rapid the rate of migration. The rate is also lower the wider the cultural distance between migrants and the indigenous. It might also be falling over time as improved international communications make it easier for migrants to remain connected, day to day, with their societies of origin. This suggests that for assimilation and fusion to work, there is a need for controls on the rate of migration that are fine-tuned to take into account its composition. Neither the indigenous nor migrants can be hectored into integration, but the indigenous must be subject to requirements that all their organizations become inclusive of migrants, while migrants may need to be subject to requirements of language learning and spatial dispersion.

The permanent cultural separation approach to migration faces different problems. It sits less comfortably with the maintenance of a common sense of national identity than the assimilation and fusion approaches. For migrants it is undemanding: instead of having to switch from one national identity to another, they can simply add citizenship of their new nation as an identifier to their other characteristics. But if the indigenous are to be relegated to the status of one cultural "community" among several, what identity are they to be given? Almost inevitably, if Bangladeshis in England are "the Bangladeshi community," and the Somalis are "the Somali community," then the indigenous become "the English." But with this development the sense of shared nationality is forfeited: this is the royal road to "England for the English." If the indigenous appropriate the national identifier, what term is left for the entirety? Yet more problematic, what role does the narrative of cultural separation offer to the indigenous community? In the prevailing official narrative, the dominant message delivered to the indigenous is "Don't be racist," "Make way," and "Learn to celebrate other cultures." As it stands, this is belittling. It may drive the indigenous into "hunkering down": the dismal sentiment, now often voiced within the indigenous English working class, that "times used to be good."

Such an uninspiring role for the indigenous is not the only one available to the cultural separation approach. It could instead be presented through a narrative in which the indigenous have a more positive role. For example, it might be that in cohabiting in the same territory, the many distinct formerly national communities are pioneers of the future "global village." The indigenous, in choosing this strategy for their territory, are the vanguard of this future. Within this narrative, the nation embodies a set of ethical principles of intercommunity equity made manifest in a set of legal obligations and entitlements that apply to all equally. It is these globally appropriate values, rather than its culture, that the indigenous community shares with others. In Britain, the closest that officialdom came to promoting such a narrative was an initiative of Gordon Brown, while prime minister, which sought to answer the question "What is Britishness?" Since Brown strongly self-identified as Scottish but needed English votes, this had a certain comic aspect to it. The obvious answer, that to be British meant to be Scottish, English, Welsh, or Northern Irish was off the menu, and the official answer turned out to be that our defining qualities were a commitment to democracy, equity, and various other appealing characteristics commonly associated with Scandinavia. Attractive as that vision might be, in the ensuing election Mr. Brown's vote share of the indigenous vote collapsed to the lowest his party had ever received.

In summary, while migration does not make nations obsolete, the continued acceleration of migration in conjunction with a policy of multiculturalism might potentially threaten their viability. Absorption has proved more difficult than anticipated. The alternative of continued cultural separation works well enough when judged by the minimalist hurdle of the preservation of social peace between groups but may not work on the more pertinent hurdles of the preservation of cooperation and redistribution within them. Such evidence as we have is that continually increasing diversity could at some point put these critical achievements of modern societies at risk.

CHAPTER 12

Making Migration Policies
Fit for Purpose

CONTRARY TO THE PREJUDICES OF XENOPHOBES, the evidence does not suggest that migration to date has had significantly adverse effects on the indigenous populations of host societies. Contrary to self-perceived "progressives," the evidence does suggest that without effective controls migration would rapidly accelerate to the point at which additional migration would have adverse effects, both on the indigenous populations of host societies and on those left behind in the poorest countries. Migrants themselves, although the direct beneficiaries of the free lunch of higher productivity, suffer psychological costs that appear to be substantial. Migration thus affects many different groups, but only one has the practical power to control it: the indigenous population of host societies. Should that group act in its self-interest, or balance the interests of all the groups?

The Right to Control Migration

Only from the wilder shores of libertarianism and utilitarianism can it be argued that migration controls are ethically illegitimate. Extreme libertarianism denies the right of governments to restrict individual freedom, in this instance the freedom of movement. Universalist utilitarianism wants to maximize world utility by whatever means. The best possible outcome would be if the entire world population moved to the country in which people were most productive, leaving the rest of the earth empty. A useful supplement to such mass migration would be if Robin Hood could rob all the rich people and transfer the money to all the poor people, although economists would caution Robin to temper robbery with concern for incentives. Evidently, neither of these philosophies provides an ethical framework by which a democratic society would wish to navigate migration policy. Indeed, they could be dismissed as the stuff of teenage dreams were they not the ethical basis for the standard economic models of migration.

Why might there be a right to control migration? To see why, push the logic of unrestricted migration to its limits. As we have seen, it would be possible for the free movement of migrants to come close to emptying some poor societies and producing majority-immigrant populations in some rich ones. The utilitarian and the libertarian are unconcerned about such a prospect: if Mali were to empty, so what? The people who used to think of themselves as Malian can now reinvent their lives elsewhere and live much better. If Angola were to become predominantly Chinese, or England to become predominantly Bangladeshi, the change of aggregate identity would be of no consequence: individuals are free to adopt any identity they choose. But most people would be uneasy with such consequences. Environmental economists have introduced the concept of "existence value": while you may never see a panda, your life is enhanced by the knowledge that it exists somewhere on the planet. We do not want species to become extinct. Societies also have existence value, arguably far more so than species and not just for their members but for others. American Jews value the continued existence of Israel, even though they may never go there. Similarly, millions around the world value Mali, the ancient society that produced Timbuktu. Neither Israel nor Mali must be preserved in aspic: they are living societies. But Mali should develop, not empty. It is not a satisfactory solution to Malian poverty if its people should all become prosperous elsewhere. Similarly, were Angola to become an extension of China, or England an extension of Bangladesh, it would be a terrible loss to global cultures.

The golden rule, do unto others what you would have them do to you, is not an unreasonable ethical check on migration policy. So, for unrestricted migration to be the moral principle for, say, African immigration to America, it must also be the principle for Chinese immigration to Africa. Yet most African societies are understandably extremely wary of unrestricted immigration. Africans experienced being taken over by the societies of others and would reject a repetition, albeit this time by the power of numbers rather than the power of the gun. In practice, even the economists who extol the billions of dollars to be gained from the free movement of labor between countries do not literally advocate unrestricted migration. They use the billions as an argument for migration restrictions that are somewhat more generous than at present. But always, at the margin of restrictions there will be economic gains left on the table; why it may be sensible to do so cannot be left implicit.

The essence of a country is not simply its physical territory. The underlying difference in incomes between rich and poor societies is due to differences in their social models. If Mali had a similar social model to France and maintained it for several decades, it would have a similar level of income. The persistence of differences in income is not inherent to differences in geography. Of course, differences in geography matter: Mali is landlocked and it is dry, both of which make prosperity more difficult. But both have been made more of a handicap than they need to be. Being landlocked is greatly compounded by the fact that Mali's neighbors also have dysfunctional social models: the war currently raging in Mali is a direct spillover of the collapse of Mali's neighbor Libya. Being dry is made more difficult by heavy reliance upon agriculture: Dubai is even drier, but it has diversified into a prosperous service economy where the lack of rainfall is of no consequence.

Functional social models are decisive, but they do not just happen: they are built as a result of decades, and sometimes centuries, of social progress. They are, in effect, part of the common property inherited by those born in the high-income societies. That that property is common to the members of a society does not imply that it must necessarily be open access to others: the world abounds in such club goods.

However, while most people might accept that the citizens of a country have some rights to restrict entry, such rights are limited and some societies have weaker rights of exclusion than others. If population density is extremely low, a right to exclude starts to look selfish. If the host population is itself recently descended from immigrants, then tough restrictions are indeed hauling up the ladder. Yet paradoxically, those countries most characterized by low density and recent occupation often have the most severe restrictions on immigration: stand forth Canada, Australia, Russia, and Israel. Canada and Australia are *the* recent immigrant societies, and both are still hugely underpopulated.[1] Yet they pioneered the restriction of immigration to the highly educated, and the move to supplement educational points systems with interviews that assess other qualities. Russia only acquired the huge and empty territory of Siberia in the nineteenth century. Much of it borders on China, one of the most heavily populated societies of earth. Yet a core principle of Russian policy has been to keep the Chinese out of Siberia. Israel is an even more recent society of immigrants. Yet immigration is so restricted that indigenous émigrés do not have the right of return.

Even in densely populated countries with a long-established indigenous majority, some rules of entry would be manifestly racist and so impermissible. Others would be inhuman. All decent societies recognize a duty of rescue, most obviously toward asylum seekers. Sometimes the duty of rescue becomes literal. Australia is currently the ultimate land of immigrant promise. As a result of the global boom in minerals its economy is booming, and a global survey of happiness has found that Australians are the happiest people on earth. Australia is far from crowded: an entire continent with a mere 30 million inhabitants, nearly all themselves the descendants of recent immigrants. Even the prime minister is herself an immigrant. Unsurprisingly, people from countries that are crowded and impoverished would like to move there, but the Australian government has imposed tough restrictions upon legal entry. The gulf between dreams and legal realities has created a market in organized illegal passage. Entrepreneurs sell people places on small boats bound for Australian territory. The results are tragically predictable. The people who buy illegal passage have no recourse against deceit and incompetence: boats sink and people drown. A debate is currently raging in Australia as to how far the duty of rescue should extend. An evident dilemma is what economists coyly term "moral hazard": if getting on a leaky boat puts someone in a position where they have to be rescued by being given residency in

Australia, then many more people will get on leaky boats. The duty of rescue can be abused. This does not release Australians from the duty of rescue: by its nature, this is a duty without an escape clause. But, if Australians have the right to restrict entry, then they have the right to delink rescue from subsequent rights of residency. A newly adopted policy is to hold rescued boat people outside Australian territory and deny them any advantage over other applicants in processing their applications for legal entry. A tougher, and arguably more humane, proposal is to tow apprehended boats back to their port of embarkation. But the game between the hopeful immigrant and the authorities need not stop there. Migrants can play dumb—literally—and destroy their papers, so that it is impossible for the authorities to identify either their country of embarkation or their country of origin. In effect, they raise the stakes: rescuing me lands you with a liability that you cannot exit except by granting me residence. Such a conscious abuse of the duty of rescue would warrant equivalent, though proportionate, responses that would not include the migrant getting what they want.

Migration is a private act usually decided primarily by the migrant, perhaps with input from the family. Yet this private decision has effects both on host societies and on societies of origin that the migrant does not take into account. Such effects, which economists call externalities, potentially infringe the rights of others. It is legitimate for public policy to factor in these effects that migrants themselves ignore.

It is therefore legitimate for the governments of host countries to limit migration, but controls affect three distinct groups: immigrants themselves, those left behind in countries of origin, and the indigenous population of host countries. Migration policies need to take all three groups into account. The sleight of hand by which utilitarian economics glibly aggregates these three effects to produce net gains in the hundreds of billions of dollars is unreasonable. So too is the xenophobe's exclusive concern for the indigenous: although the concern for others evidently weakens beyond borders, it does not evaporate.

The angry debate between xenophobes and "progressives" addresses the wrong question: is migration good or bad? The relevant question for policy is not whether migration has been good or bad overall. Rather, it is the likely effects *at the margin* should migration continue to accelerate. In answering this question, three analytic building blocks that have been set out in different parts of the book are important. It is time to bring them together.

Migrants: The Acceleration Principle

The first building block concerns migrants and is about their decisions. Its key message is that, left to the decentralized decisions of potential migrants, migration accelerates until low-income countries are substantially depopulated. The acceleration principle follows from two indisputable features of migration. One is that for a given income gap, the larger is the diaspora, the easier and hence more rapid is migration. Frédéric Docquier, currently the foremost scholar of the migration process, describes this as the most powerful single influence on migration.[2] The other indisputable feature is that migration has only small, and indeed ambiguous, feedback effects on the income gap. Immigration, until it is massive, does not significantly drive incomes down; emigration, even if massive, may not significantly drive them up. The initial income gap is so wide that if emigration were the only equilibrating force, it would continue for many decades and involve huge relocations of people.

The *acceleration principle* itself is derived from these intrinsic characteristics of the migration process. However, in practice, acceleration is compounded by two other changes in low-income countries: rising incomes and rising education. Within the relevant range, rising income will tend to increase migration even though it narrows the income gap. This is because rising income makes it easier to finance the initial investment in migration: the truly poor cannot afford to migrate. Rising education implies that any given educational hurdle used as a criterion for migration policy will be met by an increasing number of people.

The implication is that either acceleration is offset by periodic tightening of the criteria of eligibility, or the rate of migration and the size of the diaspora will both increase until finally limited by depopulation in countries of origin.

Those Left Behind: The Happy Medium

The second building block concerns those left behind and is about education and remittances. Emigration has several effects on those left behind, but the clearest, and probably the most important, are on the resident stock of educated people and on remittances. Both of these effects have only recently been well understood, and both have yielded surprising results.

Emigration of the educated does not necessarily deplete the stock of the educated. On the contrary, at moderate levels, which depend upon other characteristics of the society, emigration can lead to a net benefit—the brain gain. But whereas China and India have characteristics that naturally limit migration to rates at which there is a brain gain, the many small, poor societies face emigration rates that drain them of human capital, which is already extremely scarce. Worse, emigration of the innovative drains the society of the very skills it most needs to adopt and adapt to modernity. Similarly, in the absence of migration, remittances would be zero, so a modest rate of emigration is sure to increase them and thereby benefit those left behind. But beyond a point emigration becomes an alternative to remittances rather than a source of them. Thus, at some point the relationships between the rate of migration and their effects on education and remittances change from being positive to negative. They rise to a peak and then fall away again. The evidence is that for most small, poor countries, even the current rate of emigration is probably beyond the peak.

The implication is that from the perspective of those left behind there is a *happy medium*, a moderate rate of emigration at which the combined effects of the incentive to get education and the receipt of remittances are at their maximum. The most beneficial migration is not permanent exodus but temporary migration for higher education. Not only does this enhance the skills that are in desperately short supply, students absorb the functional political and social norms of their host country. Not only that, on returning they transmit these norms to the many people still lacking an education. But the governments of countries of origin do not control either the emigration rate or the rate of return and so are dependent upon the controls set by the governments of host countries.

Indigenous Hosts: Trade-offs

The third building block concerns the indigenous population in host societies. It is partly about direct economic effects and partly about social effects: variety, trust, and redistribution. As with those left behind, migration has numerous effects, but these are probably the most important and potentially the most persistent.

The direct economic effects on wages depend upon the scale of migration. At moderate rates of migration the effects are usually modestly positive in the short term and nonexistent in the long term. Were migration to continue to accelerate, basic economic forces would set in and drive wages substantially lower. The economic effects of sharing scarce publicly provided services such as social housing are liable to be negative for the indigenous poor even at moderate rates of migration and would become substantially negative were migration to accelerate. Other economic effects, such as overpopulation and the accentuation of boom-bust cycles, may be important in particular contexts.

Migrants increase social diversity. Diversity enriches economies by bringing fresh perspectives for problem solving, and the variety it brings with it enhances the pleasures of life. But diversity also undermines mutual regard and its invaluable benefits of cooperation and generosity. The corrosive effects of diversity are accentuated if migrants are from countries with dysfunctional social models to which they remain attached. There is therefore a trade-off between the costs and benefits of diversity. In managing this trade-off, the key information concerns how precisely both the benefits and the costs increase with greater diversity. The benefits of variety are probably subject to diminishing returns, as with any other form of variety. That is, as variety increases, the benefits keep increasing but by less and less. In contrast, the costs of moderate diversity are likely to be negligible, but beyond some level greater diversity might begin to jeopardize cooperation games and undermine the willingness to redistribute income. So the costs of diversity are likely to rise at an increasing rate. At some point, the incremental costs of diversity are therefore likely to exceed the incremental gains from variety. So the right way of posing the diversity question is not whether it is good or bad—the xenophobe versus the "progressive"—but how much is best. Unfortunately, social research is currently nowhere near the level of sophistication needed to estimate at what point diversity would become seriously costly. You may regard the implication of this ignorance as being that the concerns are scaremongering. Or you may see them as grounds for caution. Regrettably, this judgment will probably be determined by your moral priors, as Jonathan Haidt predicts, rather than by your attitude to risk. For choices concerning migration policy, limited evidence collides with strong passions. But try, for the moment, to remain dispassionate.

A Policy Package

Now bring these building blocks together. They carry a message of responsibility to the governments of host countries. The rate of migration depends upon the individual decisions of potential migrants and any policies set by these governments. Left to the decisions of migrants, migration is liable to accelerate beyond the happy medium at which those left behind gain most from it. It would also accelerate beyond the point at which host populations gain from further migration. Migration cannot be left to the decisions of individual migrants; it must be managed by governments. But migration policy is unavoidably complicated. To be fit for purpose, policy must get to grips with these complexities. On many of the issues, research is not yet at the stage where it can provide reliable answers. Meanwhile, official pronouncements have forfeited the trust of ordinary citizens by a continuous litany of complacent reassurance: recall that spectacularly erroneous forecast by the British Home Office as to likely migration from eastern Europe. But until the taboos are broken and the parameters of future policies are widely understood, such research will not even start. In chapter 5 I set out a schematic prediction of how migration policy might blunder into mistakes in the typical high-income society. I termed it the political economy of panic. I now return to precisely the initial conditions that produced that disturbing policy sequence and propose a different one.

As in the political economy of panic, the initial configuration of the migration function and the diaspora schedule implies that there is no equilibrium. In the absence of controls, migration and the diaspora will expand without limit. However, instead of leaving migration to accelerate until the point of policy panic, the government of the host country now adopts a package of policies designed around ceilings, the selection of migrants, the integration of diasporas, and the legalization of illegal immigrants.

Ceilings

At minimum, the task for migration policy is to prevent its acceleration to rates that would become damaging, both for those left behind in poor countries of origin and for the indigenous people of host countries. Migration has not yet generated such damage, so there is no need for policies of panic. But we should recognize that fundamental forces will lead migration to accelerate and that preventative policies are greatly superior to reactive ones. Indeed, I suspect that by putting effective preventative policies in place, mainstream politicians would stymie the current appeal of extremist parties to ordinary citizens and avert the conditions under which that appeal might spread. What is the rationale for ceilings? It unites enlightened self-interest and compassion.

The argument from enlightened self-interest is preventative: it does not suggest that migration has already caused net damage to high-income societies. The economic rationale is that continued accelerating migration would drive wages down for indigenous workers and seriously dilute public goods. There are practical limits to how rapidly jobs markets in high-income countries are able to generate high-productivity employment: they are already struggling. At the moderate rates of migration experienced for most of the past half-century, which happened to be coincident with prolonged boom conditions, favorable offsetting effects sustain and indeed modestly enhance wages. But these effects cannot be extrapolated to what would happen in the absence of migration controls. The social rationale is that continued acceleration would increase diversity to the point at which it undermined mutual regard.

The case from compassion is that the neediest people in the world are not the migrants from poor countries. Migrants are usually drawn from the better-off in their own countries because the poorest cannot afford the costs of migration. The neediest are the people who are left behind. This is the great moral challenge of our age, and softheadedness about migration is not the remedy. China would continue to gain from accelerating migration, but Haiti would not, and it is Haiti that we should be concerned about, not China. While migration at moderate rates helps these people, even present rates of migration are most likely beyond the happy medium at which it is most beneficial to them. At the margin, migration is already handicapping their struggle out of poverty. The argument from compassion thus implies both more urgent and more restrictive policies than the argument from enlightened self-interest.

So there is a sound case from both self-interest and compassion for ceilings on migration. Such policies are not a vestige of a bygone age: accelerating mass migration from poor societies to rich ones is a new, and indeed prospective, phenomenon analogous to global warming. As with global warming, we do not yet have an adequate research base on which to model it in the necessary detail, but it is already evident that controls will become increasingly necessary in the next few decades. Growing awareness of climate change is teaching the high-income societies to think long term and to consider the potential risks of carbon emissions. Migration policy is analogous: indeed, the two processes share the essential feature that flows in excess of a threshold accumulate into stocks. In respect of climate change, analysts have realized that the safe rate of carbon emissions is derived from the safe stock of carbon dioxide in the atmosphere. In respect of migration, the equivalent concept is the safe size of the unabsorbed diaspora. The diaspora is the accumulated stock of *unabsorbed* migrants, so it is the diaspora that measures the impact of migration on diversity. It is the degree of diversity that should be the ultimate objective of migration policy, not the rate of migration itself. Analogous to climate change, we do not know how large an unabsorbed diaspora would need to be before it significantly weakened the mutual regard on which the high-income societies depend. Of course, accelerating migration would also at some stage reduce wages, but the weakening of mutual regard is the more important danger on which to focus because it is less obvious and probably has long lags. This makes it more susceptible to serious policy mistakes: if a society stumbles into it, it is difficult to correct. People will disagree about the risks of growing diversity, just as they disagree as to whether a risk of three, four, or five degrees of global warming is acceptable. But at least in respect of climate people are now having that discussion. The same is needed in respect of diasporas: should the ceiling on diasporas as a percentage of a population be 10 percent, 30 percent, or 50 percent, bearing in mind that left to themselves diasporas will cluster heavily in some cities? For climate change we not only have the right concepts, we are increasingly measuring them. For migration policy we have neither.

Given some ceiling to the safe size of the diaspora, whatever it might be, the next key number on which policy should be built is not the rate of migration but the rate at which the diaspora is absorbed. The core insight of our workhorse was that the sustainable rate of migration that corresponds to any particular ceiling on the diaspora depends upon how rapidly the diaspora is absorbed. This rate differs massively among immigrant groups and between host societies: for example, Tongans in New Zealand have a far higher absorption rate than Turks in Germany. In most societies this key information is not even measured properly, so initially it would need to be approximated and gradually refined.

Between them, the safe ceiling on the diaspora and the rate of its absorption lead us to the sustainable ceiling on the rate of migration. A high rate of migration is only consistent with a stable diaspora if combined with a high rate of absorption. Conversely, a low rate of absorption is only consistent with a stable diaspora if the rate of migration is kept low. This ceiling on the rate of migration evidently relates to the gross flow of immigration. There is nothing outrageous about specifying a ceiling in gross terms: for example, the various lottery systems adopted in some high-income countries for controlling migration automatically specify a ceiling in terms of gross inflows. Yet the ceiling currently being debated by British politicians is for the net flow of immigration minus emigration. This bears little relation to the concept that really matters, which is the size of the diaspora. It would be pertinent only for concerns about overpopulation. I doubt that the current majority opinion in Britain that "migration is excessive" reflects anxieties about overpopulation. More likely, it reflects a vague unease that unabsorbed diasporas are getting too large. Accelerating emigration might warrant being an objective of policy in its own right: for high-income countries it is damaging to the remaining population due to the loss of skills.

Once we are able to distinguish between gross immigration and gross emigration, other important distinctions follow. Faster migration for the purpose of settlement augments the diaspora, while draining the poorest countries of talent. In contrast, faster temporary migration for the purpose of higher education does not increase the diaspora, augments vital skills in poor countries, transfers values, and trains future leaders. A parody of Soviet central planning in the old USSR recounts how a target specified in terms of heads of cattle had been met by breeding the two-headed cow. Meeting a migration target by reducing the inflow of foreign students nests in the same category of policy design.[3]

Selectivity

Having established an overall ceiling for gross migration, the next component of a fit-for-purpose public policy would be to shape its composition. The salient dimensions are household status, education, employability, cultural origins, and vulnerability.

If the right to migrate is conferred simply by a relationship or prospective relationship to an existing immigrant, all other criteria are of little moment. Dependent relatives of the diaspora will increasingly crowd out other would-be migrants as diaspora-fueled migration accelerates, and that is the end of the story. Further, generous rights to bring in relatives reduce the incentives to make remittances, the lifeline that migration provides to the poorest countries. It is therefore a crucial, albeit sensitive issue, as to how these rights are defined. I have argued that these rights only exist because the indigenous population rarely uses them. As rights, they do not meet Kant's categorical imperative test of whether something is ethical: what if everyone did that? They are only viable because, in respect of the indigenous population, the answer to Kant is "Fortunately, they don't." So the reasonable extension of these little-used indigenous rights to migrants is to confer them with the same proviso: that they should be little used. As a practical matter, this implies a lottery system in which migrants as a group receive the same proportion of immigration slots for their relatives as do the indigenous. Restricting the migration of dependents in this way opens up room for the immigration of workers. How should workers be selected?

The most obviously desirable characteristic of immigrant workers is that they should be educated or equivalently skilled. If immigrants are more educated than the indigenous population, they tend to raise the wages of the indigenous; if they are less educated, they tend to lower them, at least toward the bottom of the wage spectrum. So, based on the self-interest of host societies, policy should select potential migrants based on a threshold level of education. This is becoming increasingly common in high-income societies, although there are currently wide variations between them. As education levels continue to rise, this threshold will also need to rise. As I discussed in part 4, from the perspective of those left behind in the poorest countries, this is not ideal. The poorest countries are already suffering a brain drain, and this weakens their capacity to catch up with modernity through adopting and adapting global technologies. Further, there is some evidence that beyond a point, highly educated migrants send less money back home than those who are not so highly educated.

Beyond education comes employability. While educational criteria lend themselves to the checklist regulation of applications for immigration, they miss enormous amounts of other information that is pertinent for a working environment. Anyone familiar with universities will recognize that some of their students, and indeed some of their staff, are virtually unemployable despite being highly educated. Government visa offices are ill-equipped to elicit such information, and the degree of discretionary power that would be handed to immigration officials were they tasked with doing so would invite increased corruption. The sensible way for a society to use this information is to add a layer to the migration decision that is administered by firms. Having satisfied the criteria set by government, would-be migrants must also satisfy a firm that it wants to employ them. New Zealand and Germany both operate such a system. Employers have the incentive to vet the applicant, thereby taking into account a more balanced array of characteristics. Countries that select migrants only by means of mechanically applied points systems are liable to lose out to those that also vet, because they will attract people who meet the letter of the requirements but are otherwise unsuitable.[4]

Beyond these work-based attributes is culture: a message of this book has been that cultures matter. Culture is what separates diasporas from the indigenous, and some cultures are more distant from the culture of the indigenous population than others. The more distant the culture is, the slower will be the rate of absorption of its diaspora, and also slower will be the sustainable rate of migration. Yet, in one of the paradoxes of migration, in the absence of culturally differentiated controls, the culturally distant will be advantaged in migration decisions. Precisely because their diasporas take longer to be absorbed than the culturally proximate, these large diasporas facilitate further migration. So to the extent possible without transgression into racism, a fit-for-purpose migration policy sets the rights to migration from particular countries so as to offset these perverse effects of cultural distance. As an example of culturally targeted but politically acceptable differential controls, in both Sweden and Britain there is currently no restriction placed upon immigration from Poland, but immigration from Turkey is restricted because Turkey has not been admitted to the European Union.[5]

The last, though not the least, criterion is vulnerability. Although the status of asylum is abused, as a category it is extremely important. Helping the vulnerable is unlikely to confer economic benefits on the indigenous population. That is not its rationale. By helping the most stressed societies, the high-income societies retain their self-respect. However, there is scope for reforming the asylum process. A fit-for-purpose migration policy would target asylum on those few countries in the throes of civil war, brutal dictatorship, minority persecution, or equivalent severe social disturbance. For the citizens of such countries asylum would be granted swiftly and generously. But this liberality would be combined with time-bound rights of residence: when peace is restored, people would be required to return. The rationale for this rider is that postconflict countries face an acute coordination problem. Though they are desperately short of skilled people, individual members of the diaspora are reluctant to return. Only if many people return together are the prospects of the country sufficiently promising for return to be other than quixotic. Analytically, we are back to the discussion of chapter 3: the difficulties of coordinating cooperation. But whereas there we were concerned with the fragility of existing cooperation in the high-income societies, now we are concerned with how to get coordination started in some of the poorest. The governments of postconflict states usually try despairingly to attract their diasporas back to the country, but they lack the means to engineer a coordinated return. Only the host governments of asylum-seeking migrants have this power. In the interests of these societies at the bottom of the global heap, they should use it. The purpose of asylum in conflict situations is not to confer a permanently transformed life onto the fortunate minority who are able to get out but to preserve the country's critically important skilled and politically engaged people until it is safe for them to return to rebuild their society. The duty of rescue does not absolve the high-income societies from the duty to think through the implications of their policies.

Integration

Controlling the size and composition of migration is not the only means of containing diversity and stabilizing the size of the diaspora. The other means is to increase the rate of absorption. This opens slots in the diaspora, enabling migration to fill them up. The rate at which diasporas are absorbed depends in part upon the choice between multiculturalism and assimilation.

Absorption has turned out to be more difficult than social scientists and policymakers initially imagined. In part the switch to multiculturalism was probably a psychological response to this failure: "What cannot be eschewed must be embraced." But for any ceiling on diversity, the lower the rate of absorption the lower must be migration, so multiculturalism has a clear cost. It is premature to give up on integration. A fit-for-purpose migration policy therefore adopts a range of strategies designed to increase the absorption of diasporas. The government cracks down hard on racism and discrimination on the part of the indigenous population. It adopts Canadian-style policies of requiring geographic dispersion of migrants. It adopts America-in-the-1970s-style policies of integrating schools, imposing a ceiling on the percentage of pupils from diasporas. It requires migrants to learn the indigenous language and provides the resources that make this feasible. It also promotes the symbols and ceremonies of common citizenship.

Most people who consider themselves progressive want multiculturalism combined with rapid migration and generous social welfare programs. But some combinations of policy choices may be unsustainable. Electorates have gradually learned to be skeptical of the alluring policy combination of low taxes, high spending, and stable debt offered by rogue politicians. One level up in economic sophistication, an important insight of modern international economics is "the impossible trinity": a government that permits the free movement of capital and sets its own monetary policy cannot also set the exchange rate. In consequence, the free movement of capital has belatedly been recognized by the International Monetary Fund as inappropriate for some countries. There may, perhaps, be an equivalent impossible trinity arising from the free movement of people. It may prove unsustainable to combine rapid migration with multicultural policies that keep absorption rates low and welfare systems that are generous. The evidence pointing to such an impossible trinity is sketchy, but be wary of outraged dismissals: social scientists are not immune from systematically biased reasoning.

Legalizing Illegal Immigration

All controls inevitably induce evasion. Currently, those who successfully evade migration controls become illegal residents, and this illegality gives rise to serious problems such as crime and the black economy. Debates on what to do about illegal immigrants have been as damagingly polarized as the larger migration debate. Social liberals want a one-off granting of full legal status; social conservatives oppose this on the grounds that rewarding evasion would encourage more of it. The result has been deadlock: nothing has been done and meanwhile illegal immigrants have accumulated: in America twelve million of them, in Britain nobody even knows. As I write, the Obama administration is beginning to wrestle with the problem.

The policy package offers an effective and straightforward approach that meets the reasonable concerns of both camps but will presumably outrage the fundamentalists in both. To meet the reasonable concerns of social liberals, it recognizes that evasion is unavoidably a continuing process, so that future flows of illegal immigrants need to be addressed as well as the accumulated stocks. Any granting of rights that claims to be once-and-for-all is a piece of political deception. The package also recognizes that once border controls have been evaded, so that people have succeeded in entering the country illegally, all such migrants must be granted sufficient legal status to be able to work within the official economy. Otherwise, illegal immigrants are a source of further illegality. To meet the reasonable concerns of social conservatives, it involves a penalty for evasion relative to legal entry, does not increase overall migration, and tightens the process for dealing with migrants who choose to remain illegal.

The approach is to maintain and indeed perhaps upgrade border controls, but to grant all those who despite these controls enter the country an initial status of guest workers. This status permits them to work and automatically places them in a queue to become permanent, fully legal immigrants. While guest workers, they would have an obligation to pay taxes but would not be entitled to social benefits: in using public services they would have the same rights as tourists. The slots to convert them into fully legal immigrants would count toward the overall ceiling on legal migration, so that illegal immigration would reduce legal migration rather than be supplementary to it. This would give the pro-migration lobby a strong incentive to support effective border controls. Finally, to strengthen the incentive to register, those illegal immigrants who chose not to do so would be subject to deportation without appeal if detected.[6]

Would such an approach dangerously increase the incentives for illegal migration? I think not. We can straightforwardly deduce that, despite the large stock of illegal migrants in many countries, existing controls are largely effective. The economic incentives to migrate from poor countries are so substantial, and diasporas already sufficiently well established, that were the controls not effective, migration flows would have been far greater. Consequently, the flow of illegal migration is likely to be fairly insensitive to minor changes in incentives such as those I have proposed. The road to the status of a fully legal migrant would still be hard and long, typically requiring many years of taxation without benefits. If governments wanted to make the status of guest worker less attractive, those convicted of crimes could be subject to deportation without appeal. Would the proposed approach breach human rights? Only if the controls on migration themselves are judged to do so. If the controls are legitimate, then any policies that are forgiving of migrants who evade them are more humane than leaving them without any legal status.

How the Package Works

This package of ceilings, selection, integration, and legalization can be evaluated using our workhorse model. In may be worth flipping back to Figure 5.1, which depicts the political economy of panic that responds so damagingly to the initial absence of equilibrium. Figure 12.1 starts from exactly the same position: as in Figure 5.1, there is initially no equilibrium.

But now the policies of ceilings combined with selective migration flatten the migration function, twisting it clockwise. Meanwhile, the policies of accelerated integration steepen the diaspora schedule, twisting it counterclockwise. As a result, the two lines now intersect: equilibrium is restored. With this package, migration initially accelerates but then stabilizes; similarly the diaspora initially grows but then stabilizes. The result of the package is superior to the political economy of panic in four important

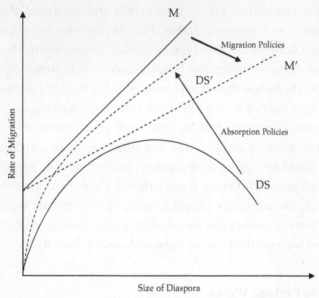

Figure 12.1 The Political Economy of Selection and Integration

respects. In the long run the migration-diaspora combination is better. Comparing Figures 12.1 and 5.1, for a common size of the diaspora in equilibrium, the rate of migration is higher, and conversely, for a common rate of migration, the size of the unabsorbed diaspora is smaller. Thus, the host society can choose to have both a higher rate of migration and a smaller diaspora. This is an improvement because the economic gains are generated by labor migration, while the social costs are generated by the unabsorbed diaspora. We also get to equilibrium rapidly, whereas the panic sequence might take a century. Further, the path to equilibrium avoids a prolonged detour involving wild swings in both the rate of migration and the size of the diaspora. Finally, the pool of illegal (and therefore unabsorbed) migrants that accumulates during the political economy of panic is entirely avoided.

Two lessons can be drawn from this straightforward application of the model. One is that the pertinent array of policies for successful migration is quite wide. If some desired ceiling on diversity is the objective, then the rate of absorption as well as migration matters. The other is that appropriate policies need to be set early in the migration process with a view to the long term. Climate change is not the only policy that needs long-term thinking. In Britain, the Office of Budgetary Responsibility has recently put out an analysis suggesting that if Britain adopted a higher rate of net immigration, the per capita growth rate of GDP during the next three years might increase by around 0.3 percentage points. With due respect to the team that produced this forecast, it is categorically how not to think through migration policy.

How might such a policy package affect the groups that matter for migration?

There is no reason to expect that the migration rate that the policy package would generate would be ideal for those left behind in poor countries of origin. Indeed, we do not currently have the evidence even to estimate what such a rate of migration would be. But we know that for many poor countries even the current rate is excessive: a somewhat slower rate of emigration would probably benefit them. It also seems likely that the savage reduction in migration that would be risked by the political economy of panic would switch it to being inadequate. Hence, since selection and integration would result in a faster rate of migration than that, it would likely be an improvement from the perspective of the poorest societies.

From the perspective of the indigenous population of the host society, the policy package is considerably superior. The sustainable rate of migration is higher, enabling the economy to continue to benefit from the modest economic gains thereby implied, and the social costs of an excessive, unabsorbed diaspora are avoided.

From the perspective of the existing stock of migrants, the political economy of panic is unattractive in both economic and social respects. In economic terms existing migrants are the big losers from further migration, and so during the anxiety phase of accelerating migration they would be squeezed by competition from new entrants. Socially, during the ugly phase of tightening restrictions and mounting social costs, they would be the ones at risk of xenophobia. The package of selection and integration does, however, place demands upon migrants: they are discouraged from remaining in a comfort zone of cultural separation. They are required to learn the indigenous language and send their children to integrated schools, and their right to bring in relatives is limited.

No migration policy can benefit everyone. In the package I have proposed the losers are those potential migrants who in the absence of the proposed policies would in the near future have migrated. The policies of selection and integration indeed imply that the sustainable rate of migration is higher, so that would-be migrants benefit eventually, but the package avoids the phase during which migration temporarily exceeds that rate. Why is this justified? Although potential migrants have interests like anyone else, there is no reason for their interest to trump those of others, which is what happens in the absence of a fit-for-purpose policy. The indigenous populations of host countries have a right to control entry, taking into account not only their own interest but also a sense of charity to others. But in exercising charity, their chief concern should be the vast group of poor people left behind in countries of origin, rather than the relatively tiny group of fortunate people who get dramatic increases in their income through being permitted to migrate.

Conclusion: Converging Economies, Diverging Societies

Migration is a large topic and this is a short book. But few areas of public policy are more in need of accessible and dispassionate analysis. I have attempted to shake the polarized positions: the hostility to migrants, tinged by xenophobia and racism, that is widespread among ordinary citizens, opposed by the contemptuous refrain from the business and liberal elites, supported by social science academics, that open doors will continue to confer large benefits and are ethically imperative.

Mass international migration is a response to extreme global inequality. As never before, young people in the poorest countries are aware of opportunities elsewhere. That inequality opened up over the past two centuries and will close during the coming century. Most developing countries are now rapidly converging on the high-income countries: this is the great story of our time. Mass migration is therefore not a permanent feature of globalization. Quite the contrary, it is a temporary response to an ugly phase in which prosperity has not yet globalized. A century from now, the world will be far more integrated than now in respect to trade, information, and finance, but the net flow of migration will have diminished.

Although international migration responds to global inequality, it does not significantly change it. What is driving economic convergence is the transformation of the social models prevailing in poor societies. Gradually, their institutions are becoming more inclusive and less the preserve of extractive elites. Their economic narratives are shifting from the zero-sum mentality of grievance, to recognition of the scope for positive-sum cooperation. Loyalties are gradually expanding from clans to nations. Organizations are learning how to make workers more productive by combining scale with motivation. These profound changes are being achieved through adapting global ideas to local contexts. As social models strengthen and economies grow, migration from rural poverty indeed matters, but the journey is to Lagos and Mumbai, not London and Madrid.

Yet although international migration is a transient sideshow to convergence, it may leave permanent legacies. One sure legacy that is unambiguously benign is that the high-income societies have become multiracial. Given their past history of racism, the revolution in sentiments consequent upon intermarriage and coexistence has been profoundly liberating for all concerned.

But in the absence of effective migration policies, migration will continue to accelerate, and this could imply other possible legacies. The currently high-income countries could become postnational, multicultural societies. On the hopeful new view of multiculturalism propounded by Western elites, this would also be benign: such societies would be stimulating and prosperous. But the track record of culturally diverse societies is not so encouraging that this is the only possible outcome from an unlimited increase in diversity. In most societies for most of history high diversity has been a handicap. Even within modern Europe, the relatively modest cultural difference between Germans and Greeks has stretched to breaking the limited institutional harmonization achieved by the European Union. It is possible that permanently rising cultural diversity would gradually undermine mutual regard and that unabsorbed diasporas would hang onto dysfunctional aspects of the social models that prevailed in their countries of origin at the time of migration. A further possible legacy of a continuing acceleration in migration is that small, poor countries like Haiti that can offer little to their most talented people would suffer an accelerating hemorrhage of capabilities: an exodus. They are already beyond the point at which emigration is beneficial. While the fortunate would leave, those left behind might be unable to catch up with the rest of mankind.

Meanwhile, the emerging high-income societies are likely to become *less* multicultural. As part of the gradual transformation of their social models, identities will have enlarged from the fragmentation of clans to the unifying sense of the nation. In embracing the benign uses of nationalism, they will come to resemble the old high-income countries prior to migration.

Periodically, over the centuries the fortunes of societies have reversed. North America overtook Latin America; Europe overtook China. The financial crisis, with its source and effects in the high-income societies, has dented the smug complacency by which their citizens took economic superiority for granted. That most societies will catch up with the West is now accepted. But convergence may not be the end of the story. Singapore, which in 1950 was much poorer than Europe, is now much richer. If social models really are the fundamental determinants of prosperity, the rise of multiculturalism in one part of the world, coincident with its decline elsewhere, could have surprising implications.

As I finish this book I look up again at Karl Hellenschmidt. He was, before his time, the archetypical modern migrant. Leaving a small, poor village and a large, poor family, he reaped the modest rewards afforded to a low-skilled migrant in a high-income city. But my eye travels on to another photograph, to another man in middle age, who bears a family resemblance. I realize that he, not my grandfather, is the true role model for this book. Karl Hellenschmidt Jr. faced the habitual second-generation choice. Should he cling to an affectation of difference or embrace a new identity? He took the leap. Which is why you have just finished a book by Paul Collier, not Paul Hellenschmidt.

Notes

Chapter 1

1. Haidt (2012).
2. Benabou and Tirole (2011).
3. Wente (2012).
4. Dustmann et al. (2003).

Chapter 2

1. Besley and Persson (2011); Acemoglu and Robinson (2012).
2. Jones and Olken (2005).
3. Kay (2012).
4. In a brilliant new study, Timothy Besley and Marta Reynal-Querol (2012) show that in Africa remembered conflicts from as far back as the fifteenth century still cause violent conflict today.
5. Greif and Bates (1995).
6. Pinker (2011).
7. Akerlof and Kranton (2011).
8. Beatty and Pritchett (2012).
9. Beine et al. (2011).

10. Carrington et al. (1996).
11. The Dunbar constant proposes that there is a ceiling of around 150 to the number of people with whom we can maintain a meaningful relationship (Dunbar 1992).
12. For example, in a particularly careful study of the Turkish and Serbian diasporas in Germany, Koczan (2013) shows that the higher the proportion of diaspora children is in the class, the more likely a diaspora child will grow up with a strong sense of diaspora identity.
13. By convention, this point at which the two axes of the diagram meet is termed its origin.
14. To see this, suppose for a moment that the absorption rate did not depend on the diaspora: for example, every year 2 percent of the diaspora merged into the mainstream population regardless of its size. In that case, if the diaspora doubled, the number of people absorbed into the mainstream would also double. With twice as many people flowing out of the diaspora, there would be room for twice as many migrants to flow in: doubling the diaspora would double the rate of migration that kept the diaspora stable. Visually, the *diaspora schedule* would be a straight line coming out of the corner of the diagram. Now suppose, more plausibly, that the absorption rate declines as the diaspora increases. If there are 30,000 Tongalese in New Zealand, there are sufficient interactions with other members of society to support an absorption rate of 2 percent, but if there are 60,000, the typical Tongalese has fewer interactions outside the group and so the rate of absorption falls to 1.5 percent. As a result, if the diaspora doubles, the number of people being absorbed from it less than doubles.
15. It is what economists term a dynamic equilibrium.
16. Hatton and Williamson (2008).

Chapter 3
1. Clemens (2011).
2. Cunliffe (2012).

3. Besley and Reynal-Querol (2012).

4. Weiner (2011).

5. Pinker (2011).

6. Nunn and Wantchekon (2011).

7. Gaechter et al. (2010).

8. Fisman and Miguel (2007).

9. Hofstede and Hofstede (2010).

10. Shih et al. (1999).

11. Akerlof and Kranton (2011).

12. Koczan (2013).

13. See Hurley and Carter (2005), especially the chapter by Ap Dijkster-huis, "Why We Are Social Animals."

14. Candelo-Londoño et al. (2011).

15. Putnam (2007).

16. Putnam (2007), p. 165.

17. Miguel and Gugerty (2005).

18. Hirschman (2005).

19. Montalvo and Reynal-Querol (2010).

20. Pinker (2011).

21. Murray (2012).

22. Sandel (2012).

23. Alesina et al. (2001).

24. Alesina et al. (1999). Natalie Candelo-Londoño, Rachel Croson, and Xin Li (2011) provide a useful recent review of the literature and some interesting new results.

25. Belich (2009).

26. Acemoglu et al. (2001).

27. In turn, the Scots who migrated to the north of Ireland were descendants of the Scoti, a tribe that invaded the north of Britain from Ireland around the eighth century. They did not, to my knowledge, invoke a "right of return" to Ireland.

28. Nunn (2010).

29. Fleming (2011), Cunliffe (2012), and Halsall (2013) give rather different accounts.
30. Montalvo and Reynal-Querol (2010).
31. Kepel (2011).
32. Romer (2010).
33. Heath et al. (2011).
34. Herreros and Criado (2009), p. 335.
35. Koopmans (2010).

Chapter 4

1. Dustmann et al. (2012).
2. Docquier et al. (2010).
3. Grosjean (2011).
4. Corden (2003).
5. Nickell (2009).
6. Card (2005).
7. Hirsch (1977).
8. Sampson (2008).
9. Goldin et al. (2011).
10. Andersen (2012).
11. Docquier et al. (2010).
12. For an analysis that uses the 2012 British census, see Goodhart (2013).
13. Walmsley et al. (2005).

Chapter 6

1. Clemens et al. (2009).
2. McKenzie and Yang (2010); Clemens (2010).
3. Borjas (1989).
4. Van Tubergen (2004).
5. Cox and Jimenez (1992).
6. An old Yorkshire joke.
7. Yang (2011).
8. Agesa and Kim (2001).
9. Mousy and Arcand (2011).

10. Aker et al. (2011).
11. Because our work is only provisional, it has not yet been through the process of academic refereeing. The results should therefore be treated with considerable caution. Our analysis includes migration from all low- and middle-income countries for which there is data, to all countries in the OECD, and covers the period 1960–2000. Paul Collier and Anke Hoeffler, 2013, "An Empirical Analysis of Global Migration," mimeo, Centre for the Study of African Economies, Oxford University.
12. Beine et al. (2011).
13. Cited in Clemens (2011).

Chapter 7

1. Docquier et al. (2010).
2. Deaton et al. (2009).
3. Stillman et al. (2012).
4. Stillman and his colleagues add a variety of other, nonstandard psychological questions such as "peace of mind," and on these measures migration enhanced states of mind.
5. Dercon et al. (2013).

Chapter 8

1. Hirschman (1990).
2. Docquier et al. (2011); Beine and Sekkat (2011).
3. Batista and Vicente (2011).
4. Pérez-Armendariz and Crow (2010).
5. Dedieu et al. (2012).
6. Chauvet and Mercier (2012).
7. Mahmoud et al. (2012).
8. Beine et al. (forthcoming).
9. Docquier et al. (2007).
10. I turn to the evidence for this in the next chapter.
11. Spilimbergo (2009).
12. Besley et al. (2011).
13. Spilimbergo (2009).

14. Akerlof and Kranton (2011), ch. 8.
15. Mercier (2012).
16. *I Didn't Do It for You*, by Michaela Wrong (2006), provides a rare, lucid account of this little-known country.

Chapter 9

1. Thurow (2012).
2. Economists prefer a mathematically optimizing approach to probabilistic decisions, such as would be taken by a fully rational, well-informed person.
3. Docquier and Rapoport (2012); de la Croix and Docquier (2012); Batista and Vicente (2011).
4. One surprising effect that helps the poorest countries is that, controlling for other things, a country is more likely to be a net winner if it starts with few educated people. To see this, suppose that everyone is already educated: then neither the incentive effect nor the role model effect can have any traction. While this tends to help the poorest countries, the effect of size predominates.
5. Marchiori et al. (2013).
6. Docquier and Rapoport (2012).
7. Akerlof and Kranton (2011).
8. This is a variant of an idea of Besley and Ghatak (2003) about the matching of the attitudes of workers to those of the firms that employ them.
9. Akerlof and Kranton (2011), ch. 8.
10. Serra et al. (2010).
11. Wilson (1996).
12. Rempel and Lobdell (1978).
13. Yang (2011).
14. As with much concerned with migration, this outcome is not inevitable. If the migrants would have been particularly productive relative to those left behind, they may have contributed even more to others than through their remittances. But a modest increase in per capita expenditure is the most likely outcome.

15. Clemens et al. (2012).
16. Yang (2008).
17. Hoddinott (1994).
18. Yang and Choi (2007).
19. Docquier et al. (2012).
20. Beegle et al. (2011).
21. Glaeser (2011).
22. Saunders (2010).

Chapter 10

1. Ferguson (2012).

Chapter 11

1. Sandel (2012).
2. Dijksterhuis (2005).
3. Haidt's exception is the educated social elite of high-income countries who appear to suppress community and most of the other normal moral sentiments. Such "weird" people navigate their lives only by the two utilitarian moral sentiments of harm and fairness.
4. For a fascinating technical reformulation of *The Theory of Moral Sentiments*, see Benabou and Tirole (2011).
5. Zak (2012).
6. Pagel (2012).
7. Zak (2012).
8. Alesina and Spolaore (1997).

Chapter 12

1. See Corden (2003).
2. Beine et al. (2011).
3. Evidently, for student migration to be excluded from migration targets it is necessary to ensure that students return to their countries of origin upon completing their course of study. Once this is treated seriously, there are several options for effective control.

4. See Schiff (2012).
5. Turkey would be the poorest member of the Union and have its largest population and its highest birthrate, encouraged by pronatal government policies. Its entry would place extraordinary strains on social cohesion in Europe without clear benefits for Turkey itself.
6. The same penalty might also apply to tourists and students who overstayed. Clearly, these categories could not qualify for guest-worker status.

References

Acemoglu, D., Johnson, S., and Robinson, J. A. 2001. The Colonial Origins of Comparative Development: An Empirical Investigation. *American Economic Review* 91(5), 1369–1401.

Acemoglu, D., and Robinson, J. A. 2012. *Why Nations Fail: The Origins of Power, Prosperity, and Poverty*. New York: Crown Business.

Agesa, R. U., and Kim, S. 2001. Rural to Urban Migration as a Household Decision. *Review of Development Economics* 5(1), 60–75.

Aker, J. C., Clemens, M. A., and Ksoll, C. 2011. Mobiles and Mobility: The Effect of Mobile Phones on Migration in Niger. *Proceedings of the CSAE Annual Conference,* Oxford (March 2012).

Akerlof, G. A., and Kranton, R. E. 2011. *Identity Economics: How Our Identities Shape Our Work, Wages and Well-Being*. Princeton, NJ: Princeton University Press.

Alesina, A., Baqir, R., and Easterly, W. 1999. Public Goods and Ethnic Divisions. *Quarterly Journal of Economics* 114(4), 1243–1284.

Alesina, A., Glaeser, E., and Sacerdote, B. 2001. Why Doesn't the US Have a European-Style Welfare State? Harvard Institute of Economic Research Working Papers 1933.

Alesina, A., and Spolaore, E. 1997. On the Number and Size of Nations. *Quarterly Journal of Economics* 112(4), 1027–1056.

Andersen, T. 2012. Migration, Redistribution and the Universal Welfare Model, IZA Discussion Paper No. 6665.

Batista, C., and Vicente, P. C. 2011a. Do Migrants Improve Governance at Home? Evidence from a Voting Experiment. *World Bank Economic Review* 25(1), 77–104.

Batista, C., and Vicente, P. C. 2011b. Testing the Brain Gain Hypothesis: Micro Evidence from Cape Verde. *Journal of Development Economics* 97(1), 32–45.

Beatty, A., and Pritchett, L. 2012. From Schooling Goals to Learning Goals. CDC Policy Paper 012, September.

Beegle, K., De Weerdt, J., and Dercon, S. 2011. Migration and Economic Mobility in Tanzania: Evidence from a Tracking Survey. *Review of Economics and Statistics* 93(3), 1010–1033.

Beine, M., Docquier, F., and Ozden, C. 2011. Diasporas. *Journal of Development Economics* 95(1), 30–41.

Beine, M., Docquier, F., and Schiff, M. Forthcoming. International Migration, Transfers of Norms and Home Country Fertility. *Canadian Journal of Economics*.

Beine, M., and Sekkat, K. 2011. Skilled Migration and the Transfer of Institutional Norms. Mimeo.

Belich, J. 2009. *Replenishing the Earth: The Settler Revolution and the Rise of the Anglo-World, 1783–1939*. New York: Oxford University Press.

Benabou, R., and Tirole, J. 2011. Identity, Morals and Taboos: Beliefs as Assets. *Quarterly Journal of Economics* 126(2), 805–855.

Besley, T., and Ghatak, M. 2003. Incentives, Choice and Accountability in the Provision of Public Services. *Oxford Review of Economic Policy* 19(2), 235–249.

Besley, T., Montalvo, J. G., and Reynal-Querol, M. 2011. Do Educated Leaders Matter? *Economic Journal* 121(554), F205–F208.

Besley, T., and Persson, T. 2011. Fragile States and Development Policy. *Journal of the European Economic Association* 9(3), 371–398.

Besley, T., and Reynal-Querol. M. 2012a. The Legacy of Historical Conflict: Evidence from Africa. STICERD—Economic Organisation and Public Policy Discussion Papers Series 036, London School of Economics.

Besley, T. J., and Reynal-Querol, M. 2012b. The Legacy of Historical Conflict: Evidence from Africa. CEPR Discussion Papers 8850.

Borjas, G. J. 1989. Economic Theory and International Migration. *International Migration Review* 23, 457–485.

Candelo-Londoño, N., Croson, R. T. A., and Li, X. 2011. Social Exclusion and Identity: A Field Experiment with Hispanic Immigrants. Mimeo, University of Texas.

Card, D. 2005. Is the New Immigration Really So Bad? *Economic Journal* 115(507), F300–F323.

Carrington, W. J., Detragiache, E., and Vishwanath, T. 1996. Migration with Endogenous Moving Costs. *American Economic Review* 86(4), 909–930.

Chauvet, L., and Mercier, M. 2012. Do Return Migrants Transfer Norms to Their Origin Country? Evidence from Mali. DIAL and Paris School of Economics.

Clemens, M. A. 2010. The Roots of Global Wage Gaps: Evidence from Randomized Processing of US Visas. Working Paper 212, Center for Global Development.

Clemens, M. A. 2011. Economics and Emigration: Trillion-Dollar Bills on the Sidewalk? *Journal of Economic Perspectives* 25(3), 83–106.

Clemens, M. A., Montenegro, C., and Pritchett, L. 2009. The Place Premium: Wage Differences for Identical Workers across the US Border. Working Paper Series rwp09-004, John F. Kennedy School of Government, Harvard University.

Clemens, M. A., Radelet, S., Bhavnani, R. R., and Bazzi, S. 2012. Counting Chickens When They Hatch: Timing and the Effects of Aid on Growth. *Economic Journal* 122(561), 590–617.

Corden, W. M. 2003. 40 Million Aussies? Inaugural Richard Snape Lecture, Productivity Commission, Melbourne. Available at http://papers.ssrn.com/sol3/papers.cfm?abstract_id=496822.

Cox, D. C., and Jimenez, E. 1992. Social Security and Private Transfers in Developing Countries: The Case of Peru. *World Bank Economic Review* 6(1), 155–169.

Cunliffe, B. 2012. *Britain Begins*. New York: Oxford University Press.

de la Croix, D., and Docquier, F. 2012. Do Brain Drain and Poverty Result from Coordination Failures? *Journal of Economic Growth* 17(1), 1–26.

Deaton, A., Fortson, J., and Tortora, R. 2009. Life (Evaluation), HIV/AIDS, and Death in Africa. NBER Working Paper 14637.

Dedieu, J. P., Chauvet, L., Gubert, F., and Mesplé-Somps, S. 2012. Political Transnationalism: The Case of the Senegalese Presidential Elections in France and New York. Mimeo, DIAL.

Dercon, S., Krishnan, P., and Krutikova, S. 2013. Migration, Well-Being and Risk-Sharing. Mimeo, Centre for the Study of African Economies, University of Oxford.

Dijksterhuis, A. 2005. Why We Are Social Animals. In *Perspectives on Imitation: From Neuroscience to Social Science*, ed. Susan Hurley and Nick Carter, vol. 2. Cambridge, MA: MIT Press.

Docquier, F., Lodigiani, E., Rapoport, H., and Schiff, M. 2011. Emigration and Democracy. Policy Research Working Paper Series 5557, The World Bank.

Docquier, F., Lohest, O., and Marfouk, A. 2007. Brain Drain in Developing Countries. *World Bank Economic Review* 21(2), 193–218.

Docquier, F., Ozden, C., and Peri, G. 2010. The Wage Effects of Immigration and Emigration. NBER Working Paper 16646.

Docquier, F., and Rapoport, H. 2012. Globalization, Brain Drain and Development. *Journal of Economic Literature* 50(3), 681–730.

Docquier, F., Rapoport, H., and Salomone, S. 2012. Remittances, Migrants' Education and Immigration Policy: Theory and Evidence from Bilateral Data. *Regional Science and Urban Economics* 42(5), 817–828.

Dunbar, R. I. M. 1992. Neocortex Size as a Constraint on Group Size in Primates. *Journal of Human Evolution* 22(6), 469–493.

Dustmann, C., Casanova, M., Fertig, M., Preston, I., and Schmidt, C. M. 2003. The Impact of EU Enlargement on Migration Flows. Online

Report 25/03, Home Office, London. Available at www.homeoffice
.gov.uk/rds/pdfs2/rdsolr2503.pdf.

Dustmann, C., Frattini, T., and Preston, I. P. 2012. The Effect of Immigration along the Distribution of Wages. *Review of Economic Studies*, doi: 10.1093/restud/rds019.

Ferguson, N. 2012. The Rule of Law and Its Enemies: The Human Hive. BBC Reith Lecture 2012, London School of Economics and Political Science, June 7. Transcript available at http://www2.lse.ac.uk/public Events/pdf/2012_ST/20120607-Niall-Ferguson-Transcript.pdf.

Fisman, R., and Miguel, E. 2007. Corruption, Norms, and Legal Enforcement: Evidence from Diplomatic Parking Tickets. *Journal of Political Economy* 115(6), 1020–1048.

Fleming, R. 2011. *Britain after Rome*. New York: Penguin.

Gaechter, S., Herrmann, B., and Thöni, G. 2010. Culture and Cooperation. CESifo Working Paper Series 3070, CESifo Group Munich.

Glaeser, E. L. 2011. *Triumph of the City: How Our Greatest Invention Makes Us Richer, Smarter, Greener, Healthier and Happier*. New York: Penguin.

Goldin, I., Cameron, G., and Balarajan, M. 2011. *Exceptional People: How Migration Shaped Our World and Will Define Our Future*. Princeton, NJ: Princeton University Press.

Goodhart, D. 2013. White Flight? Britain's New Problem—Segregation. *Prospect*, February.

Greif, A., and Bates, R. H. 1995. Organising Violence: Wealth, Power, and Limited Government. Mimeo, Stanford University.

Grosjean, F. 2011. Life as a Bilingual. *Psychology Today*.

Haidt, J. 2012. *The Righteous Mind: Why Good People Are Divided by Politics and Religion*. New York: Pantheon.

Halsall, G. 2013. *Worlds of Arthur*. New York: Oxford University Press.

Hatton, T. J., and Williamson, J. G. 2008. *Global Migration and the World Economy: Two Centuries of Policy and Performance*. Cambridge, MA: MIT Press.

Heath, A. F., Fisher, S. D., Sanders, D., and Sobolewska, M. 2011. Ethnic Heterogeneity in the Social Bases of Voting in the 2010 British General Election. *Journal of Elections, Public Opinion and Parties* 21(2), 255–277.

Herreros, F., and Criado, H. 2009. Social Trust, Social Capital and Perceptions of Immigrations. *Political Studies* 57, 335–357.

Hirsch, F. 1977. *Social Limits to Growth*. New York: Routledge.

Hirschman, A. O. 1990. *Exit, Voice and Loyalty: Responses to Decline in Firms, Organizations, and States*. 2nd ed. Cambridge, MA: Harvard University Press.

Hirschman, C. 2005. Immigration and the American Century. *Demography* 42, 595–620.

Hoddinott, J. 1994. A Model of Migration and Remittances Applied to Western Kenya. *Oxford Economic Papers* 46(3), 459–476.

Hofstede, G., and Hofstede, G. J. 2010. National Culture Dimensions. Available at http://geert-hofstede.com/national-culture.html.

Hurley, S., and Carter, N., eds. 2005. *Perspectives on Imitation: From Neuroscience to Social Science*. Vol. 2. Cambridge, MA: MIT Press.

Jones, B. F., and Olken, B. A. 2005. Do Leaders Matter? National Leadership and Growth Since World War II. *Quarterly Journal of Economics* 120(3), 835–864.

Kay, J. 2012. The Multiplier Effect, or Keynes's View of Probability. *Financial Times*, August 14. Available at http://www.ft.com/cms/s/0/f7660898-e538-11e1-8ac0-00144feab49a.html.

Kepel, G. 2011. Banlieues Islam: L'enquete qui derange. *Le Monde*, October 5.

Koczan, Z. 2013. Does Identity Matter? Mimeo, University of Cambridge.

Koopmans, R. 2010. Trade-offs between Equality and Difference: Immigrant Integration, Multiculturalism and the Welfare State in Cross-National Perspective. *Journal of Ethnic and Migration Studies* 36(1), 1–26.

Mahmoud, O., Rapoport, H., Steinmayr, A., and Trebesch, C. 2012. Emigration and Political Change. Mimeo.

Marchiori, L., Shen, I.-L., and Docquier, F. 2013. Brain Drain in Globalization: A General Equilibrium Analysis from the Sending Countries' Perspective. *Economic Inquiry* 51(2), 1582–1602.

McKenzie, D., and Yang, D. 2010. Experimental Approaches in Migration Studies. Policy Research Working Paper Series 5395, World Bank.

Mercier, M. 2012. The Return of the *Prodigy* Son: Do Return Migrants Make Better Leaders? Mimeo, Paris School of Economics.

Miguel, E., and Gugerty, M. K. 2005. Ethnic Diversity, Social Sanctions, and Public Goods in Kenya. *Journal of Public Economics* 89(11–12), 2325–2368.

Montalvo, J., and Reynal-Querol, M. 2010. Ethnic Polarization and the Duration of Civil Wars. *Economics of Governance* 11(2), 123–143.

Mousy, L. M., and Arcand, J.-L. 2011. Braving the Waves: The Economics of Clandestine Migration from Africa. CERDI Working Paper 201104.

Murray, C. 2012. *Coming Apart: The State of White America, 1960–2010.* New York: Crown Forum.

Nickell, S. 2009. Migration Watch. *Prospect Magazine*, July 23. Available at http://www.prospectmagazine.co.uk/magazine/10959-numbercruncher/.

Nunn, N. 2010. Religious Conversion in Colonial Africa. *American Economic Review* 100(2), 147–152.

Nunn, N., and Wantchekon, L. 2011. The Slave Trade and the Origins of Mistrust in Africa. *American Economic Review* 101(7), 3221–3252.

Pagel, M. D. 2012. *Wired for Culture: The Natural History of Human Cooperation.* London: Allen Lane.

Pérez-Armendariz, C., and Crow, D. 2010. Do Migrants Remit Democracy? International Migration, Political Beliefs, and Behavior in Mexico. *Comparative Political Studies* 43(1), 119–148.

Pinker, S. 2011. *The Better Angels of Our Nature.* New York: Viking.

Putnam, R. 2007. E Pluribus Unum: Diversity and Community in the 21st Century. *Scandinavian Political Studies* 30(2), 137–174.

Rempel, H., and Lobdell, R. A. 1978. The Role of Urban-to-Rural Remittances in Rural Development. *Journal of Development Studies* 14(3), 324–341.

Romer, P. 2010. For Richer, for Poorer. *Prospect Magazine*, January 27. Available at http://www.prospectmagazine.co.uk/magazine/for-richer-for-poorer/.

Sampson, R. J. 2008. Rethinking Crime and Immigration. *Contexts* 7(1), 28–33.

Sandel, M. J. 2012. *What Money Can't Buy: The Moral Limits of Markets*. London: Allen Lane.

Saunders, D. 2010. *Arrival City: How the Largest Migration in History Is Reshaping Our World*. New York: Pantheon.

Serra, D., Serneels, P., and Barr, A. 2010. Intrinsic Motivations and the Non-profit Health Sector: Evidence from Ethiopia. Working Paper Series, University of East Anglia, Centre for Behavioural and Experimental Social Science (CBESS) 10-01.

Schiff, M. 2012. Education Policy, Brain Drain and Heterogeneous Ability: The Impact of Alternative Migration Policies. Mimeo, World Bank.

Shih, M., Pittinsky, T. L., and Ambady, N. 1999. Stereotype Susceptibility: Shifts in Quantitative Performance from Socio-cultural Identification. *Psychological Science* 10, 81–84.

Spilimbergo, A. 2009. Democracy and Foreign Education. *American Economic Review* 99(1), 528–543.

Stillman, S., Gibson, J., McKenzie, D., and Rohorua, H. 2012. Miserable Migrants? Natural Experiment Evidence on International Migration and Objective and Subjective Well-Being. IZA-DP6871, Bonn, September.

Thurow, R. 2012. *The Last Hunger Season: A Year in an African Farm Community on the Brink of Change*. New York: Public Affairs.

Van Tubergen, F. 2004. *The Integration of Immigrants in Cross-National Perspective: Origin, Destination, and Community Effects*. Utrecht: ICS.

Walmsley, T. L., Winters, L. A., Ahmed, S. A., and Parsons, C. R. 2005. Measuring the Impact of the Movement of Labour Using a Model of Bilateral Migration Flows. Mimeo.

Weiner, M. S. 2011. *The Rule of the Clan*. New York: Farrar, Straus and Giroux.

Wente, M. 2012. Michael Ignatieff Was Right about Quebec. *The Globe and Mail*, April 26. Available at http://www.theglobeandmail.com/commentary/michael-ignatieff-was-right-about-quebec/article4102623/.

Wilson, W. J. 1996. *When Work Disappears: The New World of the Urban Poor*. New York: Alfred A. Knopf.

Wrong, M. 2006. *I Didn't Do It for You*. New York: Harper Perennial.

Yang, D. 2008. International Migration, Remittances and Household Investment: Evidence from Philippine Migrants' Exchange Rate Shocks. *Economic Journal* 118(528), 591–630.

Yang, D. 2011. Migrant Remittances. *Journal of Economic Perspectives* 25(3), 129–152.

Yang, D., and Choi, H. 2007. Are Remittances Insurance? Evidence from Rainfall Shocks in the Philippines. *World Bank Economic Review* 21(2), 219–248.

Zak, P. 2012. *The Moral Molecule: The Source of Love and Prosperity.* New York: Dutton Adult.

Index

Acemoglu, Daron, 29–30, 93, 180
Afghanistan, 200
Africa. *See also specific countries*
  economic growth in, 39
  intergroup conflicts in, 64–65
  lack of trust in, 64–66
  migration policy in, 247
  national identity in, 17, 239
  public provision in, 239
  remittances to, 207
  return migration to, 201–202
  slave trade in, 65–66
African Americans, migration
  within the United States by,
  204–205
aging populations. *See* migration,
  demographic argument for

Akerlof, George, 6, 32–33, 192,
  204, 238
Alesina, Alberto, 85
Amin, Idi, 189
Andersen, Torben, 125
Angola, 94
apprenticeship programs, 127–128
Arab Spring, 35, 221–222
assimilation
  advantages of, 98–99
  in European Union countries,
    76–77
  intermarriage and, 99, 272
  language acquisition and, 70,
    98–99, 107, 242, 264, 270
  in the United States, 69, 76–77,
    242, 264

asylum, 160, 249, 262–263

Australia
detention of migrants in, 161, 250
happiness in, 249
migration policy in, 12, 51–52, 157–158, 248–250
population density in, 24, 118, 137, 249

Bangladesh, 200, 208, 214
Batista, Catia, 184–185
Belgium, 17–18, 236
Belich, James, 92–93
Besley, Timothy, 64–65, 191
Bhagwati, Jagdish, 150
Boko Haram, 222–223
"bottom billion." *See also* countries of origin
migration and, 4, 23, 179, 193, 216, 222–223
population growth and, 213–214
untapped potential of, 196, 223
Bottom Billion, The (Collier), 213
Bradford (Great Britain), 4, 36, 101–102
brain drain. *See under* countries of origin
British Medical Association, 126
British Nationalist Party, 241
Brown, Dan, 214
Brown, Gordon, 21, 130, 244

California (United States), 85–86
Cameron, David, 138

Canada
East Asian migrants in, 120–121
migration policy in, 12, 100, 157–158, 248–249, 264
national identity in, 17–18, 236–237
population density, 92, 137
Cape Verde, 184–185, 193
capital mobility, 23, 28–29, 36, 51, 121, 129–130, 265
carbon emissions, 257–258
Caribbean migration to Great Britain, 47–48
Catalonia, 235
categorical imperative, 260
charter cities, 103
Chauvet, Lisa, 185–187
Chekhov, Anton, 222
China
brain gain *versus* brain drain in, 218, 220, 252
demography in, 123
economic growth in, 39–40, 201–202
economic productivity in, 149
education emigration and, 201
education investment in, 200
governance in, 183–184
national identity and, 17
remittances to, 207
return migration and, 201–202
Russia and, 249

Clemens, Michael, 58
climate change, 257–258
Clinton, Bill, 31, 200
Collier, Charles, 3, 273
community, concept of, 232–233
Condé, Alpha, 191
Congo, Democratic Republic of, 184
Conservative Party (Great Britain), 15, 103
cooperation
    experimental games measuring, 63–64, 66–67, 74, 80, 254
    foundations of, 31–32
    free-rider problem and, 63–64, 66
    Kenya study of, 76, 239–240
    mutual regard and, 62–63, 67, 83, 87
    punishing transgression and, 63–64, 74, 79
    trust and, 32, 64, 66–67, 73–74
Corden, Max, 118
Côte d'Ivoire, 191
countries of origin. See also specific countries
    brain drain and, 117, 184, 190–191, 195–204, 217–220, 225–226, 260–261
    civil wars in, 189–190, 263
    diasporas' impact on, 180–182, 184–185, 187–189, 202–203, 221
    discrimination in, 180

    economic productivity in, 146–147, 149, 201, 204, 214, 226
    education investment in, 197–201
    education motivation for migration and, 158, 253
    elites in, 150–151
    "left behind" population in, 4, 23, 25, 217–226, 252–253, 257, 261, 270
    migration's economic impact on, 179, 195–196, 213–214, 217, 220, 269
    migration's impact on elections in, 185–187
    migration's impact on governance in, 180–190, 193, 217
    migration's impact on potential leaders of, 190–193
    migration's impact on the culture of, 187–188, 192
    outsider attitudes in, 205–206
    political institutions in, 181
    population growth in, 213–216
    proposed special supplemental tax on emigrants from, 150–152
    return migration and, 201–202, 263
    rural to urban migration within, 173–174, 215–216, 221, 272

countries of origin. (*continued*)
  social models in, 34–35, 96,
    103, 132, 147–148, 179,
    248, 254, 271
  violence in, 98, 190
cultural differences
  as distinguished from racism,
    21–22
  economic consequences of,
    34–35
  ethnicity and, 75
  value of, 95
cultural separatism, 97–98,
    100–102, 243–244
Cyprus, 167–168

Denmark, 19, 118
Descartes, René, 231–232
diaspora communities. *See also*
    migrants
  absorption rates and, 41–43,
    45–46, 87–88, 90–91,
    105–106, 109, 140–142,
    242, 258–259, 262,
    264–265, 268, 276n14
  boundaries of, 41–42
  composition of, 88–92, 164, 166
  cultural distance from host
    society and, 88–91, 141, 242,
    262
  diaspora schedules and, 45–48,
    88–90, 106, 109, 140–141,
    256, 267, 276n14

impact on countries of origin
    by, 180–182, 184–185,
    187–189, 202–203, 221
  migration equilbria and, 89–90
  Polish and Bangladeshi example
    of, 88–90
  residential concentration of,
    164, 258
  schools and, 106–107, 276n12
  sizes of, 39, 42–43, 46–48, 87,
    91, 105–106, 141–142, 199,
    258, 268
  subsequent migration and,
    162–165, 199
Docquier, Frédéric, 6, 251
Dubai (United Arab Emirates), 12,
    132–133, 248
Duggan, Mark, 79–82
Dunbar constant, 276n11

East Asia
  economic growth in, 39
  financial crisis in, 129, 210
East Asians, 119–121
economic development
  political institutions and, 29–31
  productivity and, 32–33, 35,
    149
  social norms and, 31–32
  social organizations and, 32–33
economic productivity
  in countries of origin, 146–147,
    149, 201, 204, 214, 226

in host countries, 146–147,
149, 171, 226
identity and, 32–33, 192, 203
migration and, 146–147, 149
economics, academic discipline of
development economics and, 28
growth theory and, 28
individualism and, 233–234
migration and, 38, 111
policy assessment and, 14–15
studies of trust and, 234
Egypt, 35, 200, 222
Einstein, Albert, 235
El Salvador, migrants from,
207–208
emigrants, compared to settlers,
93, 96
England. *See also* Great Britain
"England for the English," 231,
241, 243
Glorious Revolution (1688) in,
29–30, 34
national identity and, 18,
243–244
social model in, 34
Enlightenment ideals, 67
Eritrea, 160, 193
Ernsbach (Germany), 4, 41
ethical values
categorical imperative and, 260
disagreements about, 14
golden rule and, 98–99, 108,
247

Haidt on, 13–14
migration and, 13–16, 53, 58,
150, 165, 246, 260
Ethiopia, 204–205
European Union
economic redistribution in, 236
euro currency and, 19, 30–31,
240
Germany and, 30, 236, 240, 272
nationalism and, 16–18,
235–236, 272
European Union countries. *See also*
specific countries
assimilation in, 69, 76–77
attitudes toward economic
redistribution in, 85
deportation of migrants from,
134
extremist political parties in,
52–53, 241
foreign-born prison population
in, 122
inflation in, 30–31
migrants' identities in, 73
migration levels in, 51, 76, 149
proportional representation
voting systems, 52
existence value, 95, 246–247

Ferguson, Niall, 222
Fiji, 158, 180
Finland, 19, 241
Fisman, Ray, 67–68

foreign aid programs, 207,
209–210, 223–225, 236
France
economic redistribution in, 68
foreign-born prison population
in, 122
French Revolution, 34, 237
Mali and, 186
migration policy in, 37, 126
Muslims in, 101, 108–109
national identity and, 17
national identity in, 242
veil-wearing policy in, 108–109

Gaddafi, Muammar, 185
Germany
apprenticeship programs in, 127
European Union and, 30, 236,
240, 272
guest workers in, 132, 134
migration from, 3–4
migration policy in, 37, 126, 262
multiculturalism and, 70
national identity in, 17
Norway and, 240
Poland and, 240
Turkish immigrants in, 37, 70,
134, 207, 221, 259
Ghana, 200
Glaeser, Edward, 85
Glasgow (Great Britain), 100–101
Global Financial Crisis (2008), 273
global language tree, 76–77, 88

global warming. See climate
change
Glorious Revolution (England,
1688), 29–30, 34
golden rule, the, 98–99, 108, 247
"Golden Thirty Years" (1945-1975),
28, 37, 39, 51
government services
charity and, 151
marketization and, 84, 86
migration's impact on, 107,
111, 116, 125, 136, 141,
165, 264–265
public opinion regarding, 85–86
Great Britain. See also England;
Scotland
Afghanistan war and, 82
African immigrants in, 99,
100–101, 161, 243
Afro-Caribbean community in,
80, 82–83
ancestry in, 59–60, 99
Anglo-Saxon cultural diffusion
in, 94–95
anti-immigrant sentiment in,
3–4, 20–21
apprenticeship programs in, 127
Asian immigrants in, 36, 86–87
asylum policy in, 161
attitudes toward economic
redistribution in, 85
Bangladeshi immigrants in,
101–102, 243

Caribbean migrants and, 47–48, 80–81

First World War and, 3–4

foreign aid programs in, 224–225

German immigrants in, 3–4

guns in, 78–81

housing market in, 116

Islamic extremists in, 4

looting outbreak in, 81–82

migration from, 92, 129

migration policy in, 15, 20–21, 37, 48, 51, 126, 137, 259, 262, 269

Muslim immigrants and community in, 4, 82, 101–102, 108–109

National Health Service (NHS) in, 62, 126, 238

national identity and, 17–18, 241, 243–244

political parties in, 4, 15, 21, 102–103

Polish immigration to, 20–21, 262

population density in, 118

postal voting in, 102

Premium Bonds in, 197

social mobility in, 83

social networks in, 79–80

textile industry in, 36

trade policies of, 36

trust levels in, 79–80

Turkish Cypriots in, 167–168

veil-wearing policy in, 108–109

wages in, 112

Great Depression, 27, 196

Greece, 35, 236, 240

guest workers, 70, 131–134, 212–213, 266–267

Guinea-Bissau, 200

Haidt, Jonathan, 6, 13–14, 175, 233, 255

Haiti

brain drain and, 199–200, 208, 218, 220, 272

citizenship policy in, 189

earthquake (2010) in, 30, 225

outsider attitudes in, 205–206

remittances to, 208

happiness

economic factors and, 139, 171–172

of indigenous populations in host countries, 138–139

measurements of, 138–139, 172–173

of migrants, 171–174

social factors and, 139, 171–172, 234

Hellenschmidt Jr., Karl. *See* Collier, Charles

Hellenschmidt, Karl, 3–4, 273

Hirsch, Fred, 121

Hirschman, Albert, 181

Hoeffler, Anke, 148, 164
Hofstede, Geert, 68
Hookway, Chris, 6
host countries. *See also* indigenous
    populations in host countries;
    specific countries
    economic deceleration in, 51
    economic productivity in,
        146–147, 149, 171, 226
    education spending in, 226–227
    labor unions in, 37
    migration's potential future
        consequences for, 57–59, 76,
        113, 132
    poor people in, 25
    social models in, 151, 221
housing
    migration's impact on, 114–117,
        121, 165, 254
    private, 116–117, 121
    social, 114–116, 165, 254
human trafficking, 161–162
"hunkering down" (Putnam),
    74–75, 105, 108, 139, 243

ideas
    transformations from, 35–36
    transmission of, 35–37, 221–222
identity. *See also* national identity
    economic productivity and,
        32–33, 192, 203
    empathy and, 84
    formation of, 70–71

language and, 70, 73
neurological foundations of, 71
role models and, 71, 198,
    204
stereotypes and, 71–73
Identity Economics (Akerlof and
    Kranton), 238
Ignatieff, Michael, 17
immigrant exceptionalism,
    117–123, 137
income gap. *See* income
    inequality
income inequality
    capital endowment and, 28
    capital mobility and, 28–29
    factors explaining, 27–28
    global aspects of, 28, 37–40, 50
    marketization's impact on, 84,
        233
    migration and, 38–41, 44–47,
        49–50, 166, 251–252, 267,
        271
    technology's impact on, 83–84
India
    brain gain *versus* brain drain in,
        218, 220, 252
    economic growth in, 39,
        201
    education investment in,
        200–201
    migration study from,
        173–174
    remittances to, 207

indigenous populations in host
    countries
  education competition and,
    119–120
  emigration by, 128–131
  fatalism among, 119
  happiness of, 138–139
  migration policy and, 245
  migration's impact on housing
    for, 114–117, 123, 165, 254
  migration's impact on the
    happiness of, 138–139
  migration's impact on wages
    for, 111–113, 123, 129, 131,
    136, 169–170, 253–254,
    258, 261
  migration's impact on worker
    training for, 126–128
  social networks among,
    107–108, 242
  trust levels among, 74–75, 81,
    105, 141
  values of, 243–244
individualism, 231–233
Indonesia, 200
international trade, 23, 36, 271
Iraq, 193
Ireland
  economic boom in, 130
  famine in, 94, 215
  migration from, 92, 94, 215
  Protestants in, 94
Israel, 93, 247–249

Istanbul (Turkey), 216, 221
Italy, 123

Jamaica, 80, 200, 214
Japan, 12, 33, 132
Johnson, Boris, 96–97
Johnson, Simon, 93

Kahneman, Daniel, 6, 14, 78, 175
Kant, Immanuel, 260
Kenya
  cooperation study from, 76,
    239–240
  ethnic identity in, 240
  remittances and, 206
  schooling in, 196–197
Kenyatta, Jomo, 240
Keynes, John Maynard, 30, 198
Khomeini, Ayatollah Ruhollah, 188
Koopmans, Ruud, 107
Kranton, Rachel, 32–33, 192, 204,
    238

Labour Party (Great Britain), 15,
    21, 103
"ladder of life" metric, 172–174
language
  assimilation and, 70, 98–99,
    107, 242, 264, 270 and
  cultural distance and, 77
  identity and, 70, 73
  multiculturalism and, 107
Laos, 200

Latin America. *See also specific countries*
  economic growth in, 39
  migrants to the United States from, 37, 76
  remittances to, 206–207
  Spanish imperialism in, 94
Layard, Richard, 138
Leicester (Great Britain), 36
Lenin, Vladimir, 188
liberalism
  critiques of, 5
  multiculturalism and, 97, 272
  views of migration and, 13–14, 265, 271
Liberia, 200, 209
libertarianism, 232, 246
Libya, 35, 185
life expectancy, retirement ages and, 124
London (Great Britain)
  migrant population in, 101–102, 104, 116, 121, 129
  Olympics (2012) in, 241
  social networks in, 79–80
  terrorism in, 4

Malawi, 200
Mali, 185–187, 247–248
Manchester (Great Britain), 80–81
Mercier, Marion, 185–187, 192
Merkel, Angela, 5, 18, 70, 240
Mexico, 185

migrants. *See also* diaspora communities; migration
  attitudes toward migration policy among, 170
  crime and, 122
  cultural fusion and, 97, 99–100, 242–243
  cultural separatism and, 97–98, 100–102, 243–244
  discrimination against, 105, 122, 170, 270
  economic benefits of migration for, 22, 145–147, 149, 151–153, 171, 174–175, 245, 270, 273
  economic competition between, 169–170
  education competition and, 119–120
  family sizes among, 125
  happiness of, 171–174
  honor societies and, 87
  identity of, 22, 69–70, 73
  immigrant exceptionalism and, 117–123, 137
  innovations from, 117–118, 137
  isolation from host societies and, 171–172, 174–175
  mutual regard and, 72–73
  party politics and, 104–105
  political separatism and, 102

proposed special supplemental
  tax on, 150–153
remittances from, 151,
  155–156, 206–213, 217,
  219–220, 225–226, 252, 260
residential clustering of,
  100–103, 116
self-improvement narratives
  and, 69–70
small businesses of, 163
social networks among, 106,
  108, 163
trust levels among, 72–74, 87
migration. *See also* diaspora
  communities; migrants;
  migration policy
absorption rates and, 41–43,
  45–46, 87–88, 90–91,
  105–106, 109, 140–142,
  242, 258–259, 262,
  264–265, 268, 276n14
acceleration principle and,
  251–252
boom-bust economic cycles
  and, 129–131, 254
border controls and, 161, 266
bribery and, 159–160
demographic argument for,
  123–125
economic effects of, 6, 22,
  24–25, 38–39, 111–139
economic modeling of, 43–50,
  140–141

economic skills argument for,
  126–128, 131
educational motives for, 158,
  191–192, 197, 253, 260
equilibria and, 40, 43, 46–50,
  89–90, 106, 109, 140–141,
  256, 267–268
ethical values and, 13–16, 53,
  58, 150, 165, 246, 260
family support for, 155–156,
  196
feedback mechanisms and, 50,
  105–106, 182
financial costs of, 38, 40, 92,
  153–154, 166
as foreign aid, 225–227
fraud and, 160–161
globalization and, 36, 51, 271
guest worker model of,
  131–134, 142
human trafficking and, 161–162
illegal forms of, 159–162,
  249–250, 265–266, 268
impact on economic productivity
  from, 146–147, 149
impact on government services
  from, 107, 111, 116, 125,
  136, 141, 165, 264–265
income inequality and, 38–41,
  44–47, 49–50, 166, 251–252,
  267, 271
income selection and, 154–155
as investment, 153–157

migration. (*continued*)
  marginal effects *versus* total
    effects of, 218–220
  marriage and, 159, 272
  nation-shopping and, 148–149
  opposition to racism and,
    19–20, 22
  psychological costs of, 22,
    171–172, 174–176, 245
  racism and, 21–22, 25–26, 105,
    271
  role models and, 198, 202, 205
  small countries and, 199–203
  social capital and, 74–75, 82,
    90–91
  social effects of, 6, 15, 24,
    57–58, 61–70, 72–77, 79–88,
    90–109, 135–139
  stock-flow model of, 49
  as taboo subject, 13–14, 20, 26,
    52, 120, 255
  trust levels and, 74–75, 78,
    91–92, 99, 105–106, 170
  wealth as a criterion for, 121
  xenophobia and, 25–26, 52,
    105, 245, 251, 270–271
migration policy. *See also under*
    specific countries
  anti-migration approach to,
    136–137
  "anxiety phase" of, 140–141
  asylum and, 160, 249, 262–263
  businesses' role in, 262
  ceilings and, 256–260, 267–268

  culturally differentiated controls
    and, 262
  diaspora absorption phase of, 142
  education requirements and, 12,
    157–158, 164–165, 212–213,
    252, 261
  emotive perspective on, 11–12
  family reunification and,
    158–159, 164–165, 212–213,
    260
  integration and, 264–265, 270
  legalizing illegal immigration
    and, 265–267
  lotteries and, 147, 165–166,
    259, 261
  migration rates and, 50–51,
    91, 142, 166, 244, 251–252,
    254–260, 268–269, 272
  "panic" approach to, 141,
    255–256, 267–270
  pro-migration approach to, 136
  quantitative limits approach to,
    139–141
  right to control immigration
    and, 246–251, 270
  selectivity and, 260–263
  "ugly phase" of, 141
  wealth requirements and, 121
Miguel, Edward, 67–68, 76
Mo Ibrahim Index, 193
Moldova, 187
Montalvo, Jose, 77, 98, 191
moral hazard, 249–250
moral values. *See* ethical values

motivation drain, 203–206
Mozambique, 200
Mugabe, Robert, 182, 191
multiculturalism
   critiques of, 35
   as cultural fusion, 97, 99–100,
      264
   cultural separatism and, 100, 106
   impact on integration rates and,
      107, 109
   impact on language acquisition
      and, 107
   liberalism and, 97, 272
   as reaction to assimilation
      narrative, 97
mutual regard
   citizenship and, 115–116
   cooperation and, 62–63, 67,
      83, 87
   diminishing returns from, 63,
      254
   economic redistribution and,
      61–62, 68, 83–84, 87, 113,
      254
   migrants and, 72–73
   migration's impact on, 135–136,
      254, 258
   neurological foundations of, 234
   Smith on, 234
   trust and, 62, 254

narratives, Keynes on, 30, 198
National Health Service (NHS,
      Great Britain), 62, 126, 238

national identity
   criticisms of, 5, 16–18, 231
   economic redistribution and,
      18, 235–237
   migration's impact on, 242–244
   positive aspects of, 5, 18–19,
      25, 131, 242
   public sector workers and, 238
   racism and, 241
   sense of community and, 232,
      234–242
   violence and, 19, 237, 240–241
Netherlands, 24, 118, 129, 137
neuroscience, 71, 234
New York City (United States)
   diplomats case study in,
      67–68
   premier public schools in,
      119–120
New Zealand
   businesses' role in migration to,
      262
   migration example featuring,
      44–48
   migration from Tonga to, 147,
      172–173, 259
   migration policy in, 128, 147,
      173
Niger, 163
Nigeria
   levels of trust in, 65–66, 68
   migrants from, 67–69
   terrorism in, 222–223
Norway, 16, 19, 240

Notting Hill Carnival (Great Britain), 82–83
Nunn, Nathan, 65
Nyerere, Julius, 5, 239–240

Okonjo-Iweala, Ngozi, 191
"outsider values," 203–206, 238
Outtarra, Alassane, 191

Palestinian territories, Jewish settlement in, 93
Paris (France), 216
Philippines, 208, 210–211
Pinker, Steven, 6, 31–32, 65, 80, 233, 240
Plundered Planet, The (Collier), 184, 202
Poland
    European Union and, 20
    Germany and, 240
    migration to Great Britain and, 20–21, 262
poor countries. *See* countries of origin
poor people, moral obligations to, 15–16, 19, 21, 25
Portugal, 35, 130
positional goods, 121
Powell, Enoch, 20, 22, 77
Premium Bonds (Great Britain), 197
Putnam, Robert, 74–78, 81, 83, 91, 105, 107–108, 138–139

racism
    migration and, 21–22, 25–26, 105, 271
    national identity and, 241
Rajan, Raghuram, 83–84
Rand, Ayn, 232
Rawlings, Nick, 6
remittances
    duration of, 211
    "earmarking" of, 209
    effects of, 209–210, 225–226, 252–253
    effects of financial shocks on, 210–211
    migration policies' impact on, 212–213, 253
    size of, 151, 155–156, 206–207
Respect Party (Great Britain), 4, 102–103
Reynal-Querol, Marta, 65, 77, 98, 191
rich countries. *See* host countries
Robinson, James, 29–30, 93, 180
Romer, Paul, 103
Romney, Mitt, 103
Rousseau, Jean-Jacques, 64
Rule of the Clan, The (Weiner), 87
Russia, 123–124, 187, 248–249

Sahel region, 155
Sampson, Robert, 122
Sandel, Michael, 6, 84, 233, 238
São Tomé, 184

Saunders, Simon, 6
Scandinavia, 17, 19. *See also
specific countries*
Scotland, national identity in, 18,
241, 244
Scottish National Party, 241
Senegal, 185, 207–208
settlers
compared to emigrants, 93, 96
cultural diffusion and, 94–96, 98
missionaries and, 94
in poorer countries, 96
Sierra Leone, 200
Singapore, 118, 273
Sirleaf, Ellen Johnson, 191
slavery. *See* human trafficking
Smith, Adam, 233–234
social capital
bonding, 107–108
bridging, 107–108
migration's impact on, 74–75,
82, 90–91
Putnam on, 74, 82–83, 107–108
social housing. *See under housing*
social models
in countries of origin, 34–35,
96, 103, 147–148, 179, 248,
254, 271–272
definition of, 33
economic prosperity and,
179–180, 247–248, 273
in host countries, 34–35, 151,
221

social networks
in Great Britain, 79–80
indigenous populations in host
countries and, 107–108, 242
intergroup, 107–108
intragroup, 107
migrants and, 106, 108, 163
social welfare systems. *See*
government services
Somalia
migrants from, 100–101, 136
political structure in, 32
South Africa, 93, 182
South Sudan, 31, 219
Soviet Union, collapse of, 35
Spain
Catalonian separatism in, 235
democratization in, 35
migration policy in, 130
unemployment in, 31, 130
Spectator, The, 224
Spilimbergo, Antonio, 192
Sri Lanka, 188
Stalin, Josef, 35
stereotypes, 71–72, 92
Sweden, 19, 160, 262
Switzerland, 15
Sydney (Australia), 119

taboo, migration as, 13–14, 20,
26, 52, 120, 255
Tamil diaspora, 188
Tamil Tigers (Sri Lanka), 188

Tanzania
  migration study in, 215–216
  national identity in, 5, 239–240
technology
  communication and, 81, 222
  cultural transfers and, 201, 222
  economic inequality and, 83–84
terrorism, 4, 222–223
Thatcher, Margaret, 232
Theory of Moral Sentiments, The
  (Smith), 234
Thiam, Tidjane, 191
Thinking Fast, Thinking Slow
  (Kahneman), 14
Thurow, Roger, 196–197
Tonga
  migration example featuring,
    44–48
  migration to New Zealand from,
    147, 172–173, 259
Tower Hamlets (Great Britain),
  101–102
Turkey, 221, 262, 282n5
Turkish Cypriot migrants,
  167–168
Turkish immigrants in Germany,
  37, 70, 134, 207, 221, 259

Uganda, 189, 200
United Arab Emirates, 12,
  132–133, 248
United Kingdom. *See* Great Britain
United States
  African Americans in, 204–205

assimilation in, 69, 76–77, 242,
  264
attitudes toward economic
  redistribution in, 85
deportation of migrants from,
  134, 161
foreign aid programs in, 224–225
foreign-born prison population
  in, 122
Hispanic immigrants and
  community in, 37, 73, 76–77,
  98–99, 103, 122, 206–207
illegal immigrants in, 265
immigrant exceptionalism in, 117
immigration visa lottery in, 147
income inequality in, 83–84
migration policy in, 12, 37, 51,
  158, 264
national identity in, 17
nineteenth-century migration to,
  49–50, 92, 94
political institutions in, 31, 33
social mobility in, 83
social model in, 33–34
utility
  definition of, 58
  global, 25
  libertarian approach to, 168, 246
  migration and, 6, 25
  universalist approach to, 58, 62,
    115, 150, 168, 246

Venables, Tony, 6
vendettas, 65

Vicente, Pedro, 184–185
Vietnam, 200
violence
  Jamaican culture and, 80
  language distance's impact on, 77
  media depictions of, 72
  national identity and, 19, 237,
    240–241
  social norms regarding, 31–32,
    80, 233, 240

wages, migration's impact on,
    111–113, 123, 129, 131, 136,
    169–170, 253–254, 258, 261

Wantchekon, Leonard, 65
Wealth of Nations, The (Smith),
    233–234
Weiner, Mark, 87
Winters, Alan, 133

xenophobia, 25–26, 52, 105, 245,
    251, 270–271

Yang, Dean, 210

Zak, Paul, 6
Zambia, 200
Zimbabwe, 182, 200